The Westminster Standards

in Modern English

edited by

Kevin J. Bidwell

EP BOOKS
1st Floor Venture House, 6 Silver Court, Watchmead,
Welwyn Garden City, UK, AL7 1TS

www.epbooks.org
sales@epbooks.org

EP Books are distributed in the USA by:
JPL Distribution
3741 Linden Avenue Southeast
Grand Rapids, MI 49548

orders@jplbooks.com
www. jplbooks.com

© Sheffield Presbyterian Church 2017.

British Library Cataloguing in Publication Data available

ISBN 978–1–78397–209–8

Unless otherwise indicated, Scripture quotations are from The Holy Bible, English Standard Version (ESV), copyright © 2001 by Crossway Bibles, a division of Good News Publishers. Used by permission. All rights reserved.

Printed and bound in Great Britain by Bell and Bain Ltd, Glasgow

When I was being trained for the ministry I was required to render a portion of the Westminster Standards into modern English. As a test of comprehension and communication the assignment was much harder than first appeared. This volume is the product of similar pains, and those who find the Standards more intelligible as a result have a debt of thanks to pay! That debt will double as readers discover the second part of the book: scholarly reflections urging the best of puritan piety for the good of the church today. Easy-to-read texts and need-to-read essays: seize the opportunity to deepen your faith!

Rev. Dr Chad Van Dixhoorn

An updated edition of a classic standard might be a daunting task. While we hesitate to dub the fine college of authors of this volume 'The Westminster Divines 2.0,' we can heartily endorse this work and commend it to churches and leaders. Indeed, it is faithful to the original, both a compliment to the original authors, faithfulness and to these latter disciples, separated by many generations and miles but virtually indistinguishable in substance and heartbeat. For this we are profoundly grateful. Both the essays and the editorial work are fine contributions to the church.

David W. Hall, Sr. Pastor Midway Presbyterian Church and author of *Windows on Wesminster*

If anyone doubts the ongoing significance of the 17th¬century Westminster Standards, let them dip into this outstanding work that brings this classic document into words that suit the 21st-century. The introductory articles are in themselves worth the price of the book. While relativism and contemporary queries confuse reality, the solid truths of God's infallible Word as clearly formulated in the works of the Westminster divines continue to stand the test of time.

O Palmer Robertson

Contents

Preface 7

Introduction 11

Preface to *The Westminster Standards in Modern English* 17

Essays About the Westminster Standards

History

Extraordinary Providences of an Enduring Standard
(Richard D. Phillips) 21

The Westminster Standards in the Making:
Stanley Gower, a Westminster Divine (Kevin J. Bidwell)... 37

Worship

The Westminster Standards and Public Worship
(David E. Gilbert)..................................... 59

The Westminster Standards and the Christian Sabbath
(George Swinnock, with an introduction by Kevin J. Bidwell)
.... 83

The Westminster Standards and the Sacraments
(Andy J. Young).. 99

Family Worship and Church Government

The Westminster Standards and Family Worship: Maintaining
True Religion in the Home (Chad T. Bailey) 121

The Westminster Standards and Church Government
(Guy Prentiss Waters)................................. 141

The Westminster Standards in Modern English

The Westminster Standards in Modern English
  including the Creeds. 167

The Westminster Confession of Faith in Modern English . . . 171

The Westminster Larger Catechism in Modern English 227

The Westminster Shorter Catechism In Modern English. . . . 315

The Creeds. 341

    The Apostles' Creed 343

    The Nicene Creed (AD 381). 345

    The Athanasian Creed 347

    The Definition of the Council of Chalcedon (AD 451). . . . 351

Preface

Benjamin Warfield recounted the story of an army officer stationed in an American city during a time of violent riots. The officer observed a man passing through these chaotic scenes with unusual calmness and confidence. As the soldier watched the man, he was surprised to see the man approach him and abruptly query, 'What is the chief end of man?' When the officer said, 'Man's chief end is to glorify God and to enjoy Him forever,' the man replied, 'I knew you were a Shorter Catechism boy!' To this came the answer, 'That's just what I was thinking of you.'

For the last three and a half centuries, the Westminster Standards have trained generations of men and women to live with courageous peace, holy intention, and confident hope. These precious documents trace the pathway of faith and obedience that God reveals in his Word. Like a building with a thousand windows, the confession and catechisms produced by the Westminster divines radiate the clear light of Christ in every direction, inviting the reader to come and worship the Lord.

The English Parliament convened the Westminster Assembly in 1643 in the midst of great political, theological, and ecclesiastical tensions exacerbated by the reign of Charles I. Originally called to revise the Thirty-Nine Articles of the Church of England, the divines meeting at Westminster Abbey soon found themselves crafting doctrinal and ethical standards to unify the English Church and Scottish Kirk under the banner of biblical, Reformed Christianity. The Westminster Assembly had a rich heritage from which to draw, including the writings of theologians such as John Calvin, William Perkins, and James Ussher. Though both Episcopalians and Congregationalists were represented at the assembly, Presbyterians dominated its proceedings and the vision of church life that it presented in its final documents.

One of the ironies of history is that the rise of Oliver Cromwell as a military commander and eventually Lord Protector meant that the English government never officially implemented the Reformed Presbyterian system of the Westminster Standards. However, the confession, catechisms, and directories were taken up by the Scottish Kirk in earnest. Despite the brutal persecution imposed on Scottish Covenanters during the late seventeenth-century, the Westminster Standards have continued to be a vital force in Reformed and Presbyterian Christianity around the world to this day.

The queen of Westminster documents is the Westminster Confession of Faith. Completed and submitted to Parliament in December 1646, *The Humble Advice of the Assembly of Divines ... Concerning a Confession of Faith* would have Scripture proof-texts added a few months later (at the insistence of Parliament) to become the confession as we know it today. Its thirty-three chapters open up the doctrines of divine revelation, God, his decree, creation, providence, man's fall into sin and misery, the covenant of grace, Christ's saving work, the application of salvation, life of the church, and last things. It was much in demand, and by the end of the seventeenth century it had been printed in forty editions.

The theology of the confession has illuminated the minds of many people through the catechisms that accompanied it. Efforts to produce a catechism in 1645 and 1646 led the divines to realize they needed two catechisms: one simpler for children and one fuller in exposition. The Larger Catechism was substantially completed by October 1647 (with Scripture proofs in July 1648). Its 196 questions and answers provide rich instruction for teachers and preachers of God's word. Especially noteworthy are its detailed analyses of the Ten Commandments:

an entire ethical system in catechetical form. After the body of the Larger Catechism was written, the divines produced a smaller version by November 1647 (with Scripture proofs in April 1648). The Shorter Catechism presents an excellent condensation of Reformed confessional truths in 107 questions and answers for memorization and study by youth. It opens with the grand statement that introduced the army officer to his new friend, that the main purpose of human life is 'to glorify God and to enjoy him forever.'

The God-centered Christianity summarized in the Westminster Standards energizes the worship, holiness, and missions of Reformed Christians to this day. Therefore, it is a delight to see this volume come to print. May God use the modernized English edition of the Westminster Standards to help new generations to embrace their heritage of Reformation truth derived from God's holy word.

Joel R. Beeke

Introduction

The *Westminster Standards* are one of the finest summaries of the Christian faith penned by the church in her long history. Drawn up by the Westminster Assembly (1643-1653) they traditionally comprise the *Westminster Confession of Faith*, along with the 196 questions of the *Larger Catechism* and the 107 questions of the *Shorter Catechism*, and also *The Directory for the Public Worship of God* and *The Form of Presbyterial Church Government* and *The Directory for Family Worship*. In this book we will use the term *Westminster Standards* to mean the *Confession* and the *Larger and Shorter Catechisms,* which were approved by the Church of Scotland in 1648.

To many Christians this will seem to be something of historical interest only. Why is it that these doctrinal standards are so little known and used by the greater part of the church today? There are many possible answers to this question. A neglect of church history and consequent ignorance of how and why the magisterial Confessions arose is doubtless a factor. There is a contemporary lack of interest in doctrine in many parts of the church, especially where it might hinder attempts at unity. Perhaps most significantly, faced with a culture that is increasingly opposed to the idea of objective truth, some feel that the clear statements of the *Standards* are simply too provocative.

This book has been borne out of a love for the church and the honour of the Triune God through the Lord Jesus Christ. It is as a pastor, a minister of the gospel, that I write this introduction. On one occasion a university student who worshipped with us explained that she came to a saving knowledge of Christ during our catechism class. This weekly class before our morning Lord's Day service expounds the *Westminster Standards* in order to provide an explanation of what the church believes and why. This student had been brought up in a Christian home, but it was in the catechism class that she saw how the elements of biblical truth could be brought together harmoniously. Her mind was informed and her heart moved so that she was given an assurance of salvation. That got my attention!

Practically, in our local setting in Sheffield, England, we seek to disseminate these peerless statements of the Christian faith, but an immediate problem became apparent to us. The original documents, which were first produced by the Westminster Assembly in London and published in the 1640s, were available to us only in eighteenth-century English (the most common printed form of the *Standards* is the 1728 edition). As far as we were able to determine, the *Confession* and the two *Catechisms* intact, without revisions, amendments or added proof texts in modern English could not be readily found. We set out to change this, initially for our own congregational use.

What was our aim? It was simply to preserve the original integrity of these documents and their proof-texts through light editorial changes to remove the seventeenth and eighteenth-century English and to insert the common English used today. It was perhaps a naive venture because it proved to be more demanding and extensive in scope than we imagined at first, but it has been achieved. No doctrinal changes have been introduced. The numbers of people involved in proofreading, editing, formatting and encouragement in this project are more than it is possible to list. You know who you are; thank you.

Certain alterations were uncomplicated in the change from the original text to modern English. For example, where *Holy Ghost* was used it has been uniformly altered to *Holy Spirit*. Original words have been preserved where possible and occasional wording in square brackets is included for the sake of clarity. Nevertheless, some words needed to be changed. Most people would not know these words which are found in the original of the *Westminster Standards*: vouchsafes; supererogate; contemn; oblation; keeping of stews (they mean: promises; go beyond duty; disdain; offering; keeping of brothels). Our purpose in updating the language was to enhance the overall comprehension and usability of the *Standards*.

It is a personal joy for me that this project has grown. The completed *Westminster Standards* are included in this book because we want Christians to read them and church ministers and elders to teach from them. We have included a small selection of the most prominent creeds as well, with the hope that Christians will become more familiar with them (the *Apostles'*, *Nicene* and *Athanasian* creeds are included, along with the *Creed of Chalcedon*). As the project developed, the suggestion was made that we should seek to get this published for a wider audience and also include a number of essays. Our hope is that the essays will further enrich our readers and whet their appetite for the truths contained in the *Standards* themselves.

The essays have been written by a range of authors with this in common: all are ordained ministers, who labour on the frontline in pastoral and teaching ministry (the one exception is the essay on the Christian Sabbath by the Puritan George Swinnock). Working with these men in the editing and proofreading process has been an honour. It is our intention to equip readers with the historical background to the theology and practice that lay behind the *Confession* and *Catechisms*, in order to fuel further reformation of the church in our day. We have sought to include the primary emphases that underlie the *Standards*. The seven essay titles are:

Extraordinary Providences of an Enduring Standard (Richard D. Phillips, Senior minister of Second Presbyterian Church, Greenville, SC (part of the Presbyterian Church of America)).

The Westminster Standards in the Making: Stanley Gower, A Westminster Divine (Kevin J. Bidwell Minister of Sheffield Presbyterian Church (part of the Evangelical Presbyterian Church in England and Wales)).

The Westminster Standards and Public Worship (David E. Gilbert, minister of Grace Presbyterian Church, Douglasville, GA (part of the Presbyterian Church of America)).

The Westminster Standards and the Christian Sabbath (George Swinnock (1627-1673), English Nonconformist minister).

The Westminster Standards and the Sacraments (Andy J. Young, church planting minister of Oxford Evangelical Presbyterian Church, part of the Evangelical Presbyterian Church in England and Wales).

The Westminster Standards and Family Worship (Chad T. Bailey, assistant minister at Second Presbyterian Church, Greenville, SC).

The Westminster Standards and Church Government (Guy Prentiss Waters, associate professor of New Testament at Reformed Theological Seminary, Jackson, MS).

The combination of both British and American ministers writing together signals a joint desire for the recovery of truth in the wider church on both sides of the Atlantic Ocean. Each of these ministers labour in a Presbyterian church, but we do not consider the *Westminster Standards* to be exclusively Presbyterian.

We recognize that copies of the *Westminster Standards* in modern English are readily available in the USA and in use by Presbyterian denominations. The preface to the *Westminster Confession of Faith and Catechisms with Proof Texts* as adopted by the Presbyterian Church in America helpfully explains significant changes that have been made, in contrast to the original documents.[1] The Orthodox Presbyterian Church have laboured for decades to study and revise the proof texts. We do not intend to detract from this sterling work that has sought to serve the church in the USA and elsewhere. We believe provision of the original text of the *Westminster Standards* in modern

---

[1] *The Westminster Confession of Faith and Catechisms with Proof Texts*, as adopted by the Presbyterian Church in America, Preface, Lawrenceville, GA: Christian Education & Publications, 2007, pp vii-xii. It can also be accessed at http://www.pcaac.org/resources/wcf/

English, along with its unaltered proof texts, is hopefully a welcome resource for all parts of the Christian church. Our hope is that our readers will join with us in prayer for the recovery of biblically-anchored public worship and the use of these catechisms in public instruction and in family worship.

The *Westminster Larger Catechism* was specifically designed for public teaching by ministers and its doctrine envelops the doctrine of the church. We do well to remember the famed comment by Samuel Rutherford (1600-1661) as to the necessity for two catechisms instead of one; he contended at the Westminster Assembly for two, because he believed that it had been very difficult 'to dress up milk and meat both in one dish.' In other words the church needs to know, use and teach both catechisms for its spiritual vitality.

I conclude with the words of a favourite theologian, Professor John Murray (1898-1975). He wrote in an essay on 'The Importance and Relevance of the *Westminster Confession*' that: 'No creed of the Christian Church is comparable to that of Westminster in respect of skill with which fifteen centuries of Christian thought have been preserved, and at the same time examined anew and clarified in the light of that fuller understanding of God's Word which the Holy Spirit has imparted ... in the category to which the Confession belongs, it has no peer.'[1]

Our desire is that future generations will continue to enjoy the fruit of the labours of the Westminster Assembly, especially that preserved through the *Westminster Standards*. Such hope for the furtherance of Bible doctrine is anticipated in Psalm 22:30-31: *Posterity shall serve him; it shall be told of the Lord to the coming generation; they shall come and proclaim his righteousness to a people yet unborn, that he has done it.*

Kevin J. Bidwell
Sheffield, England

---

[1] John Murray, *Collected Writings of John Murray*, Volume One *Claims of Truth*, Edinburgh: Banner of Truth, 1976, reprinted 2001, 317-318.

Preface to *The Westminster Standards in Modern English*

There is something about structure that makes learning—and memorization in particular—more manageable. Years ago, as I approached the first year of law school, someone mentioned to me that an effective way to handle the complex subjects ahead was to memorize the table of contents in each of the textbooks. The idea was that, week-by-week, as information came from the lectures, the material would neatly fit into the structure outlined in each text. It was a version of thinking along with the authors and the professors, and it proved to be a helpful tool in making it through school.

And now, many years of law practice since, the procedure continues to be useful. As new principles come along, either from statutory law or case decisions, there is almost always a place to put those rules or rulings in the structure of my thinking about a subject. New concepts drop into the memorized outline at logical places.

Interestingly, the *Westminster Standards* has been a similar resource in my own life, providing a reformed framework that has proven invaluable for my personal time in the Word, in Bible teaching, and in my role as a Ruling Elder in the Presbyterian Church in America. The structure adopted by the Westminster Assembly, from beginning to end, is logical and understandable, making it equally valuable to both laymen and ordained clergy. Little wonder that the *Confession* has traveled through nearly 400 years of history with usefulness, clarity, and relevance.

Among the many reasons this is the case, one is the wisdom of its authors in the outline of the theological system it declares.

Of course, the reformed and orthodox tradition is grounded in Word and Spirit, with Christ as its cornerstone. We proclaim Christ and his benefits, not the *Confession* and its structure. But still, as it concerns the Christian faith, the *Confession* is particularly useful in organizing and presenting the truths of the Word. In that sense, it is akin to the table of contents in a textbook.

As an illustration, a thirty-something young man and I were recently interacting about a near-crippling burden of anger he had carried for many years. He believed that it began with the divorce of his parents, and his anger had simmered and grown inwardly through his school years and early adulthood. In his early 30s the anger spilled over into essentially every aspect of his life: marriage, children, co-workers, friends, even with complete strangers. He said he believed in God, but he quickly added that his recent church experience was having no impact on how he thought or felt. If God were real and in his life, he was angry about the way things turned out.

What this young man appeared to need was a clear way of thinking about the sovereign hand of God as it had worked out in his life. So in simple words we began to work through what the Bible says about God, His decrees, providence, sin, and Christ as the Mediator. In understandable terms we discussed atonement, imputed righteousness, propitiation, and expiation. We talked about sanctification, perseverance, and assurance.

Our conversation took place at the end of a conference table as we sat 90 degrees to one another. When he first began to relate his story, he rarely made eye contact, staring away from where I sat just a few feet away. As we walked through these great principles of faith—which was generally tracking relevant portions of the table of contents of the *Confession*—his gaze shifted. He began to pay attention to the paper where I was diagraming aspects of the substitution of Christ's obedience

Preface to The Westminster Standards in Modern English 19

for our failed efforts to obey, and finally he began to make eye contact in earnest.

My heart sang as this young friend laid his burden down. It brought to mind the burden-releasing experience of Christian in *The Pilgrim's Progress*. Remember the account:

> Now I saw in my dream that the highway up which Christian was to go was fenced on either side with a wall; and that wall was called 'Salvation.'
>
> *In that day shall this song be sung in the land of Judah; We have a strong city; salvation will God appoint for walls and bulwarks* Isaiah 26:1.
>
> Up this way, therefore, did burdened Christian run; but not without great difficulty, because of the load on his back.
>
> He ran thus till he came at a place somewhat ascending; and upon that place stood a cross, and a little below, in the bottom, a sepulchre. So I saw in my dream, that just as Christian came up to the cross, his burden loosed from off his shoulders, and fell from off his back, and began to tumble; and so continued to do till it came to the mouth of the sepulchre, where it fell in, and I saw it no more.
>
> Then was Christian glad and lightsome, and said, with a merry heart,
>
> 'He hath given me rest by his sorrow, And life by his death.'
>
> Then he stood still awhile to look and wonder; for it was very surprising to him, that the sight of the cross should thus ease him of his burden. He looked therefore, and looked again, even till the springs that were in his head sent the waters down his cheeks.

In a timeless way Bunyan's seventeenth-century allegory communicates with powerful, though to some degree, dated diction. My early-30s friend may at some point take up *The Pilgrim's Progress*, make his way through it, see its message, and find inspiration in it, but at the time of our conversation what he needed was a clear twenty-first-century word about the framework of faith in plain English. That reality has given me great enthusiasm for *The Westminster Standards in Modern English*.

The organizational system of the *Confession* is both timeless and helpful, and now this amplified text will make its usage doubly beneficial for believers who want for themselves, and for others with whom they interact, a clear word concerning the Christian message.

Joseph H. Fowler
Douglasville, Georgia
May 31, 2016

Extraordinary Providences of an Enduring Standard

Rev. Dr Richard D. Phillips

In a sharp irony from church history, one of the decisive events of the English Civil War occurred eight years before the first ringing of cold steel. In the 1630s, many Puritans were fleeing to escape the religious tyranny of Archbishop William Laud, England's chief prelate under King Charles I. Venting his considerable spite towards the Puritans, Laud in 1634 seized a convoy of ships headed for New England and prohibited the dispirited passengers from leaving. For this reason, the man who would later oversee Laud's execution was barred from exiting the country. By Laud's capricious malice, young Oliver Cromwell was forced off his ship back onto English soil, later to lead Parliament's army in victory over the royalists and to direct the condemnation not only of Laud but also of Charles I.[1]

This incident involving the Puritans' future battle captain is just one of many extraordinary providences that were instrumental in shaping the *Westminster Confession of Faith* and *Catechisms*. Every doctrinal standard is of course a product of its times, and often the influence of local events will determine its value to the church. When it comes to the *Westminster Standards*, the remarkable setting of the English Civil War and

---

[1] Cited from Philip Schaff, *The Creeds of Christendom*, Volume 1, Grand Rapids: Baker, 1983, 714.

the seventeenth century as a whole served to give it an enduring quality the like of which is not likely to be repeated. To recount the sovereign hand of God over the *Westminster Standards* is important today, when some members of Presbyterian and Reformed churches would doubt how well a 370 year-old document could serve as our doctrinal yardstick. Occasionally, we hear calls for a new confession or the admission of more modern statements of faith to come alongside the *Westminster Confession*. However, if we will travel back to the years after Cromwell was kept in England, years of civil and spiritual conflict that sharpened both the Puritan sword and spirit, we may remember what a singular set of circumstances has given us the most excellent of all Reformed confessions, the value of which will endure until Christ comes again.

In celebrating the powerful circumstances by which God provided the *Westminster Standards*, we must take care to place such providences on a categorically lower plane than those involved in the inspiration and preservation of Holy Scripture. In both its inspiration and its revelation, the Bible involves a naked supernaturalism that sets it uniquely above every other authority. When it comes to the *Westminster Standards*, the working of God is cloaked by natural historical events which combined to provide a remarkably valuable resource to his church. According to Benjamin B. Warfield, the *Westminster Confession* stands at the high-water mark of a long process of doctrinal conflict which had the effect of clarifying and perfecting the church's grasp of biblical teaching. Especially in the Reformation age that preceded Westminster, 'the gem of the gospel was cut and polished, and it is on this account that the enunciation of the gospel in the Reformed Confessions attains its highest purity.'[1] As the culminating expression of the Reformation's dogmatic achievement, 'the *Westminster*

---

1   Benjamin Breckinridge Warfield, *Selected Shorter Writings,* ed John E. Meeter, Volume 2, Phillipsburg: P&R, 1973, 661.

Confession, the product of the Puritan conflict, reaches a perfection of statement never elsewhere achieved.'[1]

The aim of this chapter is to highlight four extraordinary providences involved in the production of the *Westminster Standards* that contribute to their enduring relevance and these should inspire us to grateful appreciation for their unsurpassed expression of biblical doctrine.

An Extraordinary Partnership of Church and State

The Westminster Assembly would never have met except for the long-developing alliance between the English Parliament and the Puritan divines during the tumultuous first half of the seventeenth century. This alliance was forged in the resolve of the Stuart dynasty to assert an absolute monarchy on the nation. James I and his son Charles I sought to summon and dissolve Parliaments at their whim, thus disenfranchising the representative element of national government. At the same time, they sought control over Britain's churches via the Archbishop of Canterbury and his appointed prelates. As early as 1604, in the Hampton Court Conference, newly crowned James I rebuffed the requests of Puritans for moderate church reform and debuted his signature motto: 'No bishop, no king.' From that moment, there could be no doubt that royal autocracy and episcopal tyranny would march hand-in-hand. The result was a partnership between Parliament and Puritans that was heartfelt and determined. In 1640, when the so-called Long Parliament refused to be dissolved by the over-reaching Charles I, these champions of representative government pitted themselves not only against the king's throne but also the bishop's chair.

This brief summary of many dramatic events had the momentous result of Parliament summoning in 1643 an assembly of divines to establish a new foundation for a national church. Determined to rid the nation of haughty bishops, they also feared the suspected Roman Catholicism of the king and his court and

---

[1] Ibid.

loathed the Arminian theology of Laud and his bishops. Thus two great aims motivated the summoning of the Westminster Assembly: the removal of bishops and the defense of Calvinism against Arminian and Roman Catholic theology. These aims coincided precisely with the interests of the Puritans and their pastor/theologians. Thus a most effective and, rare in history, doctrinally harmonious marriage was consummated between Parliament and the Puritan divines in the Westminster Assembly.

Parliament's idea called for an assembly 'of the most grave, pious, learned, and judicious divines of this island' to give advice on the further reformation of England's church.[1] The formal summons went forth on June 12, 1643, gathering the assembly at Westminster Abbey to assist Parliament in erecting a new church government 'as may be most agreeable to God's holy word, and most apt to procure and preserve the peace of the Church at home, and nearer agreement with the Church of Scotland, and other Reformed Churches abroad.' Additionally, the assembly was to act 'for the vindicating and clearing of the doctrine of the Church of England from all false calumnies and aspersions.'[2] The Westminster Assembly therefore consisted of a national endeavor to determine a proper biblical government for the church and to defend Reformed theology from its challengers.

Charged and resourced by the national legislature, the assembly was thus formed of 120 of the most eminent churchmen in the nation (with representatives from every county, the great universities, and the city of London). Starting in July 1643, this body met most weekdays until its last numbered session in 1649 (although the assembly maintained some functions until 1653).

If we consider the possibility of erecting a similar body of theologians today to establish a comprehensive doctrinal standard, we will realize that an endeavor of this scope is not

---

[1] December 1641 motion of Parliament, cited from Robert Letham, *The Westminster Assembly: Reading Its Theology in Historical Context*, Phillipsburg: P&R, 2009, 30.

[2] Cited from William Beveridge, *A Short History of the Westminster Assembly*, ed J. Ligon Duncan, III, Greenville, SC: Reformed Academic Press, 1993, 105-106.

only unlikely but actually inconceivable. Consider the study committees that are created by even the larger Reformed denominations today, which involve a small number of participants who may meet a handful of times and correspond over a series of months. Or consider how unlikely it would be today for a national legislature to invest such a commitment with the aim of upholding and defending biblical truth and practice. The reality is that the establishment of the Westminster Assembly by act of Parliament, thus with the full support of the national government (excepting the king and his party), was an extraordinary providence that facilitated a work of truly enduring value. How rare was the sincere union of the state with the church to promote truly biblical doctrine and practice, and how uncommon it was that both Parliament and Puritans were invested in the cause of biblical truth even at the risk of their lives. Other examples exist of a national assembly, supported and upheld by the government—the Council of Nicaea and the Synod of Dort come to mind, both of which join Westminster in their historic significance—but they belong to a past era the like of which is unforeseen today. The result was, in the words of Chad Van Dixhoorn, 'a truly remarkable text in the history of Christianity,' in which 'all who peruse its pages will find a sure-footed summary of truth for life.'[1]

An Extraordinary Deliverance from Secular Control

The Westminster Assembly's collaboration between church and state involved grave problems, however, along with the benefits. In fact, the assembly was not truly a partner to Parliament but rather a servant. The assembly's charter was 'to consult and advise' the politicians, who alone held the authority to approve and implement its final results. Critics of Westminster waste little time pointing out the ultimate disaster that could only result from this arrangement. Indeed, when Cromwell's

---
[1] Chad Van Dixhoorn, *Confessing the Faith: A Reader's Guide to the Westminster Confession of Faith*, Edinburgh: Banner of Truth, 2014, xviii.

Protectorate gave way to the restoration of the Stuart monarchy in 1660, the marriage between the *Westminster Standards* and the rebel Parliament resulted in the abject failure of its formal aims. Not only did a Presbyterian and Reformed Church of England cease to exist, but it left hardly even a memory in the national consciousness. Some years ago, a friend of mine visited Westminster Abbey and approached the curator for permission to enter the famed Jerusalem Chamber, where the assembly did its work. When asked why, my friend answered with enthusiasm for the great Westminster Assembly. To this, the curator of Westminster Abbey replied that he had never heard of it! So much for the divines enduring achievement in their homeland!

Not only did Parliament's control over the Westminster Assembly doom its attempt to reform the national church, but it also threatened to corrupt the production of the *Confession* itself. It is good to remember that in those days the current notion of the separation of church and state did not exist. Moreover, the members of Parliament were individually and corporately committed to a biblical and Reformed cause. Yet it remained the case that an assembly of church leaders ultimately subservient to the secular authorities would not likely have provided a standard worthy of our loyalty today.

It is in this respect that a second great providence intervened to rescue the *Westminster Standards* from the very authority that had brought it into being. In the background of the assembly a great war was taking place between Parliament's army of Roundheads and the royalist Cavaliers. And, to our enduring debt as Reformed Christians, the war was going quite poorly for Parliament. 1643 witnessed a number of Royalist victories and a threat to London itself. Moreover, late in the year, Charles I worked out a treaty in Ireland that permitted not only his professional troops to return to fight in England but also threatened the appearance of armed bands of papist Irishmen roaming the land. It became steadily clear in London, therefore, that help must be secured to avoid stalemate or even a disastrous defeat.

The help that Parliament needed lay to the north, across the border in Scotland. It was with the aid of Scots arms, together with the rise of Oliver Cromwell to leadership, that Parliament was able to win the English Civil War. The Scots, however, entered the war at a price. That price was the Solemn League and Covenant, signed by Parliament on September 25, 1643, effecting not merely a military but also a spiritual alliance between the two countries. This alliance with Scotland had two revolutionary effects on the Westminster Assembly. First, instead of debating what biblical form of church government would replace the episcopal bishoprics, the assembly was now charged to establish an explicitly Presbyterian form of church government so as to foster unity with the Scottish Kirk. Second, the work of the assembly was delivered from the interference and control of Parliament over its ultimate product, the *Westminster Confession of Faith* and its *Catechisms*.

It would be historically accurate to state that, even after the intervention of the Scots, the Westminster Assembly continued under the authority and ultimate approval of the English Parliament. It would be fair to add, however, that the church commission sent south by Scotland effectively mediated on the assembly's behalf to secure Parliament's compliance. In short, the extraordinary intellectual and spiritual resources of the English Puritans at their height became partnered with Scots divines who had long since proven their valor for truth and the purity of their Reformed convictions. Loraine Boettner described the Presbyterian Church of Scotland as 'the daughter of the Reformed Church of Geneva,' due to the exile of John Knox and other Scots reformers in Geneva and their tutelage under the great reformer John Calvin. Boettner observed that as a result, the Scottish Reformation 'was far more consistent and radical than in England, and it resulted in the establishment of a Calvinistic Presbyterianism in which Christ alone was recognized as the head of the Church.'[1] And what divines the

---

1 Loraine Boettner, *The Reformed Doctrine of Predestination*, Phillipsburg: P&R, 1981, 374.

Scots sent to London! Included in their party were Alexander Henderson (after Knox considered the greatest man of the Scottish Reformation), Samuel Rutherford, and George Gillespie, each of whom deserves to be placed in the first rank of Reformed Christians, scholars, and spiritual leaders.

With the Scots commissioners joining in the assembly's deliberations and representing them before Parliament, the Solemn League and Covenant effectively freed the Westminster Assembly from harmful secular interference. After all, Parliament had now bound itself by treaty to produce a confession that would be agreeable to the Scots. This is not to say that the secular influence on the assembly ceased with the Scots' arrival. (We have already noted how Parliament's future embrace of the Stuart kings spelled demise for the *Westminster Standards* in England.) But so far as they are considered for the broader church—especially as mediated to the world by the Church of Scotland and its partners in the United States—the Solemn League and Covenant preserved the integrity of the *Westminster Confession* and *Catechisms* for the benefit of centuries to come. What an extraordinary providence was at work! Formed and facilitated on a vast scope with national resources by virtue of the English Civil War, the *Westminster Standards* were then delivered from the control of that very government by the Solemn League and Covenant and at the same time transformed into a doctrinal labor of international significance. According to Warfield, 'by the Solemn League and Covenant, therefore, the work of the Assembly of divines was revolutionized ... and the real work of the Assembly became possible.'[1]

Extraordinary Men in their Perilous Times

A consideration of the remarkable nature of the Westminster Assembly has to begin with its historical context, as we have done. But our reflection must also highlight the extraordinary divines

---

[1] Benjamin Breckinridge Warfield, *Works*, Vol. 6, 'The Westminster Assembly and Its Work,' Grand Rapids: Baker, 1932, reprint 2000, 34–35.

themselves and their singular fitness for the task committed to them. In the words of the famous Puritan Richard Baxter:

> The divines there congregated were men of eminent learning and godliness, ministerial ability and fidelity, and being not worthy to be one of them myself, I may the more freely speak the truth … the Christian world since the days of the apostles had never a Synod of more excellent divines.[1]

It is never wise to idolize men in their gifts and achievements, yet for a sober assessment of the *Westminster Confession* we should acknowledge the uncommon excellence of its authors. A great many were outstanding scholars who attained an eminence of learning that would be celebrated today. They belonged to a time that highly valued learning and was devoid of the distractions of our age. The Puritan pastors who were educated at Cambridge, the movement's cradle, began their college studies at an average age of sixteen. In addition to mastering theology, they were honed in logic, rhetoric and languages. William Beveridge describes those gathered at Westminster as 'some of the most gifted men of their day,' including scholars renowned throughout Europe.[2] Robert Letham comments: 'There is little doubt that the Assembly had biblical, patristic, and scholastic learning to spare.' He cites the example of Lazarus Seaman as a representative member, who 'carried in his pocket an unpointed Hebrew text of the Old Testament for daily reading.'[3] Describing the more heralded scholars, Philip Schaff notes William Twisse as 'full of learning and subtle speculative genius;' Cornelius Burgess as 'an eminent debater and valiant defender of Presbyterianism;' John Lightfoot as 'the greatest rabbinical scholar of his age;' and said of Thomas Goodwin, 'his great attainments in scholarship and the range and variety of his thoughts astonish us when we read his writings.'[4]

---

1 Philip Schaff, *The Creeds of Christendom*, Volume 1, Grand Rapids: Baker, 1996, 729.
2 William Beveridge, *A Short History of the Westminster Assembly*, ed, J. Ligon Duncan, III, Greenville: Reformed Academic Press, 1993, 19.
3 Robert Letham, *The Westminster Assembly*, 33.
4 Philip Schaff, *The Creeds of Christendom*, 1:740–3.

This is not to say that the Westminster divines were cloistered academics. Over eighty percent of them were active pastors serving in pulpits. Many of them were accomplished Christian educators, especially those who had honed the skill of catechism-writing that would prove so important to the Westminster Assembly. Herbert Palmer had written eight different catechisms during his prior career, enabling him to play a leading role in the preparation, prior to the drafting of the *Shorter Catechism*.

For all their great learning, the Westminster divines are more fittingly known for the fervor of their piety. William Gouge began in college his life-long habit of reading fifteen chapters of Scripture daily. Rising each morning at 4:00 a.m. for prayer and study, Gouge made the love of Christ his lifelong occupation. He wrote: 'When I look upon myself, I see nothing but emptiness and weakness; but when I look upon Christ, I see nothing but fullness and sufficiency.'[1] Joining him in the Westminster Assembly were a galaxy of writers whose devotional classics are devoured by Christians today, including Samuel Rutherford, Jeremiah Burroughs, Thomas Goodwin, and Obadiah Sedgwick.

Given the spiritual intensity of the Westminster divines, it is not surprising that they further excelled in courage and conviction. Their mere presence in the assembly was a criminal act in the eyes of the kings, and most of them had earlier acted boldly in opposing the abuses of Archbishop Laud. Several were offered plum bishoprics by the king if they would abandon the Puritan cause, yet all refused. When the tables were turned in 1662, and the restored Charles II ejected all non-conforming ministers from their pulpits and livings, almost all of the remaining members of the assembly suffered persecution rather than violate their convictions.[2]

The example of the Scots commissioner Alexander Henderson

---

[1] David Hall, *Windows on Westminster,* Norcross, GA: Great Commission Publications, 1993, 73.
[2] For more information about the lives of the Westminster divines, see William Barker, *Puritan Profiles,* Ross-Shire, Scotland: Mentor, 1996.

stands out even in this splendid company. In 1638, during the crisis that birthed Scotland's National Covenant, Henderson was moderating the General Assembly. Charles I had dispatched one of his leading soldiers, the Marquis of Hamilton, to ensure that this assembly should not act against his bishops. It turned out that this very topic was before the Scottish Assembly, so the Marquis rose and informed the presbyters that such a resolution was forbidden by the king. Henderson politely thanked the Marquis, but informed him that their allegiance to Britain's king was superseded by a higher loyalty to the Sovereign of heaven. When the motion returned to the floor, the Marquis rose, saber in hand, and ordered the assembly dissolved. Seeing that a number of members were fearfully preparing to follow the king's representative, who had stalked out of the chamber, Henderson calmly spoke again. In the words of David Hall: 'Henderson commended the Marquis for serving his sovereign faithfully; he then reminded the Assembly that they were commissioners of a greater king, and urged them to follow the example of the king's servant and representative by obeying, even to death, the words of King Jesus.'[1]

This incident reminds us that the Westminster divines brought not only their learning and piety, but they came to the assembly with their lives on the line. How different are our more comfortable but less character-forming times! Not only did the historical context of the Westminster Assembly include a slow pace of life that encouraged study and the nurture of piety in the spiritual incubator of seventeenth-century Puritanism, but the tangible dangers to life and liberty inspired clarity in the minds of outlaw theologians like those who met in the Jerusalem Chamber. Remembering those extraordinary men with thanks to God and appreciating their fertile but perilous times, we may better appreciate how careful, how faithful, how searching, and how courageous are their words which set down for posterity the sacred doctrines of Holy Scripture.

---

[1] David Hall, *Windows on Westminster*, 51-2.

An Extraordinary Perch Overlooking Reformation History

A final characteristic of the Westminster Assembly that is seldom appreciated is their remarkable unity in the faith which they were called to express. The fact is that the Westminster divines were not summoned to work out amidst controversy what doctrines would be taught in the churches of England. Rather, their charge was to defend and assert an already established Reformed faith in which every member was already steeped. The strong differences of view when it came to church government—with the well-identified Presbyterian, Independent, and Erastian parties—should not convey the impression of general discord. When it came to the theology which occupies the great majority of the *Westminster Confession* and *Catechisms*, they were unified in a way that has seldom been repeated in generations since. This commitment to Reformed orthodoxy permeated not only the Puritans, but extended widely throughout the Church of England, including its then-existing doctrinal creed, in full harmony with the great Reformed churches of Continental Europe.[1] Warfield writes: 'The doctrine of the Church of England was everywhere recognized as in itself soundly Reformed, and needing only to be protected from corrupting misinterpretations.'[2]

One reason for this depth and breadth of doctrinal unity among the Westminster divines was the historical perch from which they overlooked the greatest doctrinal century in church history, the sixteenth century with its amazing Reformation. Preceding them in close historical proximity were the examples and writings of Martin Luther, Huldrich Zwingli, John Calvin, Martin Bucer, and Heinrich Bullinger, to name only the most

---

[1] It is true that radicals and fanatics abounded in the church scene at the time of Westminster. Yet, far from infiltrating the Assembly, the evident danger of these excesses served further to unify the divines. See Samuel T. Logan, Jr., 'The Context and Work of the Assembly' in *A Commemoration of the Westminster Assembly*, John L. Carson & David W. Hall eds, Edinburgh: Banner of Truth, 1994, 27–46.

[2] B. B. Warfield, *Works*, 6:13.

eminent names from a galaxy of great preachers, writers, and scholars. Moreover, the previous great Reformation confessions had erected a vantage point from which the Westminster divines could soberly consider nuance and pursue balance in working out doctrinal issues. The previous century had seen the First and Second *Helvetic Confessions*, the *Scots Confession*, the *Heidelberg Catechism*, and the *Belgic Confession*, among many more, all of which merit our study today. The seventeenth century had begun with the Synod of Dort, an equal to the Westminster Assembly in the eminence of its scholars. While the *Canons of Dort* did not express the kind of comprehensive standard envisioned at Westminster, it did work out in detail many of the primary controversies asserted against Calvinist doctrine. The divines also looked back on the titanic struggles of the English Reformation, benefiting from both its *Thirty-Nine Articles* and Archbishop Ussher's *Irish Articles*. From this providential viewpoint, the Westminster divines were not only the most well-equipped scholars to articulate a sound and comprehensive doctrinal system but they were also granted the best perspective from which to do so.

Consider the contrast with the state of theology in our own twenty-first century. If Reformed scholars today look back over our previous century or so, we see division not unity, the splintering of faith rather than its consolidation, widespread retreat before worldly assault rather than heroic advance, and the spread of error throughout our churches, ranging from fanaticism to humanistic skepticism. Even among Reformed churches adhering to the Reformation-era standards, our tendency to split rather than unite testifies to a time of doctrinal weakness. In God's will, many profitable perspectives have resulted from our troubled modernity and postmodernity, including genuine advances in areas of biblical theology. By necessity, we have been honed in the arts of polemics and the science of apologetics—worthy endeavors in their proper sphere. But the task of authoritative doctrinal consolidation is outside our reach. For the task to which the Westminster Assembly was given—that of synthesizing and perfecting the Reformed confession of faith arising from the Protestant Reformation—their age was singularly fashioned by God in equipping them to perform an enduring service to the church.

Because the Westminster divines were not debating the doctrine of the church, their labors and skills were devoted to perfecting the formulations and language of Reformed doctrine. Warfield comments: 'Doctrinally they were in complete fundamental harmony, and in giving expression to their common faith needed only to concern themselves to state it truly, purely, and with its polemic edges well-turned out towards the chief assailants of Reformed doctrine, in order to satisfy the minds of all.'[1] Van Dixhoorn hails the *Westminster Confession* as 'the wisest of creeds in its teaching and the finest in its doctrinal expression,'[2] precisely because of the providential setting in which such remarkably capable men labored. Moreover, the unity and the deep perspective with which the divines approached their work enabled them to treat not only foundational doctrines which already had been made reasonably clear, but also to take up other fundamental matters that are difficult and which require the most sober construction and expression. Examples of these challenging topics are the *Confession's* classic exposition of the decree of God and its studiously careful treatment of the sacraments.

Yet, for all these extraordinary providences—involving historical context, divine intervention, singular equipping, and theological perspective—critics will reply that the Westminster Assembly still failed: it did not establish an enduring standard of doctrine and church government for the Church of England. The answer to this challenge would be that it does not seem that God intended the *Westminster Standards* to be limited to official status in one nation. Instead, Warfield provides his assessment of the enduring achievement of the Westminster divines:

---

[1] B. B. Warfield, *Works*, Volume 6, 55–56.
[2] Chad Van Dixhoorn, *Confessing the Faith*, xix.

By the inherent power of their truth, they have held sway and won a way for themselves to the real triumph of the voluntary adhesion of multitudes of Christian men. It is honor enough for the Westminster Assembly that it has provided this multitude of voluntary adherents with a practicable platform of representative government on Scriptural lines, and a sober and sane directly of worship eminently spiritual in tone; and, above all, with the culminating Reformed Confession of faith, and a Catechism preeminent for the exactness of its definitions of faith and the faithfulness of its ethical precepts.[1]

The Window of Westminster

How should we today, especially those of us spiritually downstream from Westminster by virtue of our Presbyterian heritage, respond to these extraordinary providences of God in providing this enduring doctrinal standard? The first answer is that we should gratefully receive it, benefiting from its precepts, and faithfully uphold the doctrine we receive by means of the *Westminster Standards*. This does not mean that we should revere the *Westminster Confession* above Scripture or grant it authority to approve the Bible rather than the other way around. We must remain, in keeping with the *Confession's* teaching, Bible men and women far beyond our adherence to this or any other statement of the church. Indeed, precisely because of our higher allegiance to God's Word, we should yield to the *Westminster Standards* the influence they deserve in helping us to study the Bible, understand and teach it, and apply it practically to our lives.

Ministers of the gospel today are bound to quarrel with the *Westminster Standards* on points of varying detail and significance, and we should submit ourselves to the courts of the church for the approval of our subscription. Yet, seeing the extraordinary context in which the *Confession* was birthed, the singularly capable and godly men who labored so long and hard

---

[1] B. B. Warfield, *Works*, Volume 6, 72

on the words that speak to us still, and the uniquely profitably theological perspective from which they wrote, those who have sworn to the *Westminster Standards* should depart from it only in the most careful, humble, and hesitant manner. Rather than claiming to be humble while glibly dismissing so extraordinary a blessing from God, let us rather desire to be taught from those eminent, godly, and courageous divines before we hastily speak in the presence of their *Confession*.

The excellence of the *Westminster Confession* and *Catechisms* does not preclude their amendment, as has occurred many times in subsequent history. For instance, an American Presbyterian very likely vows a form of the *Confession* that takes a few but significant departures from the original. When such need is envisioned in the future, our awareness of just how extraordinary are these *Standards* ought to persuade us to amend with a care, expenditure of time and effort, and spirituality of mind which the Westminster Assembly itself—not to mention its subject matter of God's Word—so eminently deserves.

Finally, the extraordinary providences in the Westminster Assembly should inspire us to take up whatever work the Lord should give us in a manner that profits from their example. We see in the men of Westminster a devotion to the cause of God's Word, courage in the face of worldly scorn and threats, and personal devotion to Jesus Christ in heart and life that we may imitate to our great benefit. And if we have the great privilege of serving in the doctrinal and spiritual legacy of the *Westminster Confession*, let us aim to be worthy of the truth it so wonderfully lays bare, setting this enduring standard before us not as a painting to admire but as a window through which to more clearly see the grace and glory of its true Master, the Savior Jesus Christ.

The Westminster Standards in the Making: Stanley Gower, a Westminster Divine

Kevin J. Bidwell

Question: What is required in the third commandment?

Answer: The third commandment requires, that the name of God, his titles, attributes, ordinances, the Word, sacraments, prayer, oaths, vows, lots, his work, and whatsoever else there is whereby he makes himself known, be holily and reverently used in thought, meditation, word, and writing; by a holy profession, and answerable conversation, to the glory of God, and the good of ourselves, and others.

The Westminster Larger Catechism, Question 112.

In many ways, this answer captures the heartbeat of the work of the Westminster Assembly. This seventeenth-century assembly, which was a synod within the Church of England, with some Scottish commissioners, produced a *Confession of Faith* with 33 chapters and two robust catechisms for practical and pastoral instruction. It is pertinent to cite this answer because Rev. Stanley Gower served on a committee for the Westminster Assembly, one that was directly responsible for the catechism's answers on the Third Commandment. Both the life of Gower and the answer from this question on this particular Commandment, encapsulate the ideal of church reform, both then and now. The church must conduct all of its worship and activity in a manner that is 'holily and reverently ... to the glory of God, and the good of ourselves, and others.'

No theology or doctrine ever arises out of a vacuum. The enduring legacy of the *Westminster Standards* is the purpose of this book and essay. However, we need to grasp the context for the making of these *Standards*, in order to better appreciate the rich biblical theology they contain. This theology was forged on the anvil, with a furnace, hammer and file, metaphorically speaking. The English Civil War formed part of the background of this historical canvas, during which reformation was spreading in the church across Europe, with Roman Catholic leaders reluctantly relinquishing their religious and political power. And yet these *Standards* uphold timeless truths.

Chad Van Dixhoorn writes that 'many consider ... the *Westminster Standards*, as the finest and most enduring statements of early modern Reformed theology.'[1] Similarly, the professor of church theology, John Murray, considered the matter of 'the importance and relevance of the *Westminster Confession*.' He concluded that: 'no creed of the Christian Church is comparable to that of Westminster in respect of the skill with which the fruits of fifteen centuries of Christian thought have been preserved, and at the same time examined anew and clarified in the light of that fuller understanding of God's Word which the Holy Spirit has imparted.'[2] Our study therefore, should be the interest of every Christian and in every land.

The primary focus of this essay is to view the making of the *Westminster Standards* through the lens of a single Westminster divine. This should make our study highly personal whereby we should sense Gower's weighty pastoral concerns, and he was undoubtedly representative of his contemporaries. These concerns reflect the serious mindedness of the pastors in his

---

1 Chad Van Dixhoorn, *The Minutes and Papers of the Westminster Assembly, 1643-1652*, Volume 1, Introduction, ed Chad Van Dixhoorn, Oxford, OUP, 2012, 86-87.

2 John Murray, *Collected Writings of John Murray: Volume 1 The Claims of Truth*, Edinburgh: Banner of Truth, 2001, 317.

day. This is a challenge in our time because a lively interest on the subjects of church government, reverent public worship and doctrine seem to be irrelevant in many professing Christian circles. This cannot continue. If congregations neglect these themes which are so clearly elucidated at Westminster, then it could lead to the church's spiritual impoverishment, decline and the acceptance and promotion of false teachings and worse still, potential apostasy.

The life of Gower has a personal connection for the writer: he was the founding pastor of Hill Top Chapel, Sheffield, which is now the home of Sheffield Evangelical Presbyterian Church, where I am the minister. If no theology arises out of a vacuum, the question remains as to what kind of theology should arise.

My overall aim is to awaken a lively interest in the content of these *Standards*, but I intend to give a range of practical, pastoral and theological lessons for further consideration. If the church anticipates the blessing of the Triune God, then we have to act in accordance with the expectations of our God, as revealed in Scripture. In 1 Samuel 2:30, the Lord says *that those who honour me I will honour*. To honour the Lord therefore, in matters of worship, government and doctrine is indeed for 'the glory of God, and the good of ourselves, and others.' It is a sensible aspiration to believe that the *Westminster Standards* can serve the church for the furtherance of these ends, in our day, and in succeeding generations.

Stanley Gower: An Introduction

This Westminster divine, Stanley Gower (bap. 1600?–1660[1]) wrote an attestation for no ordinary theological treatise, one which was authored by no ordinary theologian. It was for John Owen, for his essay 'The Death of Death in the Death

---

[1] Jacqueline Eales, 'Gower, Stanley (bap. 1600?, d. 1660)', *Oxford Dictionary of National Biography*, Oxford University Press, 2004.

of Christ.'[1] This fact alone should whet our appetite to know more of this Presbyterian minister. He is worthily esteemed as a 'Puritan divine of considerable eminence' by William H. Goold, the editor of *The Works of John Owen*.[2] However, our central reason for focussing on Gower is because he was involved in the discussions and the production of all of the *Westminster Standards*, as part of the Westminster Assembly. Therefore, to understand his theological trajectory, is to help us understand God's providence in preparing one of the Westminster divines.

The life and ministry of Gower appears to have been one of growing stature and influence throughout what was a turbulent time. This was after all seventeenth-century England. Events in this period included the English Civil War, the rise of Oliver Cromwell, the execution of King Charles I (1649), the calling of one of the most influential synods in church history, that in Westminster (1643-52), and the restoration of the monarchy, King Charles II in 1660, and his subsequent undoing of the church reformation.

Clearly then, Gower's life spanned many events of momentous importance, events which shaped the history of the English-speaking peoples. His personal trajectory included an early association with Archbishop James Ussher, being the first minister of the Puritan congregation at Hill Top Chapel, Attercliffe (near Sheffield). This was followed by his appointment as the minister in Brampton Bryan under the patronage of Sir Robert Harley, then relocation to London as a member of the Westminster Assembly and finally a season of ministry as rector of Holy Trinity, Dorchester. His ministry concluded in this west country town, one described by David Underdown as 'the most 'puritan' place in England' at that time.[3] It was no small

---

1 John Owen, 'Two Attestations' in 'The Death of Death in the Death of Christ,' *The Works of John Owen, Volume 10*, ed William H. Goold, Edinburgh: Banner of Truth, 1959, repr. 2002, 147. This essay was first published by John Owen (1618-1683) in 1650.
2 William H. Goold, *The Works of John Owen, Volume 10*, ed William H. Goold, Edinburgh: Banner of Truth, 1967, repr. 2000, 147.
3 David Underdown, *Fire from Heaven: Life in an English Town in the Seventeenth Century*, London: Fontana Press, 1993, ix.

commendation of the regard of Gower's theological abilities by his contemporaries for him to be called to the church in Dorchester.

Early Days, Preparation and Ordination (1600-1629)

At his baptism, which is believed to have been conducted at Chesterfield, Derbyshire, on 29 March 1600,[1] Queen Elizabeth I was coming to the end of her reign. It concluded with her death in 1603. The Elizabethan reign (1558-1603) was characterized by a time of ferment and discussion concerning ecclesiology: 'ecclesiology was in the mix.'[2] The Elizabethan settlement with its Act of Uniformity in 1559 had failed to satisfy the desires of many ministers who were intent on a complete reformation and overhaul of the church away from papal practices. Meic Pearse believes that Elizabeth I pursued 'a policy of lowest common-denominator Protestantism' and that to be an 'informed and discerning Protestant in the England of the 1560s was both a disturbing and confusing experience.'[3] Questions relating to the nature of the church were unceasingly discussed, especially relating to 'what is a true and pure church?' or 'what is the ideal for a Reformed church?' and even as to whether the Church of England was really a true church.

It can be stated with some certainty that Gower was tutored in Derbyshire for eight years by the renowned Puritan minister Richard Rothwell, who prepared him for university.[4] Therefore Gower came under the influence of Church of England Puritanism at an early age, instead of the growing English separatist movement. All the while, in the background of Gower's formative years, debate on ecclesiological matters ran unabated. If the accession to the throne of James I (r. 1603-

---

1 Eales, *ODNB*.
2 Kevin J. Bidwell, *The Church as the Image of the Trinity: A Critical Evaluation of Miroslav Volf's Ecclesial Model*, Eugene, Oregon: Wipf and Stock, 2011, 61-63.
3 Meic Pearse, *The Great Restoration*, Carlisle: Paternoster, 1998, 155-7.
4 Eales, *ODNB*.

1625) offered fresh hope, then these hopes were dashed at a Convention at Hampton Court Palace in 1604, where leading figures of the church were summoned to discuss their differences. Instead, according to Nick Lunn, the king sought to 'pressure them into conformity.'[1] Lunn explains that there existed a wing among the delegates that sought a 'more thorough reformation of the church' than had been so far accomplished.[2]

Gower's entering into university life as a scholar at Trinity College, Dublin in 1621 led to him graduating with a BA in 1625. His simultaneous association with the famed James Ussher, Archbishop of Armagh was hardly insignificant. Ussher showed a keen interest in Gower's progress and he oversaw his ordination in 1627 and installed him as his chaplain. Ussher's anti-Arminian principles are well documented and upon his appointment as Archbishop in 1626 he surrounded himself with advisors of a similar persuasion.

Ussher's theological mentoring and role as a future sponsor, clearly set Gower upon a Puritan trajectory from which he never deviated. The seeds for Church of England ministry with Presbyterian tendencies, Calvinistic convictions and simplicity in public worship were undoubtedly confirmed in Gower's mind by Ussher. Prior to knowing Gower, Ussher had already written the *Irish Articles of Religion* (1615) when he was Professor of Divinity at Trinity College, Dublin. 'It is widely recognised' according to Robert Letham that Ussher 'had a strong influence on the Westminster Assembly through the *Irish Articles*.'[3] Gower would have been using these *Articles* in his work as part of the Westminster Assembly, but prior to this he gained frontline ministerial experience in two pastorates.

---

[1] Nick Lunn, 'Laurence Chadderton—Puritan, Scholar, and Bible Translator,' *Banner Magazine*, Edinburgh: Banner of Truth, 2008: 537, 4–5.
[2] Lunn, *Banner Magazine*, 5.
[3] Robert Letham,

The First Pastorate: Hill Top Chapel, Attercliffe, Sheffield (1630-34/5)

Hill Top Chapel still stands today in Attercliffe, Sheffield, with the inscription over one of the doors dating the completion at 1629. Attercliffe would have been a distinct community, around two miles east of the Sheffield of those days. Joseph Hunter's *History of Hallamshire* records that 'in the year of our Lord God 1629 certain of the chief of the inhabitants being by God's providence met together, they had a conference about building a chapel.'[1] The opening sermon was 10 October 1630, and 'being the Sabbath-day, divine service was read and two godly sermons preached by the Rev. Thomas Toller, vicar of Sheffield' from Jeremiah 7:8-10.[2]

Stanley Gower was 'elected an assistant minister in the church at Sheffield; and in 1630 he was nominated to the curacy of the newly-erected chapel at Attercliffe.'[3] He served there from 1630-35, therefore he was the founding minister of this new work. The explanation of the acceptance of his calling to Sheffield and Hill Top Chapel would appear obvious. There would have been a geographical affinity with his upbringing in neighbouring Derbyshire and this may have led to familiar connections. There would undoubtedly have been strong Puritan sympathies in Sheffield—why else consider calling a disciple of Ussher, who most likely would have provided a prized reference for the new ordinand.

His removal to his next pastorate was due to the calling of the great Puritan advocate Sir Robert Harley, probably drawn

---

1 Joseph Hunter, *Hallamshire: The History and Topography of the Parish of Sheffield in the County of York: With Historical and Descriptive Notices of the Parishes of Ecclesfield, Handsworth, Treeton and Whiston, and the Chapelry of Bradfield*, London: Lackington, Hughes, Harding, Mavor, and Jones, 1819, 240-41. This citation is put in modern English for ease of reading.

2 Jeremiah 7:8-10 *Behold, you trust in deceptive words to no avail. Will you steal, murder, commit adultery, swear falsely, make offerings to Baal, and go after other gods that you have not known, and then come and stand before me in this house, which is called by my name, and say, 'We are delivered!'—only to go on doing all these abominations?*

3 Hunter, *Hallamshire*, 243.

by Gower's theological convictions and his growing ministerial abilities. An additional attraction for Gower may well have been the turbulent political times as well. The onset of the English Civil War is generally marked as commencing on 22 August 1642 with the raising of the royal ensign by King Charles I in nearby Nottingham. Storm clouds may well have been brewing and Sheffield was known later to ebb and flow in its political loyalties between the Roundheads and Cavaliers (Royalists). However, in the providence of God we should summarize that this was a season of preparation for Gower; he was a theological divine in the making.

There are certain factors worthy of mention. Gower's initial curacy gives insight as to his theological and ecclesial leanings. The inaugural sermons at the opening of Hill Top Chapel provide a glimpse of the doctrinal foundations that were in place before Gower arrived. The doctrine of the Christian Sabbath was upheld with the practice of two services on this day for divine worship, with expositional preaching at its heart. This style of preaching, indicated by the choice of text from Jeremiah 7:8-10 by Toller, was intended to be penetrating, and in opposition to false worship practices possibly remaining in the minds of some from Roman Catholic influence. Well instructed, ordained and able preachers were expected to uphold the purity and simplicity of preached doctrine in public worship. Gower stood in this tradition from the onset of his ministerial career.

The Second Pastorate: Brampton Bryan, Herefordshire (1635-43)

Stanley and his wife Sarah must have found the Herefordshire countryside refreshing from the moment they arrived. As the new rector he was generously taken care of and three of his children were born there, Robert, Humphrey and Brilliana; two children were named after his patrons.[1] It is apparent

---

1 Jacqueline Eales, *Puritans and Roundheads: The Harleys of Brampton Bryan and the outbreak of the English Civil War,* Cambridge: CUP, 1990, repr. 2002, 57. She comments

from historical records and letters that Gower demonstrated clear principles for public worship, Christian ministry and Presbyterian church government at this time. The building blocks for these elements were firmly fixed before he became a member of the Westminster Assembly; Robert and Brilliana Harley were just as arduous as Gower in working for church reform. Gower was a non-conformist who resisted all Popish liturgical pressures and he repudiated all of Archbishop Laud's (1573–1645) moves regarding episcopacy, worship and preaching.

The non-conformity of Gower was not hidden from the state authorities and in 1637 (maybe 1638) a range of charges were made against him. It will be of great benefit to summarize these eleven charges to identify the common practice of public worship conducted by an English Westminster divine who stood mainstream in his day. The teaching of the *Westminster Confession* 'Of Religious Worship, and the Sabbath Day' (Chapter 21) had already been the practice of Gower for many years, before it was penned. He rejected the formalism of the *Book of Common Prayer*, preferring a Reformed emphasis of conceived prayer, extempore preaching and the leading of worship. Here is the summary of the charges:

> He reads the confession, but altogether neglects [to read] the absolution.
>
> He seldom or never reads the Lord's Prayer.
>
> He never reads the Litany [these were liturgical petitions read by the leader with fixed responses by the congregation].
>
> He seldom reads the [Ten] Commandments and neglects to read them at communion.
>
> He does not permit people to stand at readings from the gospels or to bow at the name of Jesus.

---

of this document in the state papers which charged Gower with wide-ranging practices and that his actions were 'long standing non-conformist practices.'

In his sermons he dissuades people from kneeling in prayer when they enter the church.

He asserts that it is not the church building that is holy, but it is when the ordinance of God is performed, that is of itself holy.

He seldom or never wears the surplice [a white linen cassock as worn by clergy or choristers] nor baptises with the sign of the cross.

The communion table has no rail and it is brought from the altar at the east end of the church into the body of the church

He did not follow the liturgical calendar or read common prayers for set days, except Christmas and New Year's Day.

He does catechise the youth that are aged 14–15 upon previous sermons with questions and answers.[1]

Many former practices within the church were deemed to be pre-Reformation relics and Gower would preach against them as being superstitious. The order of charges indicates in my mind the antithetical nature of the pre and post-Reformation practices for public worship. The first concern of the pre-Reformed ceremony was for a reading for the absolution of sins, something deemed to be essential to public worship to the disciples of Laud. Gower's points of dissent should be revisited by the contemporary church to avoid the same mistakes and he was not lukewarm in his pursuit of church reform. In 1640/1 he wrote to Robert Harley with unmistaken speech, that the church was to be purged of the 'trash and trumpery of massing ceremonies, altars, images, crucifixes, copes [caps], surplices, organs etc., instead which to make God's worship as plain and decent may be.'[2]

The simplification of public worship practices was to spiritually cleanse the temple, as it were, and this was deemed to

---

1 *The National Archives, State Papers,* TNA SP 16/381 f. 192 r-v, transcribed by Dr Joel Halcomb, history researcher with Cambridge University.
2 Eales, *Puritans and Roundheads,* 110 and 110 n.25.

be essential for the work of reform. Gower's ideas of reformation extended to church government as well, because the minister was responsible for the godly conducting of public worship. He fought many battles through his ministry, but at this time he discerned a twin problem to the establishment of Presbyterian church government principles. At the beginning of the Long Parliament in late 1640, extreme separatist ideas abounded and Gower wrote to Harley to complain in 1641. He expressed that 'on the one side papists erect their Babel amongst us; on the other side Brownists [separatists] that discourage your reformation of our Zion, whilst they contend for their independent government.'[1] Are we similarly aware of these twin dangers today, as Gower was in his day?

Gower's speech was plain and extremely direct; none could accuse him of lacking forthrightness. However, most of his energy appears to have been set against Arminian and remaining Catholic practices. He considered the church bishops to be 'Babel's bricklayers' and he advised that 'episcopacy should be abolished altogether or reduced to its "first order."' Instead he believed that 'ultimate authority should be shared with the presbyters.'[2] Gower had been shaped, moulded, and strengthened under God and with the aid of the patronage of the Harley's, the exercise of his Reformed ministry had flourished. He was chosen with John Green of Herefordshire as one of two representatives to the assembly of divines in London, and he moved there in the autumn of 1643.

The Westminster Standards in the Making: Gower at the Westminster Assembly, London (1643-48)

In various writings on the composition of the assembly, Gower does not have the prominence of some of the members. Men such as William Twisse (1578-1646) who was appointed 'prolocutor of the assembly,' Thomas Gataker (1576-1654) who

---

[1] Ibid., 68.
[2] Ibid., 107, 111.

was reputed to be 'among the finest Greek scholars of his day,' and the catechist Herbert Palmer (1601-1647) clearly draw the attention of historians and scholars.[1]

Does this logically infer that less famous members such as Gower were not able scholars and ministers? While Gower is not so well known to us today, there is every indication that he was a very well respected and prominent minister in his own time. In the providence of God, this period saw Calvinistic Presbyterian convictions and profound ministerial qualities flourish in England. The modern lack of knowledge of Gower is no basis for a realistic assessment, indeed his theological convictions should stir the hearts of all those who are interested in the recovery of a purified church in England and elsewhere. J.I. Packer considers the period between 1550-1700 to be one when the English Puritans were analogous to a forest of 'California Redwoods,' and 'another breed of [theological] giants.'[2] There are probably many other Christian ministers from this period who are worthy of more detailed research.

During Gower's time in London 'he was appointed as preacher in the staunchly Presbyterian parish of St Martin Ludgate and was invited to preach before the houses of parliament on several occasions.'[3] The work of an assembly member was to be extremely busy for Gower, as it was for many, combining parish ministry with long week days of theological debate and discussion. Chad Van Dixhoorn states: 'Of the three main tasks of parliament's assembly, the first two were revolutionary in nature: "settling ... the government and liturgy" of the church "as shall be most agreeable to the Word of God."'[4] Van Dixhoorn clarifies that the 'third task of the synod was stated with sharp

---

1 William Beveridge, *A Short History of The Westminster Assembly*, revised and edited by J. Ligon Duncan III, Greenville: Reformed Academic Press, 1993, 19-20.
2 J. I. Packer, *Among God's Giants: The Puritan Vision of the Christian Life*, Eastbourne: Kingsway, 1991, 11.
3 Jacqueline Eales, 'Stanley Gower' in *Oxford Dictionary of National Biography*, Oxford: OUP, 2004.
4 Chad Van Dixhoorn, *The Minutes and Papers of the Westminster Assembly, 1643-1652*, Volume 1, Introduction, ed Chad Van Dixhoorn, Oxford, OUP, 2012, 7.

difference in tone. The assembly was to "vindicate" and "clear" the church's doctrine.[1] Gower's work was set, along with 119 other divines.

The first documents that were produced by the assembly were the *Directory of Church Government and the Ordination of Ministers (jus divinum)* and the *Directory for the Public Worship of God*. It is not insignificant that the word 'liturgy' was dropped in favour of a 'Directory' to avoid wooden and unbiblical impositions in worship. Gower had already reached clear principles upon most matters of ecclesiology before he left Herefordshire but such intense theological debate in London must have further sharpened his thinking and conclusions. There were three standing committees to do assembly business and Gower served on the first. He worked with the likes of Dr Thomas Goodwin, Dr William Gouge and twenty-seven other able men. Gower's name is not overly prominent in the early records of the minutes, but he is appointed with two other men to prepare the *Confession of Faith*, with the finally agreed scriptural proof texts to be presented to parliament.[2] This is no small commendation of his abilities.

With respect to the debate on church government, Robert S. Paul highlights that 1 Timothy 5:17 was the locus of much interest in relation to the proposition of a division in the eldership into preaching and ruling elders.[3] It is well documented that the assembly was not homogenous, but consensus was sought through voting. Paul outlines that the Scottish Commissioners and dissenting brethren (Carter, Bridge, Goodwin, Nye, Simpson, Burroughes and Phillips) were firmly in favour of ruling elders. Others leaned towards a single office of minister, but Burgess, Gower, Bathurst and later, Gataker

---

[1] Ibid., 8.
[2] Chad Van Dixhoorn, *The Minutes and Papers of the Westminster Assembly, 1643–1652*, Volume 4, 384 (Session 763, December 26, 1646, Munday morning, and 504 (Session 828, Aprill 15, 1647, Thursday morning).
[3] Robert S. Paul, *The Assembly of the Lord: Politics and Religion in the Westminster Assembly and the 'Grand Debate'*, Edinburgh: T & T Clark, 1985, 163–174.

were willing to accept ruling elders as a 'prudential decision for the church.'[1] In my opinion this signals that Gower was balanced, and theologically mainstream in the assembly on this point, while being judicious. The examination of ministers was a substantial part of the work of the assembly, perhaps too little spoken of, and in October 1644 Gower was 'appointed by parliament to be one of the ministers authorized to ordain clergymen in London.'[2]

One prominent record that we have of a Gower sermon preached before parliament was on the 31 July 1644, titled: 'Things Now-a-Doing: or The Churches Travaile of the Child of the Reformation Now-a-Bearing.' This was a rather typical elongated Puritan sermon title and the text was from Daniel 12:10 (and Matthew 24:21, 23–25.). This opportunity appears to have been afforded him due to his patronage by Sir Robert Harley who was a member of the House of Commons. However, it is not unjust to report that this was not one of Gower's theological high points. This sermon confusedly surmized from Daniel's prophecy that the year 1650 would mark the ushering in of great spiritual prosperity and the crushing of anti-Christian forces. We therefore concur with Joel R. Beeke and Mark Jones that 'the Puritans did not excel in eschatology'[3] and Gower fits that summary.

One of the rich legacies of the Westminster Assembly was the production of the two catechisms. Originally the work of the committee was intended to produce a single catechism, but a key step was the decision to produce two catechisms instead. It was acknowledged that 'it had been very difficult ... to dress up milk and meat both in one dish.'[4] In the early stages of the completion of the *Shorter Catechism* when Herbert Palmer

---

1   Ibid., 166 and 166 n.132.
2   Eales, ODNB.
3   Joel R. Beeke & Mark Jones, *A Puritan Theology*, Grand Rapids: Reformation Heritage, 2012, 6.
4   W. Robert Godfrey, 'The Westminster Larger Catechism' in *To Glorify and Enjoy God: A Commemoration of the 350th Anniversary of the Westminster* Assembly, eds John L. Carson and David W. Hall, Edinburgh: Banner of Truth, 1994, 130.

was the chairman, Gower belonged to the committee.[1] John R. Bower records that a catechism committee 'was first convened in 1643' but it was in December 1646 that its 'membership swelled to no fewer than eleven members;' in August, 1647 Stanley Gower and Edmund Calamy were added.[2] There were eleven sub-committees appointed to work on the Ten Commandments and Mr Profitt and Mr Gower laid out the general rules for expounding the third Commandment.[3]

Gower was a mid-level leader in the Westminster Assembly, one who appeared to grow in stature as his ministry matured. 'In 1648 he was in the Isle of Wight as a member of the delegation of ministers sent to persuade the king [Charles I, who was executed on 30 January 1649] to accept a Presbyterian settlement' according to Eales, 'when he was approached by the townsmen of Dorchester to be their minister.'[4] The minutes of the assembly simply record their consent to approve him as Rector of Holy Trinity, Dorchester, as of 26 December, 1648. Things moved fast in those days when decisions were made. The majority of the assembly business was complete and Gower's participation spanned more than five years, during which all the lasting and historic *Westminster Standards* and associated documents were crafted.

The Final Pastorate: Holy Trinity, Dorchester, Dorset (1649-60)

Gower had been called to a town which Underdown described as

---

[1] William Carruthers, *The Shorter Catechism of the Westminster Assembly of Divines*, London: Publication Office of the Presbyterian Church of England, 1897, 31.
[2] John R. Bower, *The Larger Catechism: A Critical Text and Introduction,* Grand Rapids: Reformation Heritage Books, 2010, 16–17.
[3] Ibid., 33. Van Dixhoorn, *The Minutes and Papers of the Westminster Assembly, 1643–1652*, Volume 4, 542, Gower is mentioned in reference to the debate on the catechism question 'What was the state of Christ's humiliation?,' WLC, Q.46; 685, 10 September 1647, Gower gives a report of the last questions of the catechism.
[4] Eales, *NDB*.

the 'the most "Puritan" place in England.'[1] Gower's predecessor at Dorchester was the famed Puritan divine John White (1575-1648) who had laboured there for 43 years and he had been part of the assembly of divines as well. The calling to such a prominent ministerial post underscores the value which his peers ascribed to his pastoral acumen and abilities. The religious background in England at the time of his installation was fluid, to say the least. There were Quakers on the rise with radical charismatic teachings of immediate personal revelation, Separatists gaining ground, the national dissemination of the documents from the assembly, and yet without active parliamentary endorsement of mainly Presbyterian government. Politically, the nation was awash with all kinds of ideas under Cromwell's watch, while the issue of King Charles I remained unresolved and radical army elements threatened stability.

Gower began his ministry on 24 January 1649, while on 1 January 1649 Charles was put on trial. The king was executed on 30 January in London, and on 6 February parliament abolished the monarchy. It is difficult for our generation to understand the impact of the regicide on the nation. Alongside all this, the year 1650 had been anticipated by Gower and others as a kind of millenarian 'new beginning.' Undoubtedly 1649 would have been a period of great expectancy, exacerbated by the January events. In London this would have been a challenging time for Gower as a minister, but the move to Dorchester no doubt helped.

In this season of ministry Gower enjoyed a measure of stability, as much as those times probably allowed, and he could lead the people of God to worship in an acceptable manner before God. In Dorchester, the 'familiar liturgy had gone. Instead of Common Prayer, Gower... used the Presbyterian service book, the Directory.'[2] So there followed eleven years of stable ministry, which afforded Gower the opportunity to publish some works of which three are certainly worthy of mention. These are

---

[1] Underdown, *Fire from Heaven*, ix.
[2] Ibid., 218

his preface to the posthumous publication of James Ussher's *Eighteen Sermons Preached in Oxford, 1640: Of Conversion unto God, Of Redemption and Justification by Christ* (published in 1659): his preface to *David's Psalms in Metre: Agreeable to the Hebrew* by Rev. John White (published in 1655): and last but no means least, his preface to John Owen's *The Death of Death in the Death of Christ* (published in 1650).

His association with James Ussher, John White and John Owen speaks of Gower's stature and influence in the church. His preface to Ussher's sermons explains that it was by this worthy that he was firstly examined and admitted into the University of Dublin above forty years previously. Secondly, it was Ussher who took care of him while he studied and thirdly, by him he was ordained, put into the ministry as a chaplain, Ussher finally approving his call to Hill Top Chapel, near Sheffield. In the preface to Ussher's sermons, Gower expresses his desire that the 'Lord would raise up successors,' ones with the same 'life and doctrine as this burning and shining light.'[1]

The preface by Gower to the *Psalms in Metre* represents his desire for the singing of psalms in public worship according to 1 Corinthians 14:15, 'I will sing with the Spirit, and I will sing with the understanding also.' Gower exhorts Christians to sing psalms as part of their duty as Christians under the New Testament. Gower's preface is filled with devotional warmth in commending not only White's work, but of the singing of the psalms and the perpetuity of the fourth commandment, the Christian Sabbath. It is to be hoped that in our day there would be a recovery of the singing of metrical psalms in public worship. Something of Gower's humility is perceived as he styles himself in his concluding words, as Ussher's 'unworthy successor.'

The polemical work by Owen, *The Death of Death*, was designed to show that the notion of a universal atonement is both unscriptural and destructive. Gower's attestation is outstanding in its perception, clarity and his use of plain speech. Here is a sample. 'There are two rotten pillars on which the

---

1 Gower's preface to Ussher's Sermons

fabric of late Arminianism ... doth principally stand. The one is, that God loves all alike ... The other is, that God gives ... Christ, the great gift of his eternal love, for all alike to work out their redemption.' He concludes with penetrating analysis that 'the former destroys the free and special grace of God, by making it universal; the latter gives cause to man of glorying in himself rather than in God.' He speaks boldly when he refers to Arminianism as 'this cursed doctrine,' but also there is a sense of his personal humility when he concludes by describing himself as 'the unworthiest of the ministers of the gospel.'[1]

Dorchester was a Presbyterian town and it is likely that the majority of his congregation were Presbyterian royalists who would not have upheld ecclesiastical bishops, but they would have upheld the office of king. It was at Dorchester on 10 May 1660 that King Charles II was proclaimed. In this same year, the 'unworthiest of the ministers of the gospel' Stanley Gower died. He probably would not have understood that after his death the Restoration would mark the end of the work of church reform, not only in Dorchester, but throughout England. The millenarian ideals were shattered and faithful believers faced a fresh wave of persecution in what followed. Nevertheless, Gower's abiding legacy was his work along with other divines in producing the *Westminster Standards*. They are perhaps the greatest definition of the Christian faith in the English language, or even in any language.

The Westminster Standards for in Modern English

Presbyterianism was adopted in Scotland, and through that nation especially, this apostolic pattern for doctrine, worship, and government by elders, has been disseminated around the world, not least through what became the United States. Would Gower be satisfied with the outcome today? Despite the resurgence of interest in Reformed teaching in recent decades,

---

[1] Stanley Gower, 'Attestation Touching the Ensuing Treatise' for 'The Death of Death in the Death of Christ' in *The Works of John Owen, Volume 10*, 147.

I think that in comparison with the ideals of Gower, there is little room for apathy. The missionary vision of the Presbyterian Puritans must be seen as an abiding impetus for church reform until the return of Christ.

In closing, there are three areas in which I would like to draw attention. It is appropriate to allow the message of these *Standards* to shape our thinking regarding our pursuit of church reform, and these are specifically in relation to the church's communication, covenantal duties and at prayer.

I. The Church's Communication

Question: What are the outward means whereby Christ communicates to us the benefits of redemption?

Answer: The outward and ordinary means whereby Christ communicates to us the benefits of redemption are, his ordinances, especially the Word, sacraments, and prayer; all of which are made effectual to the elect for salvation.[1]

It can seem as if the tables are turned in some quarters and there sometimes appears to be an all-consuming pursuit of some in asking: 'how are we to communicate to the lost world?' This is probably the wrong question to ask and the wrong starting point. The *Shorter Catechism* asks the right leading question and it supplies the much-needed answer. The means of communication are 'outward and ordinary,' they are sufficient to communicate the benefits of Christ's mediation and atonement and this is to be through 'the Word, sacraments and prayer.' It is almost as if this simplicity and clarity is so staggeringly plain that for some people it seems insufficient. However, the Holy Spirit blesses the appointed means and we must not reduce the means to only 'Word and sacrament' but more correctly to the 'Word, sacraments and prayer.'

---

[1] The *Westminster Shorter Catechism*, Question 88.

II. The Church's Covenantal Duties

Under the gospel, when Christ, the substance, was exhibited, the ordinances in which this covenant is dispensed are the preaching of the Word, and the administration of the sacraments of Baptism and the Lord's Supper: which, though fewer in number, and administered with more simplicity, and less outward glory; yet, in them, it is held forth in more fullness, evidence, and spiritual efficacy, to all nations, both Jews and Gentiles; and is called the New Testament. There are not therefore two covenants of grace, differing in substance, but one and the same, under various dispensations [administrations].[1]

Such a statement expounds the 'essence of divinity' which is communicated through the 'outward and ordinary means.' Christ, the substance (Colossians 2:17-18, Hebrews 10:1-3), is exhibited in the covenant of grace, though the gospel means are administered with 'simplicity, and less outward glory.' We are not to adopt an idea that spiritual methods equal ineffectiveness. It requires faith to maintain a covenant loyalty to hold fast to the Word, sacraments and prayer. When these means are truly held forth, they will convey the New Testament fullness and be spiritual efficacious. The importance and stress needs to be upon maintaining the purity of these means and a refusal to be drawn away to 'outward glory.' This has been a perpetual snare through the history of the church.

III. The Church at Prayer

Question: What do we pray for in the second petition?

Answer: In the second petition, (which is, Your kingdom come,) ... we pray, that the kingdom of sin and Satan may be destroyed, the gospel propagated throughout the world ... the church furnished with all gospel-officers and ordinances, purged from corruption ... that the ordinances of Christ may be purely dispensed, and made effectual to the converting of those that are

---

[1] The *Westminster Confession of Faith*: 'Of God's Covenant with Man' Chapter 7:6

yet in their sins, and the confirming, comforting, and building up of those that are already converted ...[1]

Prayer must be a vital component to the upholding of the peace, purity and growth of the church on earth. The second petition of the Lord's Prayer rightly understood and prayed, provides impetus, hope and motivation for the church at prayer. How we yearn for the day when the gospel is widely propagated, the church is furnished with 'gospel-officers' and the 'ordinances of Christ' are 'purely dispensed.' This revival of this petition upon the lips of Christians is needful for genuine gospel advances.

Finally, let us ponder the words of the prophet Amos, as cited by James at the Council at Jerusalem in Acts 15:13-17:

> James replied, Brothers, listen to me. Simeon has related how God first visited the Gentiles, to take from them a people for his name. And with this the words of the prophets agree, just as it is written, 'After this I will return, and I will rebuild the tent of David that has fallen; I will rebuild its ruins, and I will restore it, that the remnant of mankind may seek the Lord, and all the Gentiles who are called by my name, says the Lord, who makes these things known from of old.'

The establishment of the apostolic pattern of New Testament congregations had at its heart sound doctrine, administered by sound elders for true worship. The rebuilding of the *tent of David*, that is pure and reverent worship of God, is a vital task for every age.

May we be energized and envisioned to labour in our own day, as Gower and others did in theirs. Our task will never be fulfilled until that final day when the heavens burst open, the great trumpet is heard and the Son of Man comes again for his church. May we pray for the Lord to raise up gospel successors, men who are equipped with the soundness of the doctrines that emanate from the *Westminster Standards*. May the government of the church be discussed again to guard against errors. May

---

[1] The *Westminster Larger Catechism*, Question 191.

a simplicity and reverence of the worship of the Father, and of the Son, and of the Holy Spirit be sought, through the pure preaching of sound doctrine, the right administration of the sacraments and prayer for the glory of God.

The Westminster Standards and Public Worship

David E. Gilbert

For nearly a century, prior to the call by Parliament of the Westminster Assembly in 1643, Thomas Cranmer's *Book of Common Prayer* (1549) governed public worship for the Church of England. Among the range of topics regulated by it—from requirements regarding baptism to prohibitions concerning burial—the *Book of Common Prayer* mandated a specific liturgy for public worship for the Church of England, the deviation from which might result in fines, imprisonment, and potential charges for treason.[1]

From Liturgy to Directory

In June 1643, following eighteen months debate, Parliament called the assembly of theologians to address a series of issues aimed at reforming the Church of England. More than one hundred men were summoned to undertake the work, the initial emphasis of which dealt with the doctrinal framework of the *Thirty-Nine Articles* of the Church of England. However, some six months after the labors of the assembly commenced, the divines undertook the work of revising the liturgical structure

---

[1] J.V. Fesko, *The Theology of the Westminster Standards*, Wheaton, IL: Crossway, 2014, 336-338.

of the *Book of Common Prayer*. With the second commandment in view, and aiming for pure worship by the Word of God, the assembly decided against the mandated liturgy of the *Book of Common Prayer*, and instead they spent virtually all of 1644 developing *The Directory for The Public Worship of God*.[1] Parliament approved the *Directory* on 3 January 1645.

Although the *Book of Common Prayer* advanced the goal of the first Reformers to remove 'vain, erroneous, superstitious, and idolatrous' practices in the public worship of God, the church had learned by 'long and sad experience' that the liturgy mandated in the *Book of Common Prayer* proved offensive and the source of much mischief. It did so by urging the reading of all prayers, by requiring 'many unprofitable and burdensome ceremonies'[2] sympathetic to the Roman Catholic Church, by leading some proponents of it to hold that God could be worshiped only by following the prayer book, and by hindering preaching and causing a superstitious people to become hardened in their ignorance of saving knowledge and true piety.

Having so concluded, and standing on the foundation of the first Reformers, the divines built upon the earlier work with further reformation. Specifically, the ceremonies of the former liturgy were laid aside in favor of those things prescribed in the Scriptures. With the adoption of the *Directory*, the church would have direction 'in those things that contain the substance of the service and worship of God.'[3]

The Regulative Principle of Worship

The burden of the divines was to free the worship of God from all practices that were not divinely instituted. Accordingly, as

---

[1] Chad Van Dixhoorn, ed. *The Minutes and Papers of the Westminster Assembly 1643–1652*, vol. 1, Oxford: Oxford University Press, 2012, 28.

[2] Westminster Assembly, *The Directory for the Public Worship of God*, 'The Preface,' Discussed by Mark Never and Sinclair Ferguson, Fears, Ross-shire: Christian Focus, 2008, 79–82.

[3] Westminster Assembly, *The Directory for the Public Worship of God*, 'The Preface.'

stated by the assembly some two years after the approval of the *Directory*, 'the acceptable way of worshiping the true God is instituted *by Himself*, and so limited by His own revealed will, that He may not be worshiped according to the imaginations and devices of men, or the suggestions of Satan, under any visible representation, or any other way not prescribed in the holy Scripture.'[1]

The *Westminster Confession* Chapter 21.1 is perhaps the clearest expression of what is referred to as the regulative principle of worship. Westminster declared that there must be scriptural warrant for everything done in worship. That warrant may be found in positive commands, in examples, or derived from good and necessary consequence.[2] The worship of the Triune God cannot be directed by our own opinions, our theories, even our tastes. Or as another put it: 'As a principle, this attention to biblical prescription usefully keeps us from promoting in our churches any activity that sounds practical, appears beautiful, smells wonderful, feels comfortable or tastes vaguely theological, but that is not prescribed in the Bible.'[3] The regulative principle then is simply *sola Scriptura* applied to worship. If the Word of God is 'the only rule of faith and obedience,'[4] then the Word must direct every aspect of worship by the people of God. To insist that God's people worship by the Word is to acknowledge three vital principles: the authority of God, the sinfulness of man, and the liberty of conscience.

The Authority of God

Genesis 1 sets forth the majesty, power, and authority of God. He speaks and all things come into existence. He rules over all in transcendent holiness (Exodus 15:11; Isaiah 6). The prophets

---

[1] WCF 21.1
[2] J. Ligon Duncan III 'Does God Care How We Worship?' in *Give Praise to God*, ed. Philip Graham Ryken, Derek W.H. Thomas, and J. Ligon Duncan III, Phillipsburg, NJ: P & R Publishing, 2003, 23.
[3] Chad Van Dixhoorn, *Confessing the Faith: A reader's guide to the Westminster Confession of Faith*, Edinburgh: The Banner of Truth Trust, 2014, 277.
[4] WLC 3.

describe at great length the incomparability and inscrutability of God (Isaiah 40-46; Jeremiah 10). Jeremiah declares *There is none like you, O* LORD; *you are great, and your name is great in might. Who would not fear you, O King of the nations? For this is your due; for among all the wise ones of the nations and in all their kingdoms there is none like you* (Jeremiah 10:6-7).

In view of God's exalted majesty and the creaturely existence of all men, how can man undertake to approach him with worship crafted by the wisdom of men?[1] God's thoughts are not our thoughts. His ways are not our ways. Indeed, his thoughts and ways are much higher than ours (Isaiah 55:8-9). If worship is to be pleasing to the glorious Triune God, he must direct it. As the authority over all, the infinite and holy God must tell finite and sinful man how to approach him.[2]

The Sinfulness of Man

Man's sinful pattern since the Garden has been *to exchange the truth about God for a lie* (Romans 1:25). Noting man's bent towards idolatry, John Calvin concluded that 'man's nature, so to speak, is a perpetual factory of idols.'[3] Calvin's words declare what is plain from Scripture, whether in Genesis 3, in Israel's sordid history, or in Romans 1. Man is totally depraved. His whole nature is corrupt. Man is 'utterly indisposed, disabled, and made opposite unto all that is spiritual good.'[4]

Clearly then the worship of man will be tainted with sin. Deceitful hearts (see Jeremiah 17:9) will always err. Accordingly, the *Westminster Confession* declares that God must tell us how to worship. He prescribes how he must be approached. He instructs sinners in the way (Psalm 25:8).

---

[1] WCF 7.1 describes the Creator/creature distinction.
[2] J. Ligon Duncan III 'Foundations For Biblically Directed Worship,' in *Give Praise to God*, ed. Philip Graham Ryken, Derek W.H. Thomas, and J. Ligon Duncan III, Phillipsburg, NJ: P & R Publishing, 2003, 53-54.
[3] John Calvin, *Institutes of Christian Religion*, ed. John T. McNeill, trans. Ford Lewis Battles, 2 vols, Philadelphia: Westminster, 1960, 1.11.8 (1:108).
[4] *Westminster Larger Catechism* 25.

The Liberty of Conscience

The burden of both the Reformers and the divines is to let Scripture alone speak concerning the elements of worship, with nothing further to bind the people of God's conscience as they worship. For example, Westminster divine George Gillespie stated that Paul made clear in Colossians 2:20-22 that God's people are not subject to the regulations of the world according to human precepts and teachings.[1] To submit to church practices not rooted clearly in Scripture would be to make ourselves servants of men and not God. Such servitude, he concluded, is tyranny.

Therefore, in the *Westminster Confession of Faith*, chapter 20 'Of Christian Liberty, and Liberty of Conscience,' the divines asserted that 'God alone is Lord of the conscience, and has left it free from the doctrines and commandments of men, which are, in anything contrary to his Word; or beside it, in matters of faith, or *worship*. So that, to believe such doctrines, or to obey such commands, out of conscience, is to betray true liberty of conscience ...'[2]

Liberty of conscience would thus be destroyed if the elders of the church were to add to any element of worship without biblical warrant. Such conduct would be binding the consciences of the people to follow an unbiblical standard.

Similarly, James Bannerman has stated 'Within that sanctuary none but the Lord of the conscience may enter; and because it is his dwelling place and home, his presence protects the conscience from the intrusion of the Church.'[3]

What then does the law of God say about our worship? Where in Scripture do we find a regulating principle of worship?

---

[1] George Gillespie, *A Dispute Against the English Popish Ceremonies Obtruded on the Church of Scotland*, Edinburgh, 1660, 1.3.
[2] WCF 20.2 (emphasis supplied).
[3] James Bannerman, *The Church of Christ: A Treatise on the Nature, Powers, Ordinances, Discipline, and Government of the Christian Church*, rev. ed, Edinburgh: The Banner of Truth Trust, 2015, 260-261.

Scriptural Foundation of the Regulative Principle

Numerous texts set forth God's regulation of our worship. For example, in the first commandment given to Moses God stated that he alone was to be the object of worship for all mankind. In the following commandment the Lord spoke clearly to Israel concerning what was acceptable worship:

> You shall not make for yourself a carved image, or any likeness of anything that is in heaven above, or that is in the earth beneath, or that is in the water under the earth. You shall not bow down to them or serve them, for I the LORD your God am a jealous God, visiting the iniquity of the fathers on the children to the third and fourth generation of those who hate me, but showing steadfast love to thousands of those who love me and keep my commandments.

Simply put, the Lord was never to be worshiped by means of images. When Israel met the Lord on Sinai, they saw no form that they might use to project an image or likeness of him. Doing so, God explained to Moses, would ignite his wrath (Deuteronomy 4:15-32). By necessary inference, therefore, resorting to man's own ideas in worship, rather than carefully doing those things the Lord prescribes, will also arouse the anger of the Lord. Worship must be done God's way, not according to our imagination.

Accordingly, the divines wrote in the *Larger Catechism* 109 'The sins forbidden in the second commandment are, all devising, counseling, commanding, using, and anywise approving, any religious worship not instituted by God Himself.' As Moses stated in Deuteronomy 12:32, *Everything that I command you, you shall be careful to do. You shall not add to it or take from it.*

Further support for Scripture-regulated worship is found in Leviticus 10:1, where *Nadab and Abihu, the sons of Aaron, each took his censure and put fire in it and laid incense on it and offered unauthorized fire before the LORD*, which he had not commanded them (emphasis supplied). These sons of Aaron did not offer a fire contrary to God's command; they offered fire having no command to do so by the Lord whatsoever. *And fire came out from before the* L*ord and consumed them, and they died before the* L*ord* (Leviticus 10:2). The Lord explained his judgment upon them in these terms: *Among those who are near me I will be sanctified* [or treated as holy] (Leviticus 10:3).[1] Nadab and Abihu came with innovation, so arousing the jealousy of the Lord, who must be worshiped according to his commandment only.

The same principle of Scripture-regulated worship is carried forward into the New Testament, notwithstanding the fact that worship no longer takes place in the tabernacle or the temple. For example, in Matthew 15 the Pharisees accused Jesus of breaking the tradition of the elders by permitting his disciples to eat without first ceremonially washing their hands. Jesus answered *And why do you break the commandment of God for the sake of your tradition? For God commanded, 'Honor your father and your mother,' and, 'Whoever reviles father or mother must surely die.' But you say, 'If anyone tells his father or mother, 'What you would have gained from me is given to God,' he need not honor his father. So for the sake of your tradition you have made void the word of God* (Matthew 15:3-6).

Jesus thus exposed the practice of the Pharisees of taking away from God's word by adding to it,[2] further declaring 'You hypocrites! Well did Isaiah prophesy of you, when he said: *This people honors me with their lips, but their heart is far from me; in vain do they worship me, teaching as doctrines the commandments of men* (Matthew 15:7-9). This indictment from the Lord was that the Pharisees' external behavior betrayed an internal problem. While they appeared serious about, and zealous for,

---

[1] Moses had done precisely that, treating the Lord as holy all throughout the construction of the tabernacle. Exodus 39 alone repeats nine times that things were done as the Lord commanded Moses. Exodus 39:1; 5; 7; 21; 26; 29; 31; 32; 42. One could also consider how the instructions for the Tabernacle were given in Exodus 26-30 and then repeated as the work was accomplished in Exodus 36-40. There was no deviation from the Lord's instructions.

[2] Their rule of *korban* (given to God) supplanted the fifth commandment by permitting a person to devote an article to God and thus free himself from supporting his parents.

God's law, in reality they replaced it with man-made regulations. Their zeal was superficial, contrived, and empty. Their disregard for the law of God manifested a shameful lack of love for him.

The stinging rebuke from Jesus in this passage demonstrates his concern about the *way* God is worshiped. He cannot be honored with mere human prescriptions or with rules having merely an appearance of sincerity. God must be worshiped in the way he prescribes. To do otherwise dishonors God.

Jesus further underscored this principle in John 4. There he pressed the confused Samaritan woman about matters of eternal life, and in the course of the discussion he brought her moral bankruptcy fully to light: she had been married five times and was living in an immoral relationship with yet another man. As Jesus pressed her regarding her condition, she attempted to avoid the further exposure of her sin by redirecting the conversation to the Samaritan principal place of worship on Mount Gerizim, as opposed to Jerusalem for the Jewish people. Jesus responded with these familiar words:

> *Jesus said to her, 'Woman, believe me, the hour is coming when neither on this mountain nor in Jerusalem will you worship the Father. You worship what you do not know; we worship what we know, for salvation is from the Jews. But the hour is coming, and is now here, when the true worshipers will worship the Father in spirit and truth, for the Father is seeking such people to worship him. God is spirit, and those who worship him must worship in spirit and truth'* (John 4:21–24).

In the course of explaining that a time had come when no one place on earth will be the place of worship,[1] Jesus revealed the idolatry of both this woman and her people. He stated clearly *You worship what you do not know; we worship what we know, for salvation is from the Jews* (John 4:22).

Jesus made two significant statements concerning worship in this passage. First, he declared that ignorance is culpable. Worship separated from truth leaves the purported worshipers

---

1 See WCF 21.6

empty by presenting them with nothing other than a god of their own making.[1] Second, Jesus stated that worship and salvation are integrally related. To worship in ignorance is to be separated from the God and the salvation he provides.

Notwithstanding this frank assessment of the Samaritan woman's spiritual condition, hope nonetheless remained for her. As Jesus said, *the hour is coming, and now is here, when the true worshipers will worship the Father in spirit and truth, for the Father is seeking such people to worship him* (John 4:23). What is the Father doing through his Son? What is the aim of Jesus' ministry, of his death and resurrection? It is to seek worshipers.[2] It is to rescue sinners from blindness that they might boast in the Lord.

It is noteworthy that Jesus' words in John 4 speak specifically to public worship. Even though there is a degree to which 'all of life is worship,' the biblical worship model anticipates the act of public worship where the people of God, ransomed from sin and wrath, join to proclaim the greatness of God (Psalm 34:1-3). Peter explains *you are a chosen race, a royal priesthood, a holy nation, a people for his own possession, that you may proclaim the excellencies of him who called you out of darkness into his marvelous light* (1 Peter 2:9). His message is that worship, extolling the glory of God, is the primary duty of the corporate people of God, assembled together, and not just alone in private worship. We are saved to proclaim.

If, therefore, salvation drives the believer to worship, and if redemption compels God-directed praise, two questions immediately follow: how are believers to worship God, and what is the acceptable way of worshiping him? In addressing the wrongly worshipping woman, Jesus said *true worshipers will worship the Father* in spirit and truth, *for the Father is seeking such people to worship him* (John 4:23).

---

[1] John Calvin puts it this way, 'unless there be knowledge, it is not God that we worship, but a phantom or idol.' See John Calvin, *Commentary on the Gospel According to John*, Grand Rapids, MI: Baker Book House, 2009, 159.

[2] Terry L. Johnson, *Reformed Worship: Worship That Is According to Scripture*, Greenville, SC: Reformed Academic Press, 2000, 15.

Worshipping the Father *in truth* means that we approach him through the blood and righteousness of Jesus Christ in the enabling power of the Spirit.[1] Worshipping the Father *in spirit* means we worship out of the spiritual life given by the Holy Spirit in accord with his truth.[2] And *spirit and truth worship* anticipates a right conception about who God is—namely, that he alone is God. He will not give his glory to another and his praise to idols (Isaiah 42:8). There can be no adoration of angels or bowing to images (Colossians 2:18; Exodus 20:3-6). And we worship him as the Triune God—the Father, and the Son, and the Holy Spirit.[3]

But we must not only know who God is to worship, we must know how he is to be worshiped. To replace God's Word with clever ceremonies steps out of line with the truth. The Scriptures, therefore, must direct our worship.

The Elements of Worship

The question naturally follows, what are the elements of public worship? What do believers have as the authority for their worship practices? In the *Confession* Chapter 21, 'Of Religious Worship, and the Sabbath Day,' the divines include the following as the parts of ordinary worship: prayer, with thanksgiving; the reading of the Scriptures with godly fear; the sound preaching and conscionable hearing of the Word; singing of psalms with grace in the heart; and the due administration and worthy receiving of the sacraments instituted by Christ.

In addition to these ordinary elements there are extraordinary elements (biblical patterns of worship that may or may not be part of the worship of God's people every Lord's Day): oaths, vows, solemn fastings, and thanksgiving upon special occasions.[4]

---

1 Ephesians 2:18
2 D.A. Carson, *The Gospel According to John,* Grand Rapids, MI: William B. Eerdmans Publishing Company, 1991, 225.
3 WCF 21.2
4 WCF 21.3-5

The *Confession's* framework in chapter 21 is not to be understood as a mere proposal for available worship practices to be supplemented with such additional activities as a minister considers fitting. It is a directory of what Scripture mandates for public worship by his people.

Prayer

The first of the elements is prayer, with thanksgiving. The *Confession* 21.3 denotes the description 'with thanksgiving' which comes from Paul's command to the Philippians, *Do not be anxious about anything, but in everything by prayer and supplication* with thanksgiving, *let your requests be made known to God* (Philippians 4:6). In everything, in private worship, in family worship, and in public worship, prayers and supplications must be lifted up to God with thanksgiving. He is the God who hears prayer (Psalm 65:2). He commands us to cast our cares on him (1 Peter 5:7). He gives us access through Christ in one Spirit (Ephesians 2:18). Failure to pray is a grievous sin.

An examination of the life of the infant church in Jerusalem makes clear that the people continuously devoted themselves to prayer (Acts 2:42). When trouble arose, when persecution began, they prayed (Acts 4:24ff). Likewise, when they chose leaders, they prayed (Acts 6:6; 13:3). Prayer was imbedded in the fabric of the church.

The divines further directed that, as the church prayed, intercession should be made for all 'sorts of men.'[1] Paul encouraged Timothy that *prayers, intercessions, and thanksgivings be made for all people, for kings and all who are in high positions, that we may lead a peaceful and quiet life, godly and dignified in every way* (1 Timothy 2:1-2). Jesus prayed for coming generations as he made intercession for those who would believe the Gospel through the ministry of the disciples (John 17:20). The elders in Bethlehem prayed for the child that would come from the union of Boaz and Ruth (Ruth 4:12). Prayer was the lifeblood of believers throughout sacred history. However, finding no

---

1 WCF 21.4

warrant for prayers for the dead, the divines made clear that such prayers were never to be made, as was common in papist churches.[1] Indeed, the opposite is found in Scripture, when King David discontinued praying for the son born to his relationship with Bathsheba after he was informed of the young child's death (2 Samuel 12:21-23).

The divines expanded their instruction concerning those for whom prayers should be made in the *Larger Catechism* Questions 178-196 and the *Shorter Catechism* Questions 98-107. For example, *Larger Catechism* Question 186 asks, 'What rule has God given for our direction in the duty of prayer?' Answer: 'The whole Word of God is of use to direct us in the duty of prayer; but the special rule of direction is that form of prayer which our Saviour Christ taught his disciples, commonly called The Lord's Prayer.' Furthermore, in the *Directory for Public Worship*, the divines provided lengthy instructions on the minister's public prayers to be offered both before and after the sermon. The divines likewise wrote, 'And because the prayer which Christ taught his disciples is not only a pattern of prayer, but itself a most comprehensive prayer, we recommend it also to be used in the prayers of the church.' Though recommended, however, the *Directory* did not mandate the use of the Lord's Prayer in worship services.

The Reading of the Word

The second element of worship found in the *Westminster Confession*, 21.5 is 'The reading of the Scriptures with godly fear ...' Paul's exhortation to Timothy is the source for this element of worship, *Until I come, devote yourself to the public reading of Scripture, to exhortation, to teaching* (1 Timothy 4:13). Paul literally stated 'give attention to *the* reading.' The Greek word for 'the reading' is found in two other places in the New Testament (Acts 13:15; 2 Corinthians 3:14), and in each instance reference is made to the regular practice of the public reading of authoritative texts in the synagogue, namely the Law and the

---

[1] *Westminster Confession of Faith*, 21.4.

Prophets.[1] What Paul commanded Timothy to do was in no way new or innovative. The reading of the Bible had been a central part of the worship of God for centuries.

Clearly, therefore, the divines recognized the reading of Scripture to be an essential part of the worship of God, and in the *Directory of Public Worship* specific instruction is given concerning such reading. The *Directory* spells out who should read: the pastors and teachers and occasionally those who had the ministry in view.[2] It indicates what should be read: 'all the canonical books of the Old and New Testament (but none of those which are commonly called Apocrypha),' and particularly the Psalms. It recommends how much should be read: ordinarily one chapter of each Testament at every meeting and that they be read in order, although it is acknowledged that the length of the reading was a matter of pastoral wisdom. And the *Directory* provides instructions for how the Scriptures should be read: in the common tongue, out of the best translation, and distinctly, 'that all may hear and understand.'

The *Directory* also states, 'When the minister who reads shall judge it necessary to expound any part of what is read, let it not be done until the whole chapter or psalm be ended; and regard is always to be had unto the time, that neither preaching, nor other ordinances be restricted,[3] or rendered tedious.' This statement is not a direction to make exposition on the reading, as it was a practice already found among the divines.[4] Rather, the wisdom displayed concerning the timing and length of the explanatory comments is insightful: the reading of the Word should be given foremost attention, and all commentary that follows must be brief.

---

1 The regular practice of the Scripture reading is further attested in the writings of Philo and Josephus, first-century Jews. See Larry W. Hurtado, *At the Origins of Christian Worship*, Grand Rapids, MI: William B. Eerdmans, 2000, 33.
2 See WLC 156.
3 The original word was 'straitened.'
4 Richard A. Muller & Rowland S. Ward, *Scripture and Worship: Biblical Interpretation & The Directory for Worship*, Phillipsburg, NJ: P & R Publishing, 2007, 121-122.

The Preaching of the Word

The *Westminster Confession* 21.5 mentions 'the sound preaching ... of the Word.' Paul exhorted Timothy, *Preach the word; be ready in season and out of season; reprove, rebuke, and exhort, with complete patience and teaching* (2 Timothy 4:2). It is apparent from Jesus' sermon at Nazareth (Luke 4:16-21) and Paul's custom of preaching in the synagogue (cf. Acts 13:15; 14:1; 17:1-3) that preaching was a regular part of the worship of God's people. And preaching clearly predates post-exilic synagogues, as the exhortations from Moses on the plains of Moab, known commonly as Deuteronomy, constitute preaching. The same is found in numerous Old Testament evidences of preaching, from Joshua to Ezra and throughout the prophets. It is only logical to find that the New Testament church began with preaching (see Acts 2; 3; 7; 10; 13; 17).

Preaching was (and is) the foundational element of the worship of the church. Luke writes that the early believers *devoted themselves to the apostles' teaching* (Acts 2:42). And when the worship service in Acts 20:7ff is considered, Paul's lengthy sermon is prominently in view. The rationale for this practice is explained by Paul, *Faith comes from hearing and hearing through the word of Christ* (Romans 10:17), and in that context Paul was explicitly speaking of the preaching of the Word. Through this element of worship, God is pleased to cause his people to be born again (1 Peter 1:23-25) and to grow them in godliness (John 17:17; 1 Corinthians 1:18; 1 Peter 2:2-3). Recognizing the pre-eminence of preaching in worship, the divines made instructions about preaching a significant part of the *Directory*.[1]

The divines used an interesting adjective to describe preaching in worship. They referred to 'the *sound* preaching ... of the Word.' While the divines provided no Scriptural proof for their use of this particular word, there is no doubt they had in view the sound exhortations in the Pastoral Epistles. Paul told

---

[1] Rowland Ward notes that, 'Some 12 percent of the directory is taken up by a fine section on preaching.' Ibid, 125.

Timothy, *If anyone teaches a different doctrine and does not agree with the sound words of our Lord Jesus Christ and the teaching that accords with godliness, he is puffed up with conceit and understands nothing* (1 Timothy 6:3-4a). Likewise Paul commanded Timothy, *Follow the pattern of sound words that you have heard from me, in the faith and love that are in Christ Jesus* (2 Timothy 1:13).

Moreover, the word translated 'sound' literally means healthy. Paul employed metaphorical language from the medical field to describe what he understood as good preaching. Hence, the words preached must promote spiritual health and expose spiritual sickness. The words preached must equip believers to see and hear gospel truth while guarding against doctrinal error and biblical untruth. The divines sought to equip ministers in these goals by urging them to follow *the pattern of sound words*. These goals may be achieved as ministers hold to a standard of healthy doctrine, which are the truths that center on Christ Jesus. But lest we think this means that preaching only consists in declaring powerful gospel indicatives (the facts of God's grace), Paul's model was to declare *the whole counsel of God* (Acts 20:27). He did not shrink away from *anything that was profitable* (Acts 20:20), which he achieved by uniting the gospel indicatives with powerful and timely gospel imperatives.[1] He explains and applies what Christ's doctrine demands of the believer, which is at the core of healthy Christian preaching.

The Hearing of the Word

In addition to sound preaching, the divines identified in the *Westminster Confession* 21.5 the 'conscionable hearing of the Word, in obedience unto God, with understanding, faith, and reverence' as an element of worship. Although the word 'conscionable' is used substantially less frequently than in earlier eras, the term communicates the proposition that the Word must be listened to in a careful manner. That is, worshipers

---

[1] See the book of Ephesians for a clear example of how Paul uses gospel indications (Ephesians 1-3) and gospel imperatives (Ephesians 4-6), and notice the 'therefore' in Ephesians 4:1.

must have their consciences engaged when in Christian worship. We must not be mere hearers of the Word (James 1:22), those upon whom the Word of God makes no lasting impression. We must be those who hear and in whom the Word works an effect.

In the parable of the sower in Mark 4, Jesus spoke of the seed of the Word falling upon four different hearers. First mentioned was the seed which fell along a stony path and was eaten by birds. He explained that this image represents that kind of listener, who, on hearing the Word, *Satan immediately comes and takes away the word that is sown in them* (Mark 4:15). The pavement-like soil of the path is illustrative of a hard, faithless, and uncultivated heart. It is as if the seed, which is the Word of God, simply bounces away. The devil quickly moves to snatch away the Word before it can produce an impact of any description on the hearer, and the listener is left unmoved. They did not ready themselves to receive the Word, and they give no further thought to it. Sermons are nonsense to them. Indeed, their mind is focused on other things. 'I need to make that doctor's appointment this week.' 'Does my lipstick need refreshing?' 'I wonder what we are having for lunch.' Hundreds of other examples could be given. The point is that, for this kind of person, there is not 'conscionable' hearing of gospel truth. His or her mind is not engaged on the Word!

The contrast to this poor listening (and the other two negative examples in Mark 4: the rocky-ground hearer and the thorny-ground hearer) is seen in the good-ground hearer. Jesus said of those who are like good soil they *hear the word and accept it* (Mark 4:20). This word translated 'accept' is a rare word in the New Testament, but its use in Acts 15:4 illuminates the significance of it. In Acts 15 Paul and Barnabas had made their way from Antioch to Jerusalem for a church council. The circumcision question was causing contention within the church as some men had been saying, *Unless you are circumcised according to the custom of Moses, you cannot be saved* (Acts 15:1). That requirement, of course, was not the message Paul and Barnabas proclaimed on their first missionary journey. In reality,

Paul had said just the opposite. *Look, I Paul, say to you that if you accept circumcision, Christ will be of no advantage to you* (Galatians 5:2).

In God's providence, *When they [Paul and Barnabas] came to Jerusalem, they were welcomed by the church and the apostles and the elders* (Acts 15:4, emphasis supplied). The word translated 'welcomed' is the identical word translated 'accept' in Mark 4:20. The one who hears the Word properly is the one who 'welcomes it.' Such a person gladly takes it in, embraces the truth, and aims to conform his life to it. Such a person listens to the Word proclaimed so that he may understand the doctrines, be rebuked and corrected, and be trained in righteousness (2 Timothy 3:16–17). Unlike the Israelites in the wilderness, the good-ground hearer listens with faith.

The author of Hebrews states that some of the Exodus generation did not benefit from the message they heard *because they were not united by faith with those who listened* (Hebrews 4:2). The good news had been proclaimed to these people, but they did not appropriate by faith the promises of God. They did not believe God would care for the needs they would have on the journey, or that he would provide the rest they required. They possessed evil, doubting hearts of unbelief and never humbled themselves to welcome and appropriate God's Word.

Such illustrations from the Word led the divines to see that 'conscionable' hearing is the kind of hearing required in worship. The believer must tremble before the Word. The believer must obey God by taking heed to what he says. In truth, conscionable listeners labor alongside the minister to hear, appropriate, and apply the truths spoken from the Word. The conscionable hearer prepares himself to listen, prays for understanding, and pays attention with great diligence. The conscionable hearer loves the Word as it comes to his soul, believing it to be the life-giving, soul-transforming, heart-rejoicing Word of God.[1]

---

[1] It's hard to improve upon the *Larger Catechism* answer to Q.160 'What is required of those that hear the Word preached? A. It is required of those that hear the Word preached, that they attend upon it with diligence, preparation, and prayer; examine

Singing

Together with ears eager to listen to God's Word, those who worship in spirit and truth must have mouths ready to praise the Lord. Genuine worship anticipates and requires the 'singing of psalms with grace in the heart.'[1] The people of God who have been drawn up from the miry bog have a song of praise to God in their mouths (Psalm 40:2-3). God's gracious deliverance produces joyful, singing hearts. After Israel passed through the Red Sea and Pharaoh's army was destroyed, Moses led the people of Israel in song (Exodus 15), After the Lord used Deborah, Barak, and Jael to be the tools of his salvation, Deborah and Barak sang (Judges 5). After David was rescued from the prolonged pursuit of Saul, he sang before his Deliverer (1 Samuel 22; Psalm 18)!

God's mighty acts, his flawless character, and the particulars of his providence demand, and will produce in true worshippers, exultation. Thus, the Psalmist says, *Praise the Lord! Praise God in his sanctuary; praise him in his mighty heavens! Praise him for his mighty deeds; praise him according to his excellent greatness ... Let everything that has breath praise the Lord! Praise the Lord* (Psalm 150:1-2, 6). The language of praise in the Psalms alone is extensive. The response to our God for his stupendous power, unflappable sovereignty, unsearchable holiness, and indelible grace is to sing to his name.

The preparation and preservation of the sacred hymnbook, the collection of the 150 psalms, demonstrates the Lord's call for his people to lift their voices in song. Terry Johnson puts the logic of singing psalms crisply, 'God wrote the psalms. He wrote them to be sung. Therefore, we ought to sing them.'[2] Paul underscored this injunction, telling the church that when

---

what they hear by the Scriptures; receive the truth with faith, love, meekness, and readiness of mind, as the Word of God; meditate, and confer of it; hide it in their hearts, and bring forth the fruit of it in their lives.'

1 *Westminster Confession of Faith*, 21.5.
2 Terry L. Johnson 'Restoring Psalm Singing to our Worship,' in *Give Praise to God*, ed. Philip Graham Ryken, Derek W.H. Thomas, and J. Ligon Duncan III, Phillipsburg, NJ: P & R Publishing, 2003, 258.

they assemble for worship there must be singing (1 Corinthians 14:26), and that those who are filled with the Spirit should be *addressing one another in psalms and hymns and spiritual songs, singing and making melody to the Lord with your heart* (Ephesians 5:19). Paul further explained that singing serves not only to give thanks to God but also as a means of instructing God's people. *Let the word of Christ dwell in you richly, teaching and admonishing one another in all wisdom, singing psalms and hymns and spiritual songs, with thankfulness in your hearts to God* (Colossians 3:16). Though it may seem otherwise, singing is a means of teaching God's people.

Not unexpectedly, the phrase, *psalms, hymns, and spiritual songs* has been the source of much controversy, especially in light of the call in *Westminster Confession of Faith* 21.5 for worshippers to engage in the 'singing of psalms with grace in the heart.' The criticism of some that follows is that proper singing is exclusively from the Psalms. However, Matthew Poole, a well-known seventeenth-century Presbyterian commentator, writing one generation after the Westminster Assembly, distinguished between these three words and provided helpful, revealing insights on the word 'psalm' in Colossians 3:16. Poole notes that the word 'psalm' may be understood 'more generally, as the genus, noting any holy metre, whether composed by the prophets of old, or others since, assisted by the Spirit extraordinarily or ordinarily.'[1] His view is that believers are not confined to the biblical psalter for lyrics in worship.[2]

'Singing psalms with grace in the heart' does not exclude hymnody, therefore, but it most certainly does mean the church

---

[1] Matthew Poole cited in Nick Needham, 'Westminster and Worship: Psalms, Hymns? And Musical Instruments?,' in *The Westminster Confession of Faith into the 21st Century*, Vol. 2, ed. Ligon Duncan, Ross-shire, Scotland: Mentor, 2005, 249.

[2] Thomas Manton, an eminent Westminster divine, demonstrates such a view in his commentary on James 5:13 *Is anyone among you suffering? Let him pray. Is anyone cheerful? Let him sing praise [or let him sing a psalm].* Manton writes, 'I confess we do not forbid other songs; if grave and pious, after good advice they may be received into the Church.' *The Complete Works of Thomas Manton*, Vol. 4, ed. Thomas Smith, London: James Nisbet Co., 1871, 572.

ought to regularly engage in the robust singing of the Psalms. Thomas Manton noted that 'Scripture psalms not only may be sung, but are fittest to be used in the church, as being indited [written] by an infallible and unerring Spirit.'[1]

And as Christian worship engages in faithful singing, the divines anticipated that believers do so 'with grace in the heart.' This phrase is a quotation of Colossians 3:16 rendered with an accurate sense in the ESV *with thankfulness in your hearts to God*. The appropriate response to the grace of God in Christ is to express gratitude to God in song. Thus, in the *Directory for Public Worship*, the divines state the following in the section 'Of Singing of Psalms': 'It is the duty of Christians to praise God publicly, by singing of psalms together in the congregation, and also privately in the family. In the singing of psalms, the voice is to be tunably [signing in tune] and gravely [seriously] ordered; but the chief care must be to sing with understanding,[2] and with grace in the heart, making melody unto the Lord.'[3]

The Sacraments

The final element of the ordinary religious worship of God is 'the due administration and worthy receiving of the sacraments instituted by Christ.'[4] Christ instituted two sacraments in the Church, Baptism (Matthew 28:18-20) and the Lord's Supper (Mark 14:22-25), and it is precisely these two sacraments which the church historically and routinely practiced (Acts 2:38-42; 1 Corinthians 11:23-32).

The phrase 'the due administration ... of the sacraments' requires that the sacraments be dispensed only by a minister of the Word lawfully ordained.[5] Jesus' instruction to baptize, found in the Great Commission was given to men he had called to labor full-time in the ministry of the Word. This is equally

---

1 *The Complete Works of Thomas Manton*, 4:574.
2 1 Corinthians 14:15
3 Colossians 3:16; Ephesians 5:19
4 *Westminster Confession of Faith* 21.5.
5 WCF 27.4

the case with respect to the distribution of the elements in the Lord's Supper. When the apostles, the original stewards of the mysteries of God (1 Corinthians 4:1), died and the office of apostle ceased, Christ provided the gift of pastor/teachers (Ephesians 4:11). To these full-time men, those called and ordained to preach the Word, the administration of the sacraments has been entrusted.[1]

Furthermore, the lawfully ordained minister of the Word is given further instructions in the administration of each sacrament. In baptism, water (not mixed with oil)[2] must be applied in the name of the Father, and of the Son, and of the Holy Spirit (Matthew 3:11; 28:19-20). The divines likewise stated in the *Westminster Confession of Faith* 28.3 that 'Dipping of the person into the water, is not necessary; but, Baptism is rightly administered, by pouring, or sprinkling water upon the person.' While not excluding immersion as a permitted mode of baptism, the divines made clear that baptism of any sort represents symbolic washing as a sign and seal of regeneration (Titus 3:5-6), cleansing (Acts 2:38), and union with Christ (Romans 6:1-4). That may be with a little water (Ezekiel 36:25), or a lot of it. Under no circumstances, however, was baptism to be administered more than once to any person.[3]

With respect to the Lord's Supper, the divines specified what constitutes 'due administration.' *Westminster Confession* 29.3 states 'The Lord Jesus has, in this ordinance, appointed His ministers to declare His word of institution to the people; to pray, and bless the elements of bread and wine, and thereby to set them apart from a common to an holy use; and to take and break the bread, to take the cup, and (they communicating also themselves) to give both to the communicants; but, to none who are not then present in the congregation.'

---

[1] Guy Prentiss Waters, *How Jesus Runs the Church*, Phillipsburg, NJ: P & R Publishing, 2011, 94-95.
[2] Chad Van Dixhoorn, *Confessing the Faith: A Reader's Guide to the Westminster Confession of Faith*, 369.
[3] WCF 28.7

As to those to whom baptism may be administered, it is not disputed that those who make a profession of faith should be baptized. However, great dispute has arisen over the assertion of the divines that 'the infants of one or both believing parents are to be baptized.' Nevertheless, in view of the continuity of the covenant of grace (Genesis 17:7-14; Galatians 3:14; Acts 2:38-39), the connections between circumcision and baptism (Colossians 2:11-12), the household baptisms of Acts (Acts 10:2, 44-48; 16:14-15; 16:30-34; 18:8; see also 1 Corinthians 1:14-16), Paul's designation of the children of a believer as holy (1 Corinthians 7:14), and Jesus' blessing of the children (Matthew 19:13-15), the divines rejected any views to the contrary and held confidently to the view that children ought to be baptized.[1] *Shorter Catechism* 95 was written to address this issue. 'To whom is baptism to be administered? Answer: Baptism is not to be administered to any that are out of the visible church, till they profess their faith in Christ, and obedience to him; but the infants of such as are members of the visible church are to be baptized.'

The worthy receiving of the Lord's Supper has been equally disputed. But once again the divines are clear. The *Shorter Catechism* asks in Question 97 'What is required to the worthy receiving of the Lord's Supper? Answer: It is required of those who would worthily partake of the Lord's Supper, that they examine themselves of their knowledge to discern the Lord's body, of their faith to feed upon him, of their repentance, love, and new obedience; lest, coming unworthily, they eat and drink judgment to themselves.' With this statement, the ignorant and the scandalous (those who do not understand the content of the Christian faith and those whose manner of life contradicts their profession of faith), are excluded from the table.[2] This is what the Lord requires (1 Corinthians 11:27-29).

---

[1] For a full treatment of infant baptism see Robert R. Booth, *Children of the Promise: The Biblical Case for Infant Baptism*, Phillipsburg: P & R Publishing, 1995.

[2] WLC Q.173 'May any who profess the faith, and desire to come to the Lord's supper, be kept from it? Answer: Such as are found to be ignorant or scandalous,

Summary

As we consider the nature of public worship, believers may confidently recognize that the inerrant Word is the final authority concerning each aspect of our approach to him. Nothing must take place in the public worship of God which has not been instituted by the Word. In this sense, it may be said that Christian worship is actually quite simple. Prayer books and crafty rituals are unnecessary. Consciences need not be bound by the whims and innovations of men. The clear principles of the Bible provide the framework.

This does not mean that every worship service looks like every other, but it does suggest that public worship in spirit and truth will be built around the biblical principles that serve as a sweet aroma to our God and King. As one pastor has helpfully and succinctly stated, in worship, we 'read the Bible, preach the Bible, pray the Bible, sing the Bible, and see the Bible.'[1] Such is the teaching of the *Westminster Confession*, and may we who love the Lord continue this biblical pattern in our worship today.

---

notwithstanding their profession of the faith, and desire to come to the Lord's supper, may and ought to be kept from that sacrament, by the power which Christ hath left in his church, until they receive instruction, and manifest their reformation.'

1 J. Ligon Duncan III 'Foundations For Biblically Directed Worship,' in *Give Praise to God*, ed. Philip Graham Ryken, Derek W.H. Thomas, and J. Ligon Duncan III, Phillipsburg: P & R Publishing, 2003, 65.

The Westminster Standards and the Christian Sabbath

George Swinnock (Introduction by Kevin J Bidwell)

Question: What is required in the fourth commandment?

Answer: The fourth commandment requires of all men the sanctifying or keeping holy to God such set times as he has appointed in his Word, expressly one whole day in seven; which was the seventh from the beginning of the world to the resurrection of Christ, and the first day of the week ever since, and so to continue to the end of the world; which is the Christian Sabbath, and in the New Testament called *The Lord's Day*.

Question: How is the Sabbath or the Lord's Day to be sanctified?

Answer: The Sabbath or Lord's Day is to be sanctified by a holy resting all the day, not only from such works as are at all times sinful, but even from such worldly employments and recreations as are on other days lawful; and making it our delight to spend the whole time (except so much of it as is to be taken up in works of necessity and mercy) in the public and private exercises of God's worship: and, to that end, we are to prepare our hearts, and with such foresight, diligence, and moderation, to dispose and seasonably dispatch our worldly business, that we may be the more free and fit for the duties of that day.[1]

---

1 The *Westminster Larger Catechism*, Questions 116 and 117.

An Introduction to the Subject of the Christian Sabbath: Kevin J. Bidwell

Have you ever met someone who has suffered from burn-out? Perhaps you have had to endure the painful steps of rebuilding your life following the after-effect of a burn-out. The recovery process takes time and patience in order to be fully reorientated after such a trial. As Christians we may wonder 'why has this happened to me?' Without wanting to belittle in any way other spiritual advice to those who have suffered or might do so, I want to consider the often neglected yet clearly biblical truth of the Christian Sabbath or Lord's Day.

The Sabbath is not primarily an antidote to stress and burn-out but it includes that, and I have little doubt of its practical and spiritual benefits for the church. There was unanimous approval of this doctrine and its practice among the Westminster Assembly and the *Westminster Standards* provide abundant proof of this. Why then has the practice of the Sabbath fallen upon such hard times among evangelicals in our generation?

Perhaps one reason for the current ignorance and neglect is our restlessness, which is in reality the product of sin. However, the lack of exposure to such practical teaching surely lies at the heart of the matter. Any true Christian desires to obey their Lord from their heart, informed by a right standard of teaching. Paul admonished the Christians in the city of Rome: *But thanks be to God, that you who were once slaves of sin have become obedient from the heart to the standard of teaching to which you were committed, and, having been set free from sin, have become slaves of righteousness* (Romans 6:17–18). So my aim here is to introduce this subject and to remove the common mistake that to remember the Sabbath is legalism, while also promoting godliness through its joyful observance.

On mentioning the Ten Commandments, many will have heard the reply, 'we are not under law but under grace,' or perhaps more directly been told that these commands are not for the church today. With one sentence, such a person has sought to release themselves from the plain teaching of God's Word and to walk openly into a path of manifest disobedience to him. Legalism is adding commandments or rules to the Word of God, but the Sabbath Day of rest is not a man-made rule or addition. It is the plainly stated will and gift of the Lord, one which began in the Garden of Eden and which continues until the second coming of the Lord Jesus Christ. The Saviour taught that *the Sabbath was made for man, not man for the Sabbath* and so this day, its God-ordained weekly rhythm was made for man as provision from his Creator. Who would want to turn down such a gift from God? The Lord went on to proclaim that *the Son of Man is lord even of the Sabbath* (Mark 2:28). Quite clearly then, to submit to Jesus Christ and to confess him as Lord, is to be one who treasures the Sabbath as something which his Lord has laid claim to.

The fourth of the Ten Commandments simply requires God's people to *remember the Sabbath day to keep it holy* (Exodus 20:8-11). This Commandment was not a new one, in fact it had originated back in the Garden of Eden. The first day that Adam enjoyed in the earthly paradise was a Sabbath Day of worship, communion with God and rest. However, after the resurrection of Jesus Christ, the Day was moved forward, from what is now known as the Saturday (the last day of the week), to what is called today Sunday (the Lord's Day, which is the first day of the week). This forward-moving of the appointed day of worship signifies the forward-movement from the Old Testament to the New Testament. The Sabbath is not abolished, but in the New Testament it is strengthened as the day appointed by Christ, the main day in which he primarily communes with his church (Revelation 1:9-20). It was on the first day of the week that Christ Jesus was resurrected (Matthew 28:1, Mark 16:2, Luke 24:1, John 20:1); it was in that first Lord's Day evening that he met with the disciples together (John 20:19); and then the church met on that day thereafter for public worship (Acts 20:7, 1 Corinthians 16:2, John 1:10).

For centuries the church has held it as an established principle and doctrine, that the first day of the week is the God-appointed day for public worship. In recent decades this day has come under attack, so that many professing Christians worship in one service and probably give less than half of their day to worshipping the Living God. We worship God in the church by the command of God. The divine order for healthy Christianity is worship first and then service second (Matthew 4:10). Though all life is to be lived for the glory of God, all of life is not worship. Worship is a conscious act, one to be practiced especially in the corporate setting in the church, on the day appointed by God himself. R. Scott Clark rightly contends against the contemporary church when he asks the question: 'Whatever happened to the second service?'[1] Quite simply, the Lord commands us to set apart as holy the whole of the Lord's Day and the practice of two services enables us to structure our day for worship and spiritual nourishment. We must not forget that from a biblical perspective, preaching is the high point of worship, not singing. In the act of the preaching of sound doctrine, the Lord addresses us and we respond back with prayer and singing.

As Christians we are to be renewed in repentance and faith throughout our Christian lives. The Word of God comes and shakes our opinions, the Holy Spirit persuades us of the truth and we are then brought to a crossroads where we respond by either hardening ourselves against the truth or by submitting to it. My hope is that some people reading this essay will have their consciences awakened to their spiritual duties, but also to acknowledge what they are missing out on by not taking the Lord's Day as the gift from God to them. Reading Isaiah 58:13–14 will then make sense: *... and call the Sabbath a delight and the holy day of the Lord honourable; if you honour it, not going your own ways, or seeking your own pleasure, or talking idly; then you shall*

---

[1] R. Scott Clark, 'Whatever Happened to the Second Service?' in *Recovering the Reformed Confession: Our Theology, Piety, and Practice,* Phillipsburg: P and R, 2008, 293–342.

take delight in the Lord, and I will make you ride on the heights of the earth ... for the mouth of the Lord has spoken. A changed mind persuaded by the truth of the written Scriptures, should lead to a change in our doctrine, which should lead to a changed life.

George Swinnock was very specific on the practice and preparation for the Lord's Day by Christians, but let me also recommend some further reading. The *Westminster Standards* are deliberately placed at the end of this book—please read them. I would suggest that a starting point should be Chapter 21 of the *Westminster Confession*, 'Of Religious Worship and the Sabbath Day.' Sections 21:7 and 8 specifically explain the Christian Sabbath, with abundant Scriptural proof. The *Westminster Larger Catechism* devotes no less than seven questions to teaching the Sabbath from the Fourth Commandment (Questions 115-121). Similarly the *Westminster Shorter Catechism* devotes six questions to the same truth (Questions 57-62). These should provide a solid basis for further study, accompanied by prayer for the Holy Spirit to instruct you in the process (Psalm 119:18). Thomas Watson (c. 1620-1686), another English Puritan wrote well when he stated that 'this commandment was engraved in stone by God's own finger, and it will be our comfort to have it engraved on our hearts.'[1] May we learn of Christ, the one who delighted in each of the Sabbaths through his life.

The seventeenth-century Puritans excelled in their teaching on the Sabbath. They wrote with clarity, pastoral warmth and a burning love for the honour of the Triune God and the head of the church, the Lord Jesus Christ. One such author on this subject was the Puritan pastor George Swinnock (1627-1673). In the first volume of Works, he wrote on 'The Christian Man's Calling' to expound the much neglected theme of godliness.[2] He deals with 1 Timothy 4:7: *Have nothing to do with irreverent,*

---

[1] Thomas Watson, *The Ten Commandments,* Edinburgh: Banner of Truth, 1692, reprinted 2000, 93.

[2] George Swinnock, 'How to Exercise Ourselves to Godliness on a Lord's-Day' in *The Works of George Swinnock, Volume 1,* Edinburgh: Banner of Truth, 1992, 222-249.

silly myths. Rather train yourself for godliness. Swinnock then proceeds to lay out pastorally and in detail what godliness looks like in practice. He devotes a whole chapter to 'How to exercise ourselves to godliness on a Lord's Day.' This excerpt below is from that particular chapter.

Swinnock works out his ideas with eight propositions but we have only included the first proposition, lightly modernized. This first proposition connects to the two questions and answers from the *Westminster Larger Catechism* cited above, most especially Question 117, in that 'we are to prepare our hearts, with such foresight, diligence and moderation' for the Sabbath. It is to the pastoral detriment of the church when such teaching is hidden from Christians. It is our hope that Swinnock's passion and pastoral gifts will stimulate a further recovery of a delighting in the Sabbath (Isaiah 58:13-14) in our own generation. It was Swinnock who probably coined the phrase describing the Lord's Day as 'the market-day of the soul' and it occurs in the excerpt below. May this introductory essay and Swinnock's teaching whet our appetite to more fully enjoy our own Sabbaths as stepping stones on the journey to heaven.

George Swinnock: 'How to Exercise Ourselves to Godliness on the Lord's Day'

An Introduction

It is because the Lord's Day is the special time for religious duties, I shall therefore, reader, give you here some particular directions for your sanctification of it, and edification by it. As of all actions, none call for more care than holy duties; so of all seasons for those actions, none commands so much caution and conscience as the Lord's Day.

The first command [of the Ten Commandments] teaches us the object of worship; the second, the matter of worship; the third, the manner of worship; the fourth, the time of worship.

That God is to be worshipped, that some time must be set

apart for that work, is moral, natural, and written on the tables of all our hearts; but that one day in seven must be consecrated to this end, is moral, positive, and written on the tables of stone.

All nations have had their seasons for sacrifice; even the heathen [Gentile nations], who worshipped dumb idols, had their festivals and holidays. It is reported of Alexander Severus, emperor of Rome, that he would on a Sabbath-day lay aside his worldly affairs, and go into the capitol [the temple of Jupiter in ancient Rome on the Capitoline Hill] to worship his gods. Among those that acknowledged the true God, the Turks have their *stata tempora*—set times of devotion—they have their Friday-Sabbath.

But to keep the Lord's Day upon a conscientious ground, and in a religious manner, is peculiar to the true Christian. In the primitive times, the observation of this day was esteemed the principal sign of a saint. Indeed, our sanctification of it is by God himself counted a sign that he has sanctified us, Exodus 31:13 (*You are to speak to the people of Israel and say, 'Above all you shall keep my Sabbaths, for this is a sign between me and you throughout your generations, that you may know that I, the Lord, sanctify you'*).

It is observable that God has fenced this command with more hedges than ordinary, to prevent our excursions [deviations].

1. It is marked with a *memento* [reminder] above other commands, *Remember the Sabbath day, to keep it holy* (Exodus 20:8), partly because of our forgetfulness, and partly because of its concernments [importance].

2. It is delivered both negatively and affirmatively, which no other command is, to show how strongly it binds.

3. It has more reasons to enforce it than any other precept, its equity, God's bounty, his own pattern, and the day's benediction [blessing].

4. It is put in the close of the first, and beginning of the second table [of the Ten Commandments], to note that the observation of both tables depends much upon the sanctification of this day (Exodus 35:1).

It is considerable also, that it is more repeated than any other of the commands: Exodus 20:8, 31:14-16, 35:2; Leviticus 16:31, 23:3, 32. God would have Israel know, in those before cited places, that their busiest times, ploughing and harvest, and the very building of the tabernacle, must give way to this precept.

On the Lord's Day we go into God's sanctuary, and his pleasure is, that we reverence his sanctuary, Leviticus 19:30. The Jews indeed made a great stir about their outward reverencing the temple. They tell us they were not to go in with a staff, nor shoes, nor to spit in it, nor, when they went away, to turn their backs upon it, but go sidling (Ezekiel 8:16); but certainly God's meaning is principally that we do, with inward reverence and seriousness, worship him in his sanctuary.

Reader, I desire you that you will take notice, that the more holy any action is, the more heedful you ought to be about it; upon which account the duties of this day require extraordinary diligence; for they have a double-dye of holiness upon them; they are double-gilt [coating as in metals such as gold]. Your task on that day, or the exercises thereof, are of divine institution, and so is the time, the day. You have God's hand and seal to the duties; he commands you to pray, hear, sing, meditate, receive the sacrament; and you have also God's hand and seal to the day, Acts 20:7; 1 Corinthians 16:1-2; Revelation 1:10. It is considerable, that in the fourth command God does not say, 'Remember the seventh day, to keep it holy', but, *Remember the Sabbath day, to keep it holy*. Further, the seventh, or a seventh is the Sabbath of the Lord your God; so, then, the morality of that command is one day of seven. The Jewish seventh day was buried in Christ's grave, though its shadow walked a little while after.

Take heed how you observe this day; God's eye is very much upon your behaviour in his house; therefore in the tabernacle, the place of public worship, it was commanded, *You shall make seven lamps, and they shall light the lamps that they may give light* (Exodus 25:37), to teach us that nothing there escapes his sight, for in his house there is always light. His eye beholds all your commission of evil, and all your omission of good there. In his sanctuary you cannot sin in secret; there are seven lamps to discover your miscarriages in the Lord's house, and therefore it requires you to be very pious [godly] in that place. Afterwards, when the temple was built, and became heir to the tabernacle, as that succeeded this in the celebration of God's worship; so also in God's observation of all the works done there: *My eyes and my heart will be there for all time' says the Lord* (1 Kings 9:3).

There is a threefold eye of God present in the assemblies of the people.

1. There is the eye of observation and inspection: God sees what uprightness and seriousness there is in your prayers and performances; God's eyes take notice of what integrity and fervency, you have in your services and sacrifices: *For my eyes are on all their ways* (Jeremiah 16:17). Whether you are praying, or reading, or hearing, or singing, his eye is upon you; and whether you perform your duties slothfully and sluggishly, or dutifully and diligently, he observes you: *his eyes see, his eyelids test the children of man* (Psalm 11:4).

2. There is the eye of favour and benediction. God's eye can convey a blessing, as well as his hand: *And I will fix my eyes upon them for evil and not for good* (Amos 9:4). And God's eye can speak his good will, as well as his heart: *My eyes and my heart will be there for all time* (2 Chronicles 7:16) that is, in my [the Lord's] house. The affection of the breast is seen at the brows. *I will look with favour on the faithful in the land* (Psalm 101:6). God's eye is in his house, to approve and bless you, if you sanctify him in ordinances. Friend, keep the Lord's Day with care and conscience, perform your duties with suitable graces, and God's eye will be upon you, you shall see his love in his pleasant and gracious looks. Jesus Christ beholds and approves the gracious performances of his people; he seems to say to them, as Paul to the Colossians: *For though I am absent in body, yet I am with you in spirit, rejoicing to see your good order and the firmness of your faith in Christ* (Colossians 2:5).

3. There is the eye of fury and indignation. God's looks will speak his anger, as well as his blows: his fury is visible by his

frowns. *I will fix my eyes upon them for evil* (Amos 9:4). God's sight can wound as deeply as his sword. Job speaks of him, *[he] sharpens his eyes against me* (Job 16:9). Wild beasts, when they fight, whet their eyes as well as their teeth. An enemy enraged looks on his antagonist as if he would look through him. He sharpens his eyes upon me, as if he would stab me to the heart, with a glance of his eye; so an expositor glosses on it. If you wait on God irreverently, worship him carelessly, and profane his day, either by physical labour or spiritual idleness, you may not expect his eye of favour, but fury. *But if you do not listen to me, to keep the Sabbath day holy, and not to bear a burden and enter by the gates of Jerusalem on the Sabbath day, then I will kindle a fire in its gates, and it shall devour the palaces of Jerusalem and shall not be quenched* (Jeremiah 17:27; Ezekiel 22:26-31). God's severity has been remarkable on the profaners of his Sabbath. The first blow given the German churches was on the Lord's Day, which they carelessly observed; on that day Prague was lost. When men disturb God's rest, God does usually deprive them of rest. The day of the Lord is like to be a dreadful day to them that despise the Lord's Day.

Truly God is as jealous in his courts under the gospel, as he was under the law. Christ, whose eyes are as a flame of fire, walks in the midst of the golden candlesticks throughout the world. He observes how holy duties are performed, and how his holy day is sanctified. *For where two or three are gathered in my name, there am I among them* (Matthew 18:20). He is in the midst of us, to behold our inward and outward carriage in his courts; he observes in praying, what confessions are made of sin, with what confusion of face, and contrition of heart, what petitions are put up for grace and pardon, with what integrity of spirit, and fervency of affection are made. He observes in hearing, whether men hear with attention suitable to that word which is able to save their souls, whether men receive the truth in the love of it, whether they resolve on subjection, and to give themselves up to that form of doctrine which is given down to them, or whether men hear sermons, as children turn over books, merely for the entertainments that are in them. *I went down to the nut orchard to look at the blossoms of the valley, to see whether the vines had budded, whether the pomegranates were in bloom* (Song of Songs 6:11). He sees the rotten bough of hypocrisy, the leaves of profession, without the fruits of an answerable conversation, he sees all your unripe, sour undigested duties.

Reader, if I were to counsel you how to spend a market-day, so that you might gain much wealth and treasure, I doubt not but you would listen to me; I am now to advise you how to spend the Lord's Day, the market-day for your soul, so that you may get the true treasure, durable riches and righteousness; I pray that you would hear and obey the directions which I have to deliver to you from the Lord for that end.

Making Preparation for the Christian Sabbath (The Lord's Day)

Make preparation for the day. There is scarcely any work which admits of any considerable perfection, but requires some previous preparation. In works of nature, the ground must be dunged, dressed, ploughed, harrowed, and all to prepare it for the seed. In works of art, the musician tunes his violin, screwing up some of his strings higher, letting some down lower, as occasion is, and all to prepare it for his lesson, and indeed without this he would make but sad music. Truly, friend, thus it is with us in matters of higher moment; hearts, like soil, must be prepared for the seed of the Word—how many a sermon hath been lost because this was lacking!—and the violins of our souls must be tuned to praise God, or otherwise they will sound but harshly in his ears.

The priests were to wash in the laver when they went into the tabernacle, and when they came near to the altar to minister, upon pain [threat] of death [if they did not do so] (Exodus 30:19–20). Signifying that to holy performances, there is required holy preparation; suitable to which is David's speech, *I wash my hands in innocence and go around your altar, O Lord* (Psalm 26:6).

When the temple was to be built, the stones were hewn, and the timber squared and fitted, before they were brought to the place where the temple stood; there was neither axe, nor hammer, nor any use of them in the temple: and what does this speak, but that the Christian must be polished and prepared to be a spiritual temple, an habitation for the God of Jacob, and also fitted for his worship, which was then in the temple.

There is no duty, but that which requires some previous disposition. A little breakfast quickens the appetite to a good dinner; duty fits the heart for duty; consider prayer. The Christian must be poor in spirit, that would prevail in prayer for spiritual riches. The vessel must be empty before it can be filled. *O Lord, you hear the desire of the afflicted; you will strengthen their heart; you will incline your ear* (Psalm 10:17). For hearing; the weeds must be plucked up before the grain be thrown into the ground. *So put away all malice and all deceit and hypocrisy and envy and all slander. Like newborn infants, long for the pure spiritual milk, that by it you may grow up into salvation* (1 Peter 2:1-2). In singing, the lungs must be good, the inwards [heart and mind] clean before the voice will be sweet and clear. *My heart is steadfast, O God, my heart is steadfast! I will sing and make melody!* (Psalm 57:7). So for the Lord's Day, the Israelites had their preparation. It was *the day of Preparation, that is, the day before the Sabbath* (Mark 15:42).

The preparation for the Lord's Day consists partly in care so as to order our worldly business, so that they may not encroach on the Sabbath; some expositors observe that the word remember, in the fourth command, enjoins a provident foresight and diligent dispatch of earthly affairs on the day before, that nothing may remain to disquiet us in, or disturb God's day of rest. There is an observable place, *if you turn back your foot from the Sabbath, from doing your pleasure on my holy day* (Isaiah 58:13), that is, from treading on my holy ground with the dirty feet of earthly affairs or affections. The Jews' preparation began at three of the clock in the afternoon, which the Hebrews called the Sabbath eve: the ancient fathers called *cœna pura* [Latin for the 'pure meal'], from the heathen (say some) whose religion taught them in their sacrifices to certain of their gods, to prepare themselves by a strict kind of holiness, at which time they had a supper, consisting of meats holy in their opinion.

The Jews were so careful in their preparation, that, to further it, the best and wealthiest of them, even those that had many servants, and were masters of families, would chop herbs, sweep the house, cleave wood, kindle the fire, and do such like things. The mariner that intends a voyage, puts his ship off from land; so truly, friend, if you would launch heavenward upon a Lord's Day, there is a necessity that the vessel of your heart be put off from the earth. When our blessed Saviour was teaching the people, he was disturbed by one that told him, *behold, his mother and his brothers stood outside, asking to speak to him* (Matthew 12:46). So when you are hearing or praying, or about any religious ordinance, what an hindrance, what a disturbance it will be for your heart to suggest to you; man, your calling, your companions, or such and such things which lie upon the spoil, through your negligence in the week days, they all stand without waiting to speak to you. If you would avoid distraction, prevent the occasions. As Isaiah said to Hezekiah, *Set your house in order, for you shall die and not recover* (Isaiah 38:1); so I say to you, set your house in order, and your heart in order, for the Lord's Day.

The main preparation of the heart for a Sabbath, lies in removing the filth of sin, and in enlivening and awakening grace. Sin must be removed. If the stomach be upset, it must be healed before it is fed, otherwise the food will not nourish and strengthen the body, but rather encourage continued upset and sickness. *Therefore, if anyone cleanses himself from what is dishonourable, he will be a vessel for honourable use, set apart as holy, useful to the master of the house, ready for every good work* (2 Timothy 2:21).

Filthiness and rampant wickedness must be laid aside, before we can receive *with meekness the implanted word* (James 1:21). When the vessel is unclean, it contaminates immediately the sweetest of liquids which are poured into it; when the heart is unclean, it loses the good, that it might have otherwise received, by the truths of God.

As sin must be cast out, so grace must be called up; grace is like fire, which needs to be gently kindled in the fireplace; so it is your duty before the Lord's Day, to kindle the fire within. Most people upon a Sabbath adorn their bodies with their best clothes; but, alas! Who clothes and dresses his soul as they ought to on this day? When, in fact, they are going to meet the blessed Redeemer!

Reader, suppose you are a person of great prominence and estate, and the king should send you a request that he would like to dine with you tomorrow, what preparation would you make for his entertainment? Would not your first work be to clean your house, by sweeping away all dust, then to clean and wash the floors, nay, for them to be rubbed, polished and everything to be neat and clean? Would you not bring out choice ornaments, then lay down your richest carpets and rugs, bring out your best plates and bone china, decorate your room with the most beautiful and costly furniture, in order to endeavour that all things are in place, something suitable for the dignity of so great a prince? I tell you, that the great King of all the world serves you notice in his Word, that on such a day, being the Sabbath, he intends to sup [commune] with you. Now, friend, what preparation will you make to demonstrate your respect to this blessed and only potentate? Can you beforehand, at least sweep away the dust of sin, and wash the room of your heart clean, adorn it with the best furniture, the graces, the embroidery of the Holy Spirit? Truly unless this be done, Christ will not think himself welcome; no, all your pretended entertainment of him, will be not only infinitely unworthy of, but also provoking to, so jealous and glorious a prince.

Believe it, your profit on a Sabbath depends not a little, upon your preparation for the Sabbath; until the matter be prepared, how can it receive the form? (Job 11:13-14). You have enjoyed many Lord's Days, and it may have done you little soul-saving good; you go to the house of God, where a table, in the preaching of the gospel, is set before you, one spread with all the sweet delicacies of pardon, love, grace, peace, and eternal life, at which others sit and feed; their souls are filled with marrow and fatness, and their mouths praise the Lord with joyful lips; but you have no appetite, who desires to eat only a little, and taste almost nothing. I dare to be the physician to diagnose for you the cause and cure of this.

The cause is, your stomach is sick, your heart is unclean; and therefore as a man that has a cold, or some disease predominant, who loses his appetite, but instead he complains sometimes of the food, sometimes of the cook, when the fault is in himself, so you cannot taste any goodness in the best spiritual food. Neither the public prayer nor the Scriptures, neither the Sabbath sermon are savoury to you. Yet you all too easily blame the preacher, saying to yourself that he does not dress the food to your taste, when actually the fault is in the foulness [sickness] of your own affections. The cure must be, to purge out this old leaven, to take some pains beforehand in cleansing your heart. When the stomach is clean, as after purging or fasting, how sweet is a piece of bread! So if you would but in secret search your soul, put away all filthiness, by a penitent confession, cleanse your heart by sincere contrition, and then frequent the public ordinances, you would find prayer sweet, preaching sweet, the sacrament sweet, every service sweet. Oh, how you would instead then love the habitation of God's house, and the place where his honour dwells.

Conclusion

Prepare to meet your God (Amos 4:12), O Christian! Betake yourself to your chamber [secret place of prayer] on the Saturday night, confess and acknowledge your unthankfulness for, and unfruitfulness under, the ordinances of God, shame and condemn yourself for your sins, entreat God to prepare your heart for, and assist it in, your religious performances; spend some time in consideration of the infinite majesty, holiness, jealousy, and goodness of God, with whom you are to have to do in sacred duties, ponder the weight and importance of his holy ordinances, how they concern your salvation or condemnation, your everlasting life or death, how certainly they will either further your unchangeable welfare, or increase your eternal woe; meditate on the shortness of the time you have to enjoy Sabbaths in; how near your life may be to its end, how speedily and how easily God may take down your earthly tabernacle, how there is no working, no labouring, no striving in heaven, to which you are hastening; and continue musing and fanning into flame the fire until it burns; you cannot imagine the good you may gain by such forethoughts, how pleasant and profitable a Lord's Day would be to you after such a preparation. The oven of your heart, thus baked in, as it were, overnight, would be easily heated the next morning; the fire so well raked up when you go to bed, would be the sooner kindled when you should rise in the morning. Therefore, if you would present your heart to God on the Saturday night, you should find it then, awakened and ready to meet with him in the Lord's Day morning.

The Westminster Standards and the Sacraments

Andy J. Young

Question: What is a sacrament?

Answer: A sacrament is a holy ordinance instituted by Christ in his church, to signify, seal, and exhibit to those that are within the covenant of grace, the benefits of his mediation; to strengthen and increase their faith, and all other graces; to oblige them to obedience; to testify and cherish their love and communion one with another; and to distinguish them from those that are without.[1]

How can I grow as a Christian? How can I know God better? How can my faith become stronger? These questions are vital yet answers to them can vary. For some the solution is found in personal devotions. Through daily Bible reading and prayer their faith is kept strong and their relationship with God deepened. Others resort to conferences where, through band-led worship and keynote speakers, they enjoy a high point in their Christian experience. Whilst personal devotions can be helpful, and conferences encouraging, we have to ask if either of these are the primary ways God intends his people to grow in faith, hope and love? The Bible gives clear answers to the above questions, and the *Westminster Standards* are arguably the most helpful summary of what the Bible teaches.[2] Acts 2:42 records the

---
[1] *Westminster Larger Catechism*, Question 162.
[2] B. B. Warfield said of the *Westminster Standards* that they are 'the richest and most precise and best guarded statement ever penned of all that enters into evangelical

early church *devoting themselves to the apostles' teaching and the fellowship, to the breaking of bread and the prayers.* The *Shorter Catechism* states: 'The outward and ordinary means whereby Christ communicates to us the benefits of redemption, are his ordinances, especially the word, sacraments, and prayer.'[1] In other words, the way God helps Christians grow is through the proper use of what are called 'the means of grace.' The public reading and preaching of God's Word, together with the sacraments of baptism and the Lord's Supper, and also prayer, combine as these means of grace.[2] As such they are the God-given, God-appointed, and God-blessed ways in which every Christian can and will grow in faith, hope and love.

Before we consider the importance of baptism and the Lord's Supper for the life of every church and Christian, we must first locate the sacraments in the context of God's grace. The *Westminster Standards* define the sacraments as 'holy signs and seals *of the covenant of grace*.'[3] As hell-deserving sinners we need Jesus Christ who is the ultimate gift of God's grace.[4] The wonderful news of the gospel is that we need God's grace and he has lavished it upon us in the person and work of Christ.

We can only answer the questions above when we realize the importance of God's grace to us in Christ. We become Christians by grace and we continue to be Christians by grace. God's grace is amazing because it takes hell-deserving sinners and makes them children of God. More, it takes those same children and changes them into the very image of Jesus Christ.[5] The sacraments are one of the ways God communicates this

---

religion and of all that must be safeguarded if evangelical religion is to persist in the world.' *Selected Shorter Writings* ed, John E. Meeter, Phillipsburg: Presbyterian & Reformed, 2001, 660

1 WLC 154. See also WSC 88
2 WCF 27.4 states clearly that 'there be only two sacraments ordained by Christ our Lord in the gospel; that is to say, Baptism and the Supper of the Lord.'
3 WCF 27.1. Emphasis added.
4 John 1:14-18
5 The *Westminster Standards* teach that both 'Justification is an act of God's free grace unto sinners' and 'Sanctification is a work of God's free grace.' See WLC 70 & 75.

grace and accomplishes this transformation, and so they are all about the grace of God in Jesus Christ. This establishes a crucial principle. Our growth as Christians is not about what we do or what we feel. It is about our reliance upon God for everything. A reliance upon a gracious God who supplies the grace we need through the means of grace he has provided.

In the context of this amazing grace we will ask five questions about the sacraments that the *Westminster Standards* clearly answer: Who? How? Where? What? and Why?

Who has Given the Sacraments?

The *Westminster Standards* states that 'Sacraments are holy signs and seals of the covenant of grace, immediately instituted by God.'[1] This is a basic, and yet profound, point. It is God himself who has instituted the sacraments. He gave them and he commanded them. To put it crudely: they are his idea.

All good parents want to provide a healthy, well-balanced and nutritious diet for their children. They buy, prepare, and provide for their family the meals they need to grow and mature. The same is true of God. He knows the spiritual nourishment that Christians need and he provides that nourishment for them. The sacraments are from God and for our good.

More specifically it is the Triune God—the Father, the Son and the Holy Spirit—who communicates grace to his people.

God the Father is the source of communicated grace

Consider the following:

> As God has appointed the elect unto glory, so has He, by the eternal and most free purpose of His will, foreordained all the means thereunto.[2]

> Man, by his fall, having made himself incapable of life by that covenant, the Lord was pleased to make a second, commonly called

---
1 WCF 27.1
2 WCF 3.6

the covenant of grace; wherein He freely offers unto sinners life and salvation by Jesus Christ ...[1]

These statements teach that God the Father has both chosen his people to get to glory, and appointed the means by which they will get there. God knew precisely how he was going to achieve his purposes. He chose to 'make use of means' to accomplish his will. We also see God was pleased to make a second covenant to save his elect people. It was God the Father who sent his Son Jesus Christ so that sinners could have life and salvation in him. It is God the Father who is the source of the grace communicated to us in the sacraments.

This highlights the objective nature of the sacraments in that they are about what God does and not what we do.[2] At the heart of God's grace, gospel and sacraments are the acts of God for his people. They are about what our God has done for us, what gifts he has given to us, how he blesses us, what he knows we need for our growth and what provision he has made for our spiritual well-being. In short, they display the indicatives of the gospel.

Jesus Christ is the substance of communicated grace

The *Westminster Standards* make this point throughout:

> It pleased God, in His eternal purpose, to choose and ordain the Lord Jesus, His only begotten Son, to be the Mediator between God and man ...[3]

> Sacraments are holy signs and seals of the covenant of grace, immediately instituted by God, to represent Christ and His benefits ...[4]

What do we need for our spiritual growth and sustenance? What spiritual vitamins and nutrients do we need to grow

---

[1] WCF 7.3
[2] Herman Bavinck states that 'Of primary importance in the Lord's Supper is what God does, not what we do.' *Reformed Dogmatics* Vol. IV, Grand Rapids: Baker, 2008, 567.
[3] WCF 8.1. See also WCF 7.6
[4] WCF 27.1

as Christians? The answer is Jesus Christ. We need more of our Saviour. He is what God gives for our growth, and what God specifically gives us in the sacraments. In baptism we receive a sign and seal of our 'in-grafting into Christ.'[1] The Lord's Supper is for the remembrance of Christ's death, the spiritual nourishment and growth of Christians 'in Him' and of their 'communion with Him'[2] and in the Lord's Supper we 'receive and feed upon Christ crucified.'[3] As the *Larger Catechism* so succinctly puts it, 'the spiritual part of both [sacraments] is Christ and his benefits.'[4]

In other words, the substance of the grace that God gives us is Jesus Christ. Think back to some of those questions we started with: How can I grow? How can I know God better? How can my faith become stronger? The answer is by knowing, loving and getting more of Jesus Christ. It is in the preaching of the Word and the sacraments that God gives us our Saviour.

The Holy Spirit is the effective cause of communicated grace

Consider two crucial sections of the *Westminster Standards* on the sacraments:

> The grace which is exhibited in or by the sacraments rightly used, is not conferred by any power in them: neither does the efficacy of a sacrament depend upon the piety or intention of him that does administer it; but upon the work of the Spirit ...[5]

> The efficacy of Baptism is not tied to that moment of time wherein it is administered; yet, notwithstanding, by the right use of this ordinance, the grace promised is not only offered, but really exhibited, and conferred, by the Holy Spirit, to such (whether of

---

[1] WCF 28.1
[2] WCF 29.1
[3] WCF 29.7
[4] WLC 176
[5] WCF 27.3

age or infants) as that grace belongs unto, according to the counsel of God's own will, in His appointed time.[1]

We must always remember that we are entirely dependent on the Holy Spirit for God's grace to be effective in our lives. As such, the Holy Spirit makes the sacraments work. He causes the grace offered in the sacraments to be effective in the lives of God's people.

This highlights the spiritual nature of the sacraments:

> Worthy receivers outwardly partaking of the visible elements in this sacrament, do then also, inwardly by faith, really and indeed, yet not carnally and corporally, but spiritually, receive and feed upon Christ crucified ...[2]

Our feeding on Christ in the sacraments is spiritual, or more precisely 'Spirit-ual'—by and with the Holy Spirit. To the unbelieving eye the rite of baptism is a mere pouring of water and the celebration of the Lord's Supper is a meagre meal. But by faith we commune with Christ by his Spirit.

Ask yourself this question: when was the last time you saw yourself grow? The answer is you did not! Yet since the day you were born to whatever height and size you are now, you have grown. Your physical growth has been imperceptible, yet inexorable. This is the same with the means of grace generally, and the sacraments specifically. Through the right and proper use of them, we will grow as Christians, yet we will not be able to observe that growth by sight. It is only as we feed on Christ by faith, and in complete dependence on the Holy Spirit to cause that growth, that we will in fact grow spiritually.

Before moving on, it is important to note the Trinitarian nature of the sacraments. Not only is baptism to be 'in the name of the Father, and of the Son, and of the Holy Spirit'[3] it is in

---

[1] WCF 28.6
[2] WCF 29.7
[3] WCF 28.2

both sacraments that 'we encounter the Holy Trinity.'[1] When we partake of the sacraments by faith we receive from God the Father his gift of God the Son by the inner working of God the Holy Spirit.

There is a direct implication from this. If the sacraments are instituted by God then we must take them seriously. They are not a suggestion or an optional extra. They are God's way of blessing his people. To ignore them is to ignore the very means our all-loving Triune God has provided for our growth and nurture. To neglect them is tantamount to a young child refusing to eat the meals his loving parents have prepared for him.

How are the Sacraments Given to Us?

The *Westminster Standards* teach that God relates to his people through covenant:

> Man by his fall, having made himself incapable of life by that covenant, the Lord was pleased to make a second, commonly called the covenant of grace; wherein He freely offers unto sinners life and salvation by Jesus Christ, requiring of them faith in Him that they may be saved, and promising to give unto all those that are ordained unto life His Holy Spirit, to make them willing and able to believe.[2]

In his covenant with us, God makes promises that he is absolutely committed to keeping. They are the very structure of his relationship with us. The way God relates to us and the way we relate to him must be within this structure. You might be wondering what this has to do with baptism and the Lord's Supper. The answer is everything.

God's covenantal dealings always included physical signs and seals of his promises. Consider the various covenants between

---

[1] Robert Letham, *The Holy Trinity In Scripture, History, Theology, and Worship*, New Jersey: Presbyterian & Reformed, 2004, p.325
[2] WCF 7.3

God and man in the Bible: with Adam, God gave the tree of life; with Noah, he gave the rainbow; with Abraham, he gave circumcision; with Moses, he gave the Sabbath day; with David, he gave kingship (Genesis 9:12-17; 17:9-14; Exodus 31:12-18; Psalm 89:20-29). The New Covenant in Jesus Christ follows the same pattern. With all the promises God gives to us in Jesus Christ we also get these two signs of those same promises: baptism and the Lord's Supper.[1] Look at what the *Westminster Standards* has to say about this:

> Under the gospel, when Christ, the substance, was exhibited, the ordinances in which this covenant is dispensed are the preaching of the Word, and the administration of the sacraments of Baptism and the Lord's Supper: which, though fewer in number, and administered with more simplicity, and less outward glory; yet, in them, it is held forth in more fullness, evidence, and spiritual efficacy, to all nations, both Jews and Gentiles; and is called the New Testament. There are not therefore two covenants of grace, differing in substance, but one and the same, under various dispensations.[2]

The sacraments are an essential part of the 'dispensing' of the New Covenant in Christ. They communicate the same substance, which is Christ, as the previous covenant dispensations, yet they do so with 'more fullness' and 'spiritual efficacy.'[3]

---

[1] Matthew 26:26-29, 28:18-20. See also WCF 27.4 & 27.5

[2] WCF 7.6

[3] See also WCF 27.5, which states, 'The sacraments of the Old Testament, in regard of the spiritual things thereby signified and exhibited, were, for substance, the same with those of the New.' This does at least three things. First, it recognises the fundamental unity in God's dealings with his people between the Old and New Testaments. Second, it understands Christ and the New Covenant era to be essentially the same as, yet at the same time, the glorious and more effective fulfilment of, all that has gone before. Third, it provides the theological basis for the baptising of 'the infants of one or both believing parents.' See WCF 28.4. If the children of believers were included in the Old Covenant dispensations, and the substance of the New Covenant is the same, then the children of believers must

As signs and seals of God's promised grace, they visibly communicate what God verbally promises, and they physically symbolize what God spiritually offers. As men and women made in the image of God we have bodies as well as souls. And so God condescends to give us physical, tangible, even edible, signs of his grace.[1] As such the salvation we have in Christ is 'earthly and physical as well as spiritual.'[2] And so Baptism and the Lord's Supper appeal to our outward senses so as to 'move the heart' and 'pierce into the soul.'[3]

Augustine and the Reformers referred to the sacraments as 'visible words' because they are inseparably bound to the Word of God.[4] The *Westminster Standards* make this clear by asserting that the efficacy of a sacrament depends both on the Holy Spirit and 'the word of institution,' and by repeatedly asserting that only lawfully ordained 'ministers of the Word' are to administer them.[5] Practically-speaking this means the sacraments should always be accompanied by the reading and preaching of God's Word. If they communicate in visible pictures the verbal promises of God, those same verbal promises need to be heard with the visible signs.[6]

This indissoluble connection between the Word and the

---

therefore continue to be included in the covenant, as so have a right to the sign of that covenant. For more on this see Cornelius P. Venema 'Covenant Theology and Baptism' in *The Case for Covenantal Infant Baptism* ed, Gregg Strawbridge, New Jersey: Presbyterian & Reformed, 2003, 201–229.

1   'But the Word signifies and seals Christ to us by the sense of hearing; the sacrament signifies and seals Christ to us by the sense of sight.' Bavinck, *Reformed Dogmatics* Vol. 4, 479
2   Robert Letham, *Baptism,* Fearn: Christian Focus, 2012, 19. For more on the physical nature of salvation and the sacraments see Letham, *Baptism,* 17ff, where he rightly corrects evangelicalisms tendency towards a physical/spiritual dualism.
3   Robert Bruce, *The Mystery of the Lord's Supper,* ed, Thomas F. Torrance, Fearn: Christian Focus, 2012, 30
4   John Calvin, *Institutes of the Christian Religion* ed. John T. McNeill, Philadelphia: Westminster Press, Vol. 2, 1281
5   WCF 27.4 & 28.2
6   Bruce argues that for a sacrament to be a sacrament it must of necessity be joined to the Word of God. See *The Mystery of the Lord's Supper,* 33-34

sacraments helps us see again the objective emphasis in the *Westminster Standards* understanding of the sacraments. Just as the gospel is to be preached and set before God's people, so too the sacraments are to be administered and set before God's people. Just as the promises of God are to be declared and heard, so in the sacraments, the visible symbols of those promises are to be seen and tasted. The sacraments 'represent Christ and his benefits'[1] and so, like the Word of God read and preached, are not primarily about me and my faith. They are about God and Christ; they are about the glorious gospel of peace; they are about the finished and accomplished work of Christ on the cross. They objectively, dramatically and visibly, set before the church their covenant God and his covenant promises. In an age when all things visual have infiltrated the evangelical church this is a timely reminder that we have the dramatic and the visible demonstration of the gospel in the sacraments. The church does not need drama, mime and graphic presentations when we already have Baptism and the Lord's Supper.

The *Westminster Standards* helpfully identify another connection and that is between the signs of the covenant and the covenant promises themselves:

> There is in every sacrament a spiritual relation, or sacramental union, between the sign and the thing signified: whence it comes to pass, that the names and effects of the one are attributed to the other.[2]

More will be said on this below: suffice to say for now that it affirms once again the importance of understanding the sacraments in relation to the covenant promises they signify. This is vital to grasp. The sacraments are inextricably connected to the covenant promises of God in Jesus Christ. God has given them to help us both understand his covenantal dealings but also to confirm us in that very same covenant.

Imagine a fiancé during their wedding service refusing to

---

1 WCF 27.1
2 WCF 27.2

accept the ring his wife-to-be was offering him, as she made promises to him. He might say, 'It is only a piece of metal! I love you and I don't need these physical signs of our love.' But he would have mistaken the significance of both the ring and of his new marriage relationship. The rings are only pieces of metal, but in that context they are so much more. They are from his wife-to-be as a symbol of their love and of their vows to each other. As she makes a public declaration of her love for, and commitment to, him, the ring she offers encapsulates the full significance of what she is saying and doing. Or imagine when a wife, in the midst of a heated argument, takes her wedding ring off and flings it at her husband. Is she simply throwing a small piece of metal at him? No—she is symbolically ending their relationship. She is threatening, in that one act, to terminate the entirety of their marriage. In that instance, and used in that way, the ring signifies their marriage.

The sacraments are the same. God offers us in the sacraments more than simply water, bread and wine. He offers in those same elements symbols of his covenantal commitment and love. As such sacraments signify and seal God's covenantal promises to us. They denote the full significance of the covenantal commitment God has for his people in Jesus Christ. In this way the sacraments point us beyond themselves to the covenant-making, covenant-keeping God of grace, who so loves his people he wants to give them these 'visible words' that confirm his written and preached words.[1]

This leads us once again to see how significant the sacraments are for the life of the church and for every Christian. They communicate to us the grace of God within the structure of the covenant of that grace. They are God's chosen ways of encapsulating his promises to us and we dare not neglect them. It is as if, when the sacraments are administered, God is saying to his people: 'I have demonstrated in the gift of my Son how

---

[1] For more on the connection between the Word and sacraments see James Candlish, *The Christian Sacraments,* Memphis: General Books, 2012, 9ff; and Calvin, Vol 2, 1278-1280.

much I love you; I have revealed to you in my Word how much I love you; here in these symbols I want you to taste and see that same love.' Who in their right mind would want to miss such a thing?

Where are the Sacraments Given?

The *Westminster Standards* locate the sacraments in the context of the gathered and worshipping church. This principle is in danger of being lost in evangelical circles today. We live in such an individualistic society this may even be shocking to some Christians. Faith is understood to be personal and private, not corporate and communal. It is about my own subjective experiences of God—whether in worship or work or wherever I choose. This can too easily be applied to the sacraments. We can view Baptism as my own personal testimony of faith. We can understand the Lord's Supper as an opportunity to have a few brief moments of 'me time' with God. The teaching of the *Westminster Standards* on the church could not be further from this. First, note how salvation in general belongs to the church:

> The visible Church ... is the kingdom of the Lord Jesus Christ, the house and family of God, out of which there is no ordinary possibility of salvation.[1]

This underlines the importance the church should have in the life of the Christian.[2] If it is in the corporate, gathered, organized and visible church that salvation is found, then it is in the context of this same church that every Christian should seek to live out their salvation. In other words we should not first think of our relationship with God in individual terms. We should think of it in relation to the church, the family of God, and therefore in corporate terms.

---

1 WCF 25.2
2 This understanding of the church is also in complete agreement with historic Christianity, see Robert Letham, *The Westminster Assembly,* New Jersey: Presbyterian & Reformed, 2009, 319-20

The Westminster Standards and the Sacraments

Second, note how the sacraments, or 'ordinances' as they are often called, are specifically given to the church:

> Unto this catholic visible Church Christ has given the ministry, oracles, and ordinances of God, for the gathering and perfecting of the saints, in this life, to the end of the world: and does by His own presence and Spirit, according to His promise, make them effectual thereunto.[1]

This means the sacraments are not something we can choose to use on our own. God has given them to his church and it is only when they are rightly used in the sphere and context of the gathered people of God that we can expect the Holy Spirit to make them effective to us. For this reason the *Westminster Standards* identify Baptism as admission 'into the visible Church'[2] and teaches that the Lord's Supper is 'to be observed in the Church.'[3]

Go back to our original questions about how we can grow. Part of the answer is with other Christians. We cannot choose how or when or even where we will grow as Christians. God has prescribed it for us and the answer is in the church and with his people.[4] As valuable as personal devotions can be, we should not view them as the primary way in which we cultivate our relationship with God. They may be highly useful means in a secondary sense, but they should always remain secondary simply because they are private and personal.[5]

---

1. WCF 25.3
2. WCF 28.1
3. WCF 29.1
4. Some want to add fellowship as a fourth means of grace. For example Wayne Grudem, *Systematic Theology*, Nottingham: IVP, 1994, 958. However, if we correctly understand the teaching of the *Westminster Standards* on the means of grace we will see that fellowship is assumed in all of them because they are understood in the context and sphere of the church.
5. Lyle D. Bierma, 'Infant Baptism in the Reformed Confessions' in *The Case for Covenantal Infant Baptism* ed, Gregg Strawbridge, Phillipsburg: Presbyterian & Reformed, 2003, 244 says 'The primary operations of divine grace take place in the church, or covenant community, through the word and sacrament.'

If you were stranded on a desert island what would you miss the most? When you returned home what would be the first thing you would do? I hope you would miss many things—your husband or wife, friends, children, parents and family. But would you miss Sunday worship? Would you look forward to attending a worship service of the church on the Lord's Day where you would gather together with God's people to meet the Triune God, and hear him speak, and bow in prayer and praise, and enjoy his presence through the sacraments?

The sacraments are given to the church, and so it is in the sphere and context of the church that we receive the fullness of God's grace with his people.

What are the Sacraments?

Having understood the sacraments as given by the Triune God, via the structure of his covenant, and to the church, we are ready now to understand what they specifically are and do. Note again how the *Westminster Standards* identify the sacraments as 'means of grace.'[1] As such they are the 'delivery systems God has instituted to bring grace.'[2] By them God gives us the grace we need.

More precisely they are 'signs and seals' of God's grace.[3] As signs they point to the grace of God in Jesus Christ, as seals they validate that grace to us in Jesus Christ.[4] As a sign, Baptism points to the reality of 'in-grafting into Christ, of regeneration, of remission of sins, and of his giving up to God ... to walk in newness of life.'[5] As a seal, Baptism validates that the recipient is united to Christ and is a member of the visible church. As a sign, the Lord's Supper points us to the body and blood of the Lord Jesus Christ which was broken and poured out for us. As a

---

1 WLC 154
2 Richard C. Barcellos, *The Lord's Supper as a Means of Grace,* Fearn: Mentor, 2013, 23
3 WCF 27.1 & 28.1. See also Romans 4:11
4 Van Dixhoorn's comments on this are particularly helpful. See 357–358
5 WCF 28.1

seal, the Lord's Supper validates to the Christian the benefits of Christ's death for him.

The sacraments are therefore more than simple rites we perform to help us remember Christ crucified. They 'offer, exhibit and confer' God's promised grace to us.[1] They are God's appointed ways of conveying the true and lasting 'benefits of Christ' to his people. Baptism is God 'in-grafting' us into Christ and the Lord's Supper is God 'feeding and nourishing us upon Christ.'

It is at this point a certain balance is struck. On the one hand, the *Westminster Standards* maintain that the sacraments actually can and do communicate the grace of God. On the other hand they insist this can only happen 'by the Holy Spirit, according to God's own will, in God's own time and only to those to whom this grace belongs.'[2] In other words the sacraments only confer the grace of God when, and to whom, God chooses. There is then a balance between God choosing to convey his grace through the sacraments, and the sacraments being dependent on God for that grace to be conveyed. This balance draws the believer to their God through the sacraments. We must use the sacraments but in so doing we must depend upon God to make them useful for us.[3]

Furthermore, given that the sacraments are instituted by the Triune God, are emblems of his covenant promises, and are given for the blessing of his body the church, then surely they will do what God intends for them to do. They will actually communicate to his people the grace we need to be his people. To put it practically, given that we have clear Scriptural and Confessional teaching on their proper administration, right use and worthy reception, we can come by faith, take God at his

---

[1] WCF 28.6 & 27.3
[2] Ibid.
[3] Think about it this way: if God did not communicate grace through means we would be left not knowing how or where or when this grace would be given. On the other hand, if God absolutely bound himself to means, they could easily become mechanical for us. This balance guards against both these errors.

word, and truly receive God's promised grace in and through them. Yes, the sacraments work as signs and seals of grace only when, and to whom, God chooses. But wonderfully the Bible is clear that God has and does choose to use them for his people's good. In short, 'God keeps his appointments.'[1]

Elsewhere the *Westminster Standards* teach that 'to all those for whom Christ has purchased redemption, He does certainly and effectually apply and communicate the same.'[2] Christ has certainly won our salvation and he certainly applies the benefits of that salvation to his people by his Word and Spirit, and through the sacraments. When God has promised us his grace, demonstrated that grace in Christ, and assures us of its effectiveness by the Holy Spirit, the issue is not whether the appointed means will do what they have been appointed to do. The issue is whether we will humbly believe the Word of God, shape our lives around those very means he has given, and by faith use them for our growth and benefit.

The above does two things. First, it holds in tension the vital theological point we have already commented upon:

> There is in every sacrament, a spiritual relation, or sacramental union, between the sign and the thing signified: whence it comes to pass, that the names and effects of the one are attributed to the other.[3]

In the sacraments we have three things: the physical sign, the reality the physical sign points to, and the relationship between the two. The physical sign and the reality signified must be kept distinct. The water of baptism is not in and of itself in-grafting into Christ; the bread and the wine are not in and of themselves the body and blood of Christ.[4] Yet at the same time they are inseparable. The water points to and authenticates in-grafting into Christ; the bread and wine point to and authenticate the

---

1 Letham, *Baptism*, 25-26.
2 WCF 8.8
3 WCF 27.2.
4 WCF 29.5 & 29.6.

body and blood of Christ. They have a 'spiritual relation.' The sign, when it is received by faith with the working of the Holy Spirit, communicates the reality—which is Christ.

Second, it draws out our faith. We should be diligent in our use of the sacraments, but in so doing look to the Christ of the sacraments. As one theologian has put it 'Faith holds the sign and the thing signified together.'[1] It is by Spirit-wrought faith that in the water, bread and wine of the sacraments we receive Jesus Christ and him crucified. By exercising faith in God and his Word we can in receiving the physical symbols of God's blessing actually receive what those symbols symbolize. As the *Belgic Confession of Faith* so graphically puts it, faith is the 'hand and mouth of our souls.'[2] In this way the objective presenting of Christ to his people in the sacraments becomes the subjective apprehending of Christ in the Christian. When I hear that God loves me from his Word, and when I taste and see that love in the sacraments, I am then led to trust more in the Christ of that love for myself.[3]

Why are the Sacraments Given?

All of the above leads us to ask one final question: Why has God given us the sacraments? The wonderful answer is union and communion. Consider how the *Westminster Standards* define both sacraments: Baptism is an 'in-grafting' or uniting to Christ; the Lord's Supper is our 'communion' with Christ.[4]

The heart of our covenant relationship with God is found in his promise *I will be your God and you will be my people* (Genesis 17:8; Exodus 6:7; Leviticus 26:12).[5] The fulfilment of

---

[1] Edmund P. Clowney, *The Church*, Downers Grove: IVP, 1995, 276.
[2] Article 35.
[3] In other words the sacraments should 'inspire, strengthen and confirm faith.' Hughes Oliphant Old, *Guides to the Reformed Tradition: Worship*, Atlanta: John Knox Press, 1984, 20.
[4] WCF 28.1 & 29.1.
[5] See also Psalm 73:26 where God is said to be his people's portion, and Deuteronomy 32:9 where Israel are said to be God's portion.

this covenant bond is in the incarnation of Jesus Christ who is himself called *Immanuel* (Matthew 1:23). The New Testament understands our relationship to Christ as a reciprocal union and communion—we are *in Christ* and Christ is *in us* (2 Corinthians 5:17; Galatians 2:20; Colossians 1:27). This union-relationship has its glorious climactic fulfilment in the new heavens and new earth when *the dwelling place of God will be with man and he will dwell with them, and they will be his people. And God himself will be with them as their God.*[1] As such, union and communion between God and his people are central to God's relationship with us, and our relationship with him.[2] God's purpose is not just to save us from our sins, but to fellowship with us as his redeemed people. This brings to a culmination all that has been noted above. The Triune God's ultimate covenantal intention is to be our God and us to be his people.

With this in mind we can see once again how important the sacraments are. If it is in Baptism we are united to Christ; and in the Lord's Supper we have communion with Christ; then the sacraments could not be more central to our relationship with God. Through them we enjoy the very heart of that relationship which is union and communion with Christ.

Moreover, the benefits of our union with Christ are communicated through the sacraments.[3] Not only do they symbolize this union, they actually offer it. It is through Baptism that we are united to Christ. It is through the Lord's Supper that we actually participate in and with Christ.[4] In other words

---

[1] Revelation 21:3.
[2] For more on this wonderful doctrine of Union with Christ see Anthony A. Hoekema, *Saved by Grace*, Grand Rapids: Eerdmans, 1994, 54–67; Richard B. Gaffin Jr., *By Faith, Not by Sight*, New Jersey: Presbyterian & Reformed, 2013; Robert Letham, *Union with Christ In Scripture, History and Theology*, Phillipsburg: Presbyterian & Reformed, 2011.
[3] Bruce helpfully argues that in the sacraments we get 'the whole Christ with His whole gifts, benefits and graces.' See *The Mystery of the Lord's Supper*, 37–39.
[4] 1 Corinthians 10:16 is a crucial verse here. See the helpful discussion in Barcellos, 45–50

the very heart of all that God has done for us in Christ is communicated to us through the sacraments.[1]

This returns us to the questions we began with: How can I grow as a Christian? How can I know God better? How can my faith be strengthened? At the heart of these questions lies the desire that every Christian has, which is to know a deeper and more meaningful relationship with God. The answer is found in Jesus Christ. The way we receive Christ is through the means of grace, of which the sacraments are a wonderful part.

To put it another way: the communion we have now with Christ by his Spirit is an anticipation of the communion we will enjoy forever in the new heavens and new earth.[2] What God will bless his people with in heaven he gives a foretaste of now on earth. The sacraments point us back to the finished and accomplished work of Christ, but they also point us forwards to the consummation of that work.[3] Even more wonderfully they give us an anticipation of that forever fellowship we will enjoy with our Saviour as we are united to him now and celebrate communion with him in his church. We celebrate Baptism now because then we will be forever with him and like him as his people. We eat and drink the Lord's Supper now because then we will sit down as the Bride of our heavenly Bridegroom at the marriage supper of the Lamb.

This begs the question: who in their right mind would disregard such a foretaste of heavenly communion? Who would miss an opportunity to enjoy now in part, what we will then enjoy in full, which is fellowship with our God?

---

[1] At this point WLC 66 must be kept in mind which teaches that only elect members of the invisible church are 'really and inseparably' united to Christ by their effectual calling. In other words, the sacraments communicate union with Christ only to those whom God chooses and calls, as already discussed above.
[2] 'Grace is glory begun or glory in the bud' cited in Barcellos, *The Lord's Supper as a Means of Grace*, 69.
[3] 1 Corinthians 11:26—The Lord's Supper is a proclamation of the Lord's death *until he comes*.

Conclusion

In conclusion we note some of the practical applications the *Westminster Standards* make on the sacraments. The rich sacramental theology of the *Westminster Standards* in no way blurs their practical usefulness. On the contrary, the biblical and theological depth of Baptism and the Lord's Supper necessarily make them relevant for the life of every Christian.

First, the *Larger Catechism* encourages every Christian to 'improve our baptisms.'[1] Understanding that Baptism is 'something that shapes the whole of the Christian life, from the very beginning to the very end,'[2] we should seek to regularly rest ourselves in the reality of what Baptism signifies, which is our union with Christ. As such Baptism should not be a one-off past event that has no bearing upon our present walk with Christ. On the contrary, every time we are tempted to sin, and every time we witness a Baptism, we should make every effort to remind ourselves of our own Baptism, and to grow into the spiritual reality that our Baptism points us to. As the German Reformer, Martin Luther, when oppressed by sin and tempted by the devil, would cry out: 'I am a baptised man,' so should we apprehend the reality of our Baptisms when tempted and hard-pressed.

Second, faith is 'ordinarily wrought' by the Word, and is 'increased and strengthened' by the sacraments.[3] This means that in times of trial, suffering and difficulty, when your faith is weak and frail, and when you are enduring periods of doubt and spiritual struggle, you should take refuge in the means of grace. To put it bluntly: when was the last time you participated in the Lord's Supper because you were struggling? Too many Christians absent themselves from the Lord's Supper during times of trial, when in fact they should do the reverse. God has provided the

---

[1] WLC 167.
[2] Old, 26. The *Directory for the Public Worship of God* instructs Ministers at a Baptism to 'admonish all that are present, to look back to their baptism; to repent of their sins against their covenant with God; to stir up their faith; to improve and make right use of their baptism, and of the covenant sealed thereby betwixt God and their souls.'
[3] WCF 14.1

means of grace to encourage, cultivate, reinforce and deepen our faith. We would do well to use them as he has directed, especially during those instances when our faith is under attack.

Third, the *Westminster Standards* warn that although Christians will persevere to the end, they can on occasion 'fall into grievous sins' and so 'incur God's displeasure, and grieve his Holy Spirit.'[1] One of the causes of this is a 'neglect of the means of their preservation' which as we have seen is the Word, sacraments and prayer. In other words, the reason why many Christians struggle to grow in their faith is because they are inattentive to the means of grace. By having a nonchalant attitude to the sacraments we are endangering ourselves. We should be warned against a blasé approach to the very ways God has chosen to bless us, and encouraged into the diligent use of them.

Fourth, the *Westminster Standards* teach that assurance of faith can be attained 'in the right use of ordinary means.'[2] Many Christians wrestle with this issue longing for a more consistent assurance of faith. We have clear help: through the regular use of the means of grace a Christian can enjoy something of this assurance. That is not to say it will come quickly or easily. You may have to 'wait long, and conflict with many difficulties.'[3] However, with a dependence on the Holy Spirit and a believing use of the very ways God has chosen to communicate his grace, such an assurance can be found.

Finally, the *Westminster Standards* define part of the use of a sacrament as 'solemnly to engage them to the service of God in Christ.' They should kindle within us an increased desire to love and serve our God, and to live a holy life for Christ. In addition they should enlarge our love for God's people. The Lord's Supper is a 'bond and pledge of their communion with Him [Christ],

---

[1] WCF 17.3
[2] WCF 18.3
[3] Ibid.

and with each other.[1] The sacraments should nurture within the life of the church a love between brothers and sisters that befits the body of Christ.

The sacraments should be an essential part of our answer to the questions we started with on how we can grow as Christians and how our faith can be strengthened. They are the Triune God's way of satisfying our hearts longing to know, love and enjoy him more. As such every Christian should seek to take every opportunity their church provides to celebrate them.

---

1 WCF 29.1. Emphasis added. See also WLC 162 on 'what is a sacrament?' which includes that they are 'to testify and cherish their love and communion one with another.'

The Westminster Standards and Family Worship: Maintaining True Religion in the Home

Chad T. Bailey

Introduction

What is the aim of your life? If you have children, what do you want them to be and do when they grow up? What is the greatest joy and highest goal of Christian parents for their children? What is to bring you most joy and satisfaction in life as a Christian? It is all too common among believers to consider education, health, money, and social status to be more important than the knowledge of God. Far too many pursue for themselves and also train their children to walk comfortably and prominently in this world instead of urging them to know and walk humbly with their God. Looking for solid joys and lasting treasures within oneself or within this world will sorely disappoint. However, the Bible has an answer to our restlessness and dissatisfaction. There is no better summary than that found in the *Westminster Catechisms*:

> Question: What is the chief and highest end of man?
>
> Answer: Man's chief and highest end is to glorify God, and fully to enjoy him for ever.[1]

---

[1] The *Westminster Larger Catechism*, Question 1.

In that most encouraging and rich High Priestly prayer, Jesus declared: *And this is eternal life, that they know you the only true God, and Jesus Christ whom you have sent* (John 17:3). The aim of the Bible is that sinners might know God and have eternal life. This is why the *Westminster Confession of Faith* begins with a chapter on Holy Scripture. For it is in the Bible alone that God can be known 'unto salvation.'[1] Knowing the only true God leads to worshiping the only true God.[2] Thus, whether you are married or single, have children or no children, are young or old, maintaining true religion in the home is both the privilege and duty of those who know God unto salvation.

All who profess the name of Christ are to glorify and enjoy God in whatever they do (1 Corinthians 10:31). While the *Westminster Standards* have much to teach the church corporately, the doctrines they teach are for every believer who seeks to walk humbly with God in their life. The specific purpose of the *Catechisms* and in particular the *Shorter Catechism*, is that the knowledge of God and his Son might flourish in every home and heart of God's people.

> Neither prayer, nor any other part of religious worship, is now under the gospel, either tied unto, or made more acceptable by any place in which it is performed, or towards which it is directed: but God is to be worshipped everywhere, in spirit and truth; as in private families daily, and in secret, each one by himself; so, more solemnly, in the public assembles, which are not carelessly, or wilfully to be neglected, or forsaken, when God, by his Word or providence, calls thereunto.[3]

Fellowship with the Triune God is the goal of the gospel (1 John 1:3) and this fellowship consists of knowing God as he has revealed himself by the Son and in his Word. The aim then of the Westminster Standards is to accurately explain the Bible that we might know our God unto salvation to the praise of his

---

[1] *Westminster Confession of Faith*, 1.1.
[2] *Westminster Confession of Faith*, 2.2.
[3] *Westminster Confession of Faith*, 21:6.

glorious grace. Such praise should fill the home of every believer. For that is a most rational thing to do in response to such saving knowledge (Romans 12:1).

For many today family worship seems a thing of the past and they would like to see it left there. Different times call for different customs, many often say. James W. Alexander, oldest son of Archibald Alexander and professor of Princeton Theological Seminary, provides a timeless rebuttal to this way of thinking. He stated plainly his belief that the practice of family worship is not antiquated nor a thing to be left in the past but is rather an ever-present outflow of genuine love for God born of the Spirit.

> I regard the neglect of family worship as springing from lukewarmness and worldliness in religion, and as a portentous evil of our day. Where piety is ardent and operative, it cannot but diffuse itself through the domestic structure.[1]

The apostle John emphatically declared as a spiritual father to the beloved Gaius, *I have no greater joy than to hear that my children are walking in the truth* (3 John 4). While this is in the context of a pastor to an adult Christian, certainly the grand desire and aim of all godly parents is here expressed for their children. The whole of the Word of God would set this forth as the duty and goal of Christian parents, to see their *little children* walking in the truth and having Christ formed in them. As John desired for his spiritual children that they may not sin but know that if they do sin they have an *advocate with the Father, Jesus Christ the righteous* (1 John 2:1), so too all Christian parents long for the children under their care to both turn from sin and rest in the Savior.

Children are a heritage from the Lord (Psalm 127:3) and as such are not our own but are precious gifts from God, which

---

[1] James W. Alexander, *Thoughts on Family Worship*, ed, Don Kistler, Pittsburgh: Soli Deo Gloria Publications, 1990, 145.

are to 'be accounted blessings, and not as burdens.'[1] It is not only a great blessing to have children but it is a greater blessing to see them walking humbly with God. The God who created the family has fixed it permanently in his sovereign Word that covenant households belong to him and should seek to worship him. The heads of households neglect their God-given duty when they fail to lead their children to worship the living and true God.

The Puritans were not the inventors of family worship, but they did champion the practice of it. Thus Thomas Manton, writing to promote family worship to the original adopters of the *Westminster Confession of Faith*, strongly declares that it is an act of 'covenant-breaking with God' to be derelict in this duty of promoting religion in the home, and perhaps much worse, it is 'betraying the souls of their children to the devil.'[2] While not the only reason, establishing and maintaining family worship or true religion in the home was a significant factor in the creation of the *Westminster Standards*. The delegates to the assembly considered the practice of family worship vital for 'cherishing piety, and preventing division and schism.' Walking humbly with God and in unity with God's people are the twin goals of family worship. It is the aim of this essay to commend that 'every Christian family ought to be as it were a little church, consecrated to Christ, and wholly influenced and governed by his rules.'[3] Consider three preliminary issues regarding a Christian household with particular regard to children.

The Guidance Covenant Children Need

First, children require leading. They are created that way.

---

[1] Matthew Henry, *Matthew Henry's Commentary on the Whole Bible, Complete and Unabridged in One Volume*, Peabody: Hendrickson, 1990, Psalm 127.
[2] Thomas Manton, 'Epistle to the Reader' in *The Westminster Confession of Faith: 1647 Edition*, Crossville: Puritan Publications, 2011, 55.
[3] Jonathan Edwards, 'Farewell Sermon' in *The Works of Jonathan Edwards, Volume 1*, Edinburgh: Banner of Truth, 1834, reps 2005, ccvi.

From their birth, they are dependent upon someone for almost everything. As sinners they will constantly struggle to follow but there is something in them on some level that not only requires but desires leadership and we must realize that one way or another they will be led—either the devil is going to train our children or we are. Better to have godly parents intentionally leading their little ones than leaving that up to the world or the evil one. This is not a matter of a certain type of education. It is possible for children schooled in the home all their life to be taught more by the devil than their parents who claim to be Christians, while children schooled outside the home can be raised by Christian parents who train up their children in the way they should go with great faithfulness. The protection and promotion and education of children is not relegated to the family alone but it does begin there and is meant by God to be the central hub of their lives. The primary location for children to be brought up in the nurture and admonition of the Lord is within the context of a family.

Charles Hodge noted the guiding influence of the theology instilled through the *Westminster Shorter Catechism* upon young Archibald Alexander in his home:

> A series of such precise, accurate, luminous propositions, inscribed on the understanding of a child, is the richest inheritance which can be given to him. They are seeds which need only the vivifying influence of the Spirit of life, to cause them to bring forth the fruits of holiness and glory. Dr. Alexander experienced this benefit to its full extent. He learned the Catechism as a matter of custom ... his mind being thus stored with truth, as soon as his moral and religious feelings were excited, they had the proper forms at hand in which to express themselves. The intellectual and emotional elements combine by a kind of elective affinity, and form that knowledge which is eternal life.[1]

---

[1] James M. Garretson, *Princeton and Preaching: Archibald Alexander and the Christian Ministry*, Edinburgh: Banner of Truth, 2005, 5

The Guarding Covenant Children Need

Second, children require protecting and guarding. According to God's will, children are born small and weak. Unlike animals, human children are born almost completely helpless. Therefore, it is obvious that they need to be guarded and helped from the beginning. The devil prowls around like a lion seeking someone to devour, writes the apostle Peter. A lion will usually go after the extremely young or old because they are easy prey. The weak are particularly vulnerable to the ferocious lions eager to make a quick and easy kill. So Satan our adversary seeks out the weak among the herd, especially the young. In the animal world, the parents must be on constant guard for predators that are looking to snatch and grab their young. We all know the stories of how protective a mother bear is towards her cubs. Now, most parents would consider themselves as protective as a bear but this usually pertains to the physical well-being of the children. But what of the spiritual well-being of our children? Jesus prayed not that we would be removed from all harmful situations to our bodies but our Savior prayed that we would be kept from the evil one (John 17:15). Much more is at stake regarding our children than their physical protection. Parents must guard the mind, heart, and soul of their little ones. Most parents do not need to be told to take care of the physical needs of their children; yet, it is too often the case that the soul of those children is neglected and left unguarded.

Thomas Manton, in his epistle to the reader for the second edition of the *Westminster Confession of Faith*, put the seriousness of the issue in plain terms:

> The devil has great malice toward the kingdom of Christ, and he knows no more succinct way to crush it in the egg than by the perversion of youth and supplanting family-duties ... now, the devil knows that it will be a blow at the root, and a ready way to prevent the succession of Churches, if he can subvert families. Then other societies and communities will not long flourish, nor

subsist with any power and vigor, for the family is the stock from which these are supplied both for the present and for the future.[1]

The Godliness Covenant Children Need

Third, the greatest need of our children is their godliness. The goal of raising our children is that they might fear the Lord and walk humbly with their God. Godliness, or living unto God, is to be the great aim of every parent that seeks to be faithful to their Master and Savior (Ephesians 6:4; 2 Timothy 1:5). We want our children to glorify and enjoy God forever. The godliness of children will not occur by osmosis and does not usually come without diligent and sound instruction. The *Westminster Standards* form a comprehensive and faithful corpus of doctrine rightly explaining the Word of God, which is meant to direct us and our children to God. In order to aid the learning of the doctrine of the *Confession*, the *Shorter Catechism* was created so that old and young could commit the teaching of the Bible to mind and heart. Benjamin B. Warfield, who was a 'shorter catechism boy' himself, describes the aim of godliness of learning not simply the *Catechism* but the doctrine it teaches. It has trained up many children in the way they should go, to live godly and holy lives. In fact, many have grown up to later thank God for such instruction in the home.

> How many have had occasions to 'thank God for that Catechism!' Did anyone ever know a really devout man who regretted having been taught the Shorter Catechism—even with tears—in his youth? How its forms of sound words come reverberating back into the memory, in moments of trials and suffering, of doubt and temptation, giving direction to religious aspirations, firmness to hesitating thought, guidance to stumbling feet: and adding to our religious meditations an ever-increasing richness and depth. 'The older I grow,' said Thomas Carlyle in his old age, 'and now I stand on the brink of eternity, the more comes

---

1 Thomas Manton, 'Epistle to the Reader' in The *Westminster Confession of Faith*.

back to me the first sentence in the Catechism, which I learned when a child, and the fuller and deeper its meaning becomes: "What is the chief end of man? To glorify God and to enjoy him forever."[1]

Though it is never meant to be a replacement for corporate worship, family worship is the best context to guard our children and guide them to godliness. But family worship is not simply for children but for all who call on the name of the Lord. Consider then the biblical foundations, theological motives, eternal benefits, continual opponents, and simple elements for establishing and maintaining true religion in the home.

Biblical Foundations of Family Worship

Maintaining Religion in the Home is Biblical

The practice of family worship has biblical foundations upon which to firmly stand, as the Westminster Assembly duly noted.[2] Religion in the home is rooted in creation. The opening words of the Bible indicate that God the Creator is to be worshiped by his creatures (Genesis 1:1). There are numerous calls to worship found in the Bible wherein creation is said to worship God (Psalm 19:1-6; 50:6; Romans 1:19-20) and all of creation is called upon to magnify its Creator (Psalm 148; 150). However, the worship of God is not merely a general command to trees and stars and animals but is specifically directed to the saints and their families (Deuteronomy 6:6-7; Psalm 78; Ephesians 6:4) so that the homes of believers are like little churches. The children of believers are to be raised *in the discipline and instruction of the Lord* (Ephesians 6:4; cf. Hebrews 11). It is a command given to Christians to raise their children specifically according to the Word and ways of the Lord, that is, to teach them to

---

[1] B.B. Warfield, 'Is the Shorter Catechism Worth While?' in *The Selected Shorter Writings of Benjamin B. Warfield*, Vol 1, Phillipsburg: P & R, 1970, 383-384.
[2] *Westminster Confession of Faith*, 21.6

worship God. And the apostle did not leave parents without adequate material for instructing their children to that chief end (Ephesians 6:1-5).

Parents who believe in the Lord Jesus and thus love God are not only given biblical commands to teach their children to worship God, they are given *precious and very great promises* (2 Peter 1:4) in Christ Jesus as well. Children should learn at an early age the Word of God that is able to *make them wise for salvation through faith in Jesus Christ* (2 Timothy 3:15). Encouraging promises are attached to raising our children in the way they should go (Proverbs 22:6). The proverbs are not meant to be guarantees, for we must remember that salvation is from the Lord. Nevertheless, it is not wrong to trust the Lord and pursue these general principles for training our children to fear or worship the Lord our God (Proverbs 22:17-21). How else would we read the book of Proverbs if we do not read them as the Lord's encouragement to live by faith and lean not on our own understanding but in all our ways to acknowledge God?

We are also given in Scripture multiple examples to commend to us the practice of family worship. Adam and Eve taught their children to worship God (Genesis 4) in light of the promise and pattern given to them (Genesis 3:15, 20). Though Cain's worship was not joined with faith, Adam and Eve had still done their duty. Abel and Seth both worshiped the Lord by faith as they were taught by their parents (Genesis 4:4, 26; Luke 3:38; Hebrews 11:4). It was a continual habit of Job to lead his children to worship God (Job 1:5). Abraham was a man who could be trusted to *command his children and his household after him to keep the way of the Lord* (Genesis 18:19). We have Joshua as yet another Biblical example and pattern of a father determined to raise his children or household to worship the Lord (Joshua 24:15). Asaph writes down for us in the book of Psalms what is meant to be an ongoing pattern of one generation telling the next generation of the *glorious deeds of the Lord* (Psalm 78). Parents have the duty to lead their children to worship God or to *set their hope in God and not forget the works of God, but keep his commandments* (Psalm 78:7). Cornelius also stands as an example or pattern for believing parents to follow in teaching their children to fear God (Acts 10:2). And one final example to note is that of Timothy. He was a man raised in the Lord by both his mother and his grandmother who intentionally taught him the Scriptures at an early age in the home (2 Timothy 3:15). The Scriptures which are able to make us wise unto salvation must be taught and understood (Acts 8:26-35), which is the very reason for the existence and use of the *Westminster Standards*.[1]

Theological Motives for Family Worship

Maintaining Religion in the Home is Good

Why practice and promote family religion in the home? It is very biblical to worship God both as individuals and families, but there are also several additional theological reasons gleaned from the Word of God.

I. The practice of family worship follows the design of God. God created parents and children. From the beginning God created and established the family and intended for godly parents to pass down the truth and the faith that their children might live unto God and walk humbly with him. There is no guarantee in this method but it is the design of God from the very beginning. Cain and Abel were both taught to bring sacrifices. They did not just learn this on their own but were taught by Adam and Eve, who also worshiped God.

II. The practice of family worship embraces the promises of God. God made promises to believers and to their children. Children were included in the promises of God made to Abraham. The covenant relationship established by God has always included children. Thus, Abraham was expected to teach his children regarding the person and work of God (Genesis 17:7; 18:19) and such a practice was intended to be continued (Acts 2:39; 10:2; Ephesians 6:4). Establishing and maintaining true

---
1 *Westminster Larger Catechism*, Questions 2-5.

religion in the home is to welcome and embrace God's promises to us and to our children.

III. The practice of family worship communicates the mercy of God. God includes entire households as recipients of mercy. Whether it is Rahab or Cornelius or Lydia, the Scriptures make it plain that while God certainly saves individuals, there is a corporate component to his overtures of grace. This most certainly does not mean that any child or member of the household is saved based upon the faith of the parents or head of the household. But the point is that God is shown to be a God who enters into a covenant relationship not simply with individuals but with households. And those in the household are to be taught the faith once delivered to the saints (Joshua 2, 6; Acts 2:39; 10:2; 16:14-15). It is an act of mercy towards children in line with God's mercy towards us that we engage in family worship and lead them in the Scriptures that are able to make them wise unto salvation through faith in Jesus Christ (2 Timothy 3:15).

IV. The practice of family worship increases the knowledge of God. God made children to learn. Children were created with a natural curiosity. It is good for children to ask questions because that is how God designed that they should learn. It is not that parents only teach their children if and when they ask questions, but it is normal for them to ask questions about everything. This is most important when it comes to the faith. God made children to learn and often through asking questions. Better they ask and learn from godly parents than an ungodly world (Joshua 4). Establishing a regular pattern of worship in the home will foster this.

V. The practice of family worship nurtures the wisdom of God. God has deemed it wise for children to listen and learn. In the book of Proverbs, there is an emphasis upon children listening and learning the way of godliness from their parents (Proverbs 1-7). God ordained that it is foolish to rebel against one's parents and wise to listen and heed their instruction (Luke 2:41-51; Colossians 3:20).

VI. The practice of family worship summarizes the will of God. God sums up life as knowing and obeying him (Ecclesiastes 12:1, 13). In the end, nothing matters more for us and our children if we have them than knowing (not simply knowing about him like the devil and demons) and loving God and walking humbly with him by faith. Our Lord Jesus says that to know God is eternal life (John 17:3). Family worship is meant to make God known to us and our children. Knowing God is to truly live and this is the will of God for his people.

VII. The practice of family worship urges our faith in God. God declares it impossible to serve two masters. Reading our Bibles and praying will remind us to whom we belong by grace. And if our children are going to serve a master, it is incumbent upon parents to direct them with all their might to serve the Lord their God with all their heart, soul, mind, and strength (Matthew 6:24). Like Elijah on Mount Carmel, family worship provides the opportunity to urge ourselves and our children to live by faith in the Lord rather than by sight as pagans.

VIII. The practice of family worship teaches the priorities of God. It was Joshua who through his determination to serve the Lord set before his children and household the right priority to have in life (Joshua 24:15). The head of the household must be determined to live in such a way and to lead the members of his household to live unto the Lord in every area of life. This determination will inevitably convey priority. What better thing can parents do for their children than to teach them to seek first the kingdom of God? Family worship teaches children that their chief end in life is to glorify God and to enjoy him forever.

IX. The practice of family worship encourages purity to God. This is not only in the context of sin but also regarding direction and devotion in life. We all, including our children, are susceptible to corruption and confusion. It is the Word of God alone that will chart a straight course for our lives. Family worship should be filled with Scripture in every way. It alone will provide the light we need in a dark and perverse world. Our way is kept pure according to God's Word, which is a lamp to our feet and a light to our path (Psalm 119:9, 105).

X. The practice of family worship fosters the love of God. We love God because he first loved us. The love of God as demonstrated in the person and work of Jesus is an overarching theme of the Bible. Worshiping God in our homes, whether we are married or single or have children or no children, is an opportunity to be reminded of God's love and to express our love in return. With regard to children, Jesus loves the little children of believers as he himself declared and demonstrated (Matthew 19:13-15; Mark 10:13-16; Luke 18:15-17). Too many parents keep their children from Christ Jesus simply by neglecting family worship. It was surely not pagans who brought their children to Jesus for a blessing. But how many Christian parents act like pagans in regard to raising their children? If Jesus expresses a desire to bless our children and states clearly that his Kingdom belongs to such, then Christian parents dare not neglect the practice of family worship.

Eternal Benefits from Family Worship

Maintaining Religion in the Home is Valuable

There are invaluable benefits to both children and parents, as well as the church and society for establishing and conducting family worship. This is not an exhaustive list but hopefully it is a compelling one to encourage religion in the home.

I. The glory of our Lord. More families worshiping God means more glory to God. Those who are new creatures in Christ love God and want to see his name magnified and his glory spread throughout all the earth. Why would parents not begin in their own home to this end? Surely, believing parents want their own children to know God and give praise to his glorious grace (Ephesians 1:3-14).

II. The joy of our children. Every parent wants their children to be happy. Typically, however, happiness derived from temporal things are most sought out for children. While education, marriage, friends, music, athletics, and work are all good things, they are not meant to satisfy more than God or even compete with God (Exodus 20:3; Ecclesiastes 2:24). Family worship gives opportunity to teach our children the solid joys and lasting treasures of knowing and walking humbly with God. As we are to rejoice in the Lord always, so we should want our children to join us in 'the science of living blessedly forever.'[1]

III. The stability of our homes. As the Word and Spirit have their way with us and our children surely the fruit of the Spirit will be evident (Galatians 5:22–23). Where there is no training, nurture and discipline according to Scripture and in the Lord, then the flesh with its passions and desires will be rampant in the home. Happy and stable is the home where God is worshiped and his Word obeyed.

IV. The good of our society. We in no way want a mere appearance of godliness whether in the home or in society (2 Corinthians 5:12; 2 Timothy 3:5). However, that society that has its citizens restrained by the Law of God is sure to be more peaceful. The Law of God will put restraints upon us and our children so that their neighbors might not fear in their presence. And how much better if the Lord should deliver our children from the *domain of darkness* and transfer them into the *kingdom of his beloved Son* (Colossians 1:13)! With the Law written upon their hearts they would surely be salt and light in this world. Who would not want neighbors governed by the Spirit, compelled by the love of Christ, and directed inwardly and outwardly by the Ten Commandments?

Children who are most established in our holy faith bring most honor to God and do most good to others. They are better church members and citizens as a result of family worship. A child taught the faith once for all delivered to the saints will be well-established and stable in life. Such children will make for

---

1 William Perkins, 'A Golden Chain' in 'Works, I:II,' J. I. Packer, *Among God's Giants*, Eastbourne: Kingsway, 1991, repr. 2000, 84. This was Perkins' description of the study of theology.

mature, stable churches and societies. The same benefits apply for all who maintain true religion.

Continual Opponents to Family Worship

Maintaining Religion in the Home is Challenging

Many households today are like *sheep without a shepherd* due perhaps to a variety of reasons. Marriage and the family, as God has designed and defined them, are under constant pressure in every land to conform to the mold of this world (Romans 12:2; 1 Peter 1:14). Opposition and suffering are normal for followers of Christ. The question is whether or not we will cave and compromise or remain steadfast in the faith. This is nowhere more evident than in the family.

The flesh, the world, and the devil are presented in the Bible as the threefold enemies of God's people. These are malevolent enemies parents are called to oppose in order to establish and maintain religion in the home. On top of these enemies, there are burdensome weights (Hebrews 12:1) that continually provide opposition to family worship, so that directing our children to the Lord becomes a burden instead of a delight. Moreover, there are many hazardous pitfalls to wisely avoid for worship in the home.

First, we must avoid *idolatry*. We are to worship God, not the family. Do not make an idol of the family. Second, we must avoid *presumption*. The family that gathers every day for worship should not presume upon the grace of God as if they could guarantee salvation. Family worship is no guarantee of salvation (Genesis 4; Hebrews 11:4). The Lord saves and neither parents nor children should think that family worship somehow saves or even obligates God to save. Third, we must avoid the pitfall of *delay*. We can make just about anything an excuse for delaying our duty. It is all too easy to fall into the dangerous pitfall of procrastination which might be due to laziness or even timidity. Do not wait until you have time or expertise. You will never be perfect in family worship. But that should not stop us from doing what is good and right. Fourth, the pitfall of *worldliness* should be avoided at all cost. It is too easy to fall prey to the love of the fleeting things of this world. Sadly, in many homes the godliness of children takes a backseat to the pursuit of worldly goods and entertainment. The love of the world is a dangerous pitfall. Fifth, we must avoid the pitfall of *discouragement*. Any parent knows the trials that come along with raising little ones. Sadly, the time-honored practice of family worship can easily fall by the wayside when trials come along and discouragement sets in. Keep this ever in mind and encourage yourself with these words:

> Doubtless many an excellent magistrate has been sent into the Commonwealth, and many an excellent pastor into the Church, and many a precious saint to heaven, through the happy preparations of a holy education, perhaps by a woman that thought herself useless and unserviceable to the Church. If only parents would begin early, and labor to affect the hearts of their children with the great matters of everlasting life, and to acquaint them with the substance of the doctrine of Christ.[1]

Simple Elements for Family Worship

Maintaining Religion in the Home is Simple

While there are certainly difficulties and challenges to practice family worship in the home, it is quite a simple thing. Maintaining true religion in the home requires hard work and effort but the elements required to do it are rather straightforward and uncomplicated. You need neither a PhD nor a seminary degree to faithfully worship God in the home. In fact, formal education is not required at all. There are really three simple elements of family worship.

1. Listen to God. The *Larger Catechism* asks the simple

---

[1] Thomas Manton, 'Epistle to the Reader' of *The Westminster Confession of Faith*.

question: 'What is the Word of God? The holy Scriptures of the Old and New Testaments are the word of God, the only rule of faith and obedience.'[1] The Bible is the living and active Word of God. That Word, being planted in the heart by the Spirit, brings forth life (1 Peter 1:23). We and our children need the Word of God hidden in our hearts and renewing our minds. There is no way for the members of our household to know God except through his Word. Eternal life will not come through the study of science or history or math but through the Word of God (John 17:3). The Bible should be read, listened to, explained, and understood in our homes with a view to obedience if we would wish to truly listen to God. Reading the Bible without comment is better than not reading it at all. However we need to understand what we read and hear.

> The Bible should be read with godly fear ... conscionable hearing ... in obedience unto God, with understanding, faith, and reverence.[2]

Both the *Larger* and *Shorter Catechisms* are meant to help us understand the Bible, which is able to make us wise unto salvation through faith in Jesus Christ (2 Timothy 3:15). Memorizing and understanding the *Shorter Catechism* will help us know what we believe and why we believe it. It will give all in the household confidence in the Lord and his Word for living in this world. And making use of the *Confession* in family worship will help teach sound, clear, certain, and useful doctrine for life and godliness. We have questions as we read and study the Bible and if we have children they are naturally inquisitive. The *Westminster Standards* are the best resources we have for aid in knowing and understanding Scripture.

II. Sing to God. There is every indication that the psalms are the songbook of the Bible. And in the New Testament we find references to songs and singing. Jesus sang with his disciples (Mark 14:26) and so parents should sing with their children.

---

[1] *Westminster Larger Catechism*, Question 3.
[2] *Westminster Confession of Faith* 21.5.

Our God is a singing God (Zephaniah 3:17; Matthew 26:30). Should his children not sing also (Ephesians 5:19; Colossians 3:16; James 5:13)? Our singing should never be half-hearted or mere formalism but should be done with 'grace in the heart.'[1] Find a good psalm book and hymnal. Pick songs that are easy and familiar at first. If you need help, then ask your pastor and church leaders for help and suggestions. Pick one or two songs each time and if you have little children, then sing a select few songs over and over until they are learned. Singing will be an ongoing activity for the people of God (Revelation 14:3; 15:3).

III. Pray to God. Communing with God is the privilege of the saints in Christ Jesus; yet, prayer is one of the most neglected elements of worship, both public and private. The writers of the *Westminster Confession of Faith* and *Catechisms* placed a high value on prayer in the life of the believer, families, and the church. Why are we to pray? To whom are we to pray? How are we to pray? These are questions we have and which the *Westminster Catechisms* explain in depth. Prayer is of such importance that they go to great lengths to explain the pattern and model of prayer we call the Lord's Prayer. Understanding even the preface and conclusion will help us in our private and family prayers.

Question: What does the preface of the Lord's prayer teach us?

Answer: The preface of the Lord's prayer (which is, Our Father who is in heaven) teaches us to draw near to God with all holy reverence and confidence, as children to a father, able and ready to help us; and that we should pray with and for others.[2]

Question: What does the conclusion of the Lord's Prayer teach us?

Answer: The conclusion of the Lord's Prayer (which is, For Yours is the kingdom, and the power, and the glory, for ever, Amen), teaches us to enforce our petitions with arguments, which are to

---

[1] *Westminster Confession of Faith*, 21:5.
[2] *Westminster Shorter Catechism*, Question 100.

be taken, not from any worthiness in ourselves, or in any other creature, but from God; and with our prayers to join praises, ascribing to God alone eternal sovereignty, omnipotency, and glorious excellency; in regard whereof, as he is able and willing to help us, so we by faith are emboldened to plead with him that he would, and quietly to rely upon him, that he will fulfil our requests. And, to testify this our desire and assurance, we say, Amen.[1]

If we have children, we should teach them how and what to pray. Our children need to hear us praying and we can also teach them to pray for things agreeable to the will of God. Jesus taught his disciples to pray and parents should teach their little disciples to pray. Prayer should fill every mouth and every home.

Conclusion

Discipleship begins in the home for the believer. The godly are to baptize their children and raise them in the nurture and discipline of the Lord. Family religion is not a practice for the spiritually elite but for the ordinary Christian. Gathering for worship in the home is the spiritual duty of godly saints and parents. Children are like arrows in a quiver for wartime (Psalm 127). The duty of Christian parents is not primarily to coddle and shield their precious gifts but to train them up in the way they should go. Like us, the bodies of our children are perishing. And yet we tend to spend much more time and energy on that which is good but perishing. Physical training is good, Paul says, but godliness is better (1 Timothy 4:8). Sadly we often live with physical well-being at the forefront instead of Christ and training in order to renounce all ungodliness. What will it profit us or our children if we foster a greater desire to gain the whole world than to have Christ and be rich towards God? Solid joys and lasting treasures are found only in Christ at the right hand of the Father (Psalm 16). Equally, there is no greater joy than to see our children walking in the truth. Thus the aim of family

---

[1] *Westminster Larger Catechism*, Question 196.

worship is to be reconciled to God in Christ, walk humbly with God by faith, be rich towards God, keep in step with the Spirit, know God which is eternal life, and glorify God and enjoy him forever.

'A most sovereign antidote against all kind of errors, is to be grounded and settled in the faith.'[1] Such a statement sums up the purpose of the *Westminster Standards* for not only adults but for their children so that they might stand firm in the faith (1 Corinthians 16:13; 2 Corinthians 1:24) and in Christ Jesus the Lord (Galatians 5:1; Ephesians 6:13; Philippians 4:1) and in the true grace of God (1 Peter 5:12) all their days.

---

1 Henry Wilkinson, Thomas Watson, Thomas Manton et al., 'To the Christian Reader Especially Heads of Families' in *The Westminster Confession of Faith, 1647 Third Edition,* http://reformed.org/documents/wcf_standards/index.html?mainframe=/documents/wcf_standards/p005-to_head_of_families.html

The Westminster Standards and Church Government

Guy Prentiss Waters

From one perspective, the *Westminster Confession of Faith* must be judged a failure. No small part of this failure may be laid squarely at the feet of its articles on church government. After extended debate that sometimes reflected significant differences among its participants, the Westminster Assembly crafted the *Confession*, and presented it to Parliament. While Parliament was pleased with the 'doctrinal part' of the *Confession*, it 'recommitted' to the Assembly 'particulars in discipline.'[1] This recommittal, in March, 1648, 'was the last positive enactment made by the English Parliament respecting the *Confession* of Faith.'[2] The *Westminster Confession of Faith* was never adopted by Parliament, and the *Confession's* articles on church government were at least partly responsible.[3] No form of the Westminster

---

1 William M. Hetherington, *History of the Westminster Assembly of Divines* 1856; repr. Edmonton, AB: Still Waters Revival Books, 1993, 284, referenced by William S. Barker, 'Lord of Lords and King of Commoners: The Westminster Confession and the Relationship of Church and State,' ed. J. Ligon Duncan III, *The Westminster Confession into the 21st Century: Essays in Remembrance of the 350th Anniversary of the Westminster Assembly, Volume 1,* Fearn: Christian Focus, 2003, 417. The 'particulars' that Parliament noted were WCF 20.4; 30; 31, ibid.
2 Hetherington, *History,* 285.
3 This non-adoption was not due to formal rejection by Parliament. Parliament never had the opportunity even to consider a revised report. As Hetherington explains,

Assembly's output would become the confessional standard of the Church of England.

From a different perspective, the *Westminster Confession of Faith* must be judged a triumph. No small part of this triumph is due to the Westminster Assembly's achievement in the realm of church government. Notwithstanding principial ecclesiological differences at the assembly, the divines drafted a document that offers a coherent statement on the nature, purpose, mission, government, and discipline of the church.[1] The divines furthermore crafted an additional statement, *The Form of Church Government,* which provided the rudiments of a manual of church operation.[2] While the *Confession's* ecclesiology would not find a home in the Church of England, the Church of Scotland eagerly embraced it. The General Assembly of the Church of Scotland approved the *Form* in 1645; the *Confession of Faith* in 1647; and the *Shorter* and *Larger Catechisms* in 1648.[3] Not only would other Scottish church bodies embrace the *Confession's* ecclesiology and polity, but Westminsterian church government would be exported to Canada, the American Colonies, and Australia in the next century.[4] At the turn of the twenty-first

---

'Parliament itself not long afterwards fell under the power of the army, and was at length forcibly dissolved by Cromwell,' ibid.

[1] The Westminster divines included advocates of episcopal, presbyterian, and independent church government, on whom see the sketch of John R. de Witt, 'The Form of Church Government,' ed. John L. Carson and David W. Hall, *To Glorify and Enjoy God: A Commemoration of the 350th Anniversary of the Westminster Assembly,* Edinburgh: Banner of Truth, 1994, 150-2.

[2] For the text of *The Form of Church-Government,* see Iain H. Murray, *The Reformation of the Church: A Collection of Reformed and Puritan Documents on Church Issues,* Edinburgh: Banner of Truth, 1965, 207-230. For its historical background, see David W. Hall & Joseph H. Hall, *Paradigms in Polity: Classic Readings in Reformed and Presbyterial Church Government,* Grand Rapids: Eerdmans, 1994, 260-1. For a concise analysis of this document, see Murray, *Reformation,* 205-6; de Witt, 'The Form of Church Government,' 162-5. De Witt has concluded that the *Form* is 'unfinished' and 'incomplete.'.

[3] Hetherington, *History,* 306.

[4] As David W. Hall and Joseph H. Hall have observed of American Presbyterianism, 'one can see the rudimentary outline of modern Presbyterian books of order from

century, the government of churches in Brazil, South Korea, Vanuatu, Ukraine, and Malawi (to name just a few) is indebted to the labors of the Westminster Assembly. The *Confession's* ecclesiological footprint is nothing short of global in its scope.

Space prevents us from undertaking anything approaching an exhaustive consideration of the *Confession's* ecclesiology. Instead, we may consider some of the leading features of it's statements on church government. We will first consider what, for the *Confession*, was the 'formal principle' of church government, that is, 'the authority of Scripture.'[1] We will then take up four heads of the *Confession's* understanding of the Bible's teaching about the church.

The Bible—A Sufficient Guide to the Church's Government

The Westminster Assembly did not believe that the church was free to devise her own government. The visible church is 'the kingdom of the Lord Jesus Christ.'[2] and, as such, is subject to her King, Jesus. As the *Confession* later states, it is the exclusive prerogative of the King to rule his kingdom how and in what way he will—'the Lord Jesus, as King and Head of His Church, hath therein appointed a government, in the hand of Church officers, distinct from the civil magistrate.'[3]

In support of this claim, the divines appealed to the Scripture. Isaiah had prophesied of Jesus that *the government shall be upon his shoulder* and *his name shall be called ... Prince of Peace* (Isaiah 9:6).[4] Furthermore, Isaiah continues, *of the increase of his government and of peace there will be no end, on the throne of David and over his kingdom, to establish it and to uphold it, with*

---
  scanning the skeletal sketch of the Westminster Assembly's Directory for Church Government,' *Paradigms in Polity,* 260.
1   De Witt, 'Form of Church Government,' 152.
2   *Westminster Confession of Faith*, 25.2.
3   *Westminster Confession of Faith*, 30.1.
4   The biblical texts in this paragraph were cited by the Westminster Assembly in support of the claims of WCF 30.1.

justice and with righteousness from this time forth and forevermore (9:7). By virtue of his accomplished death and resurrection, Jesus claimed that *all authority in heaven and on earth has been given to me* (Matthew 28:18). The Father has clothed the glorified Jesus with power and authority as the mediator of his people.

This event in the history of redemption provides the framework within which the New Testament authors understand the reign of Christ. An important passage in this connection is referenced by the Westminster Assembly in its Preface to the *Form of Church Government*, Ephesians 1:20-23:

> [The Father] raised [Christ] from the dead and seated him at his right hand in the heavenly places, far above all rule and authority and power and dominion, and above every name that is named, not only in this age but also in the one to come. And he put all things under his feet and gave him as head over all things to the church, which is his body, the fullness of him who fills all in all.

Paul says here that Jesus was exalted in his resurrection and ascension to a position of plenipotentiary authority over the whole creation. This authority encompasses nothing less than *all things*, but has a special point of reference. That point of reference is *the church*, which alone is Jesus' *body*. Jesus' headship over the church, Paul writes later in this letter, finds expression in Jesus' provision of church officers, by whose ministry the church grows *to the measure of the stature of the fullness of Christ* (Ephesians 4:13).[1]

Christ, then, is the living head of his church. But if he has appointed a government for the church, where is this government to be found? The *Confession's* answer to this question was 'the Bible.' In the Bible, we have a sufficient guide to the church's government. The assembly affirmed this conviction in the *Westminster Confession of Faith* 1.6, 'the whole counsel of God concerning all things necessary for His own glory, man's salvation, faith and life, is either expressly set down in Scripture, or by good and necessary consequence may be

---

1 The 'Preface' to the *Form* also cites Ephesians 4:11.

deduced from Scripture.' The *Confession* offers an important qualification to this statement by acknowledging that 'there are some circumstances concerning the worship of God, and government of the Church, common to human actions and societies, which are to be ordered the light of nature, and Christian prudence, according to the general rules of the Word, which are always to be observed.'[1]

What are the Westminster divines saying here? They are saying that the Bible (Scripture) provides 'the whole counsel of God concerning all things necessary for' a range of concerns. These concerns must include 'the government of the Church' as the *Confession's* qualifier indicates.[2]

But in what sense is the Bible a sufficient guide for the church's government? First, the *Confession* affirms that the mind of Christ concerning the church's government is found in the Bible and in the Bible alone. The church's King would not have the church look elsewhere than the Bible to discern what the church's government is.

Second, the church may access the 'whole counsel of God' in Scripture in one of two ways—by the express statements of the Bible or by what may be necessarily deduced from the teaching of Scripture. Such deductions do not carry less weight than what is expressly stated in the Bible. Each is the authoritative teaching of the Bible. Ascertaining the teaching of the New Testament concerning the church's government, then, does not merely consist of compiling passages that explicitly address ecclesiastical order. It requires that one carefully study, weigh, and draw out the implications of many passages, comparing the results of one passage's study with another. When one does this, it will be discovered that the New Testament has much to say about the church's government.

---

1 *Westminster Confession of Faith*, 1.6.
2 The acknowledgment that there are 'some circumstances concerning ... government of the church' qualifies the opening statement of WCF 1.6. This appended qualifier, then, confirms that Westminster understood the church's government to be included in the 'all things' of that opening statement.

Third, the *Confession* recognizes that the Bible does not prescribe every conceivable detail of the church's government. There are certain circumstantial matters pertaining to both government and worship that are left to the church's discretion to order. What is a 'circumstance?' A 'circumstance' is a practical detail attending 'an action, without which it can either not be done at all, or cannot be done with decency or decorum.'[1] While the church needs biblical warrant for a given action, the circumstantial details surrounding that action are left to the church's prudential judgment. An example may illustrate the point. The Scripture commands elders to meet together to make decisions on behalf of the church. Instances of circumstances surrounding that action include—how often that council of elders should meet; how many elders are necessary to constitute a quorum for that council; or what rules of parliamentary procedure they should follow when they conduct business. While the Scripture does not prescribe these circumstantial details, it is impossible for the elders to conduct their meeting unless there is some consensus about such matters.

The *Confession* lays down clear criteria for the defining and handling of 'circumstances.' They must be 'common to human actions and societies.' That is to say, they must not be specific or peculiar to the church as the church. They must be 'ordered' by three standards—'the light of nature, and Christian prudence, according to the general rules of the Word.'[2] The church, then, must consider carefully how biblical principles may apply even to apparently insignificant circumstantial matters. Even so, the particular circumstantial details of the church's government will differ from time to time and from place to place. While

---

[1] Thomas E. Peck, *Notes on Ecclesiology,* Richmond: Presbyterian Committee of Publication, 1892, 122.

[2] In support of its doctrine of circumstances, the *Confession* appeals to Paul's counsel delivered in the course of a lengthy discussion of the order of the church's public worship—*let all things be done for building up* (1 Corinthians 14:26); and *all things should be done decently and in order* (1 Corinthians 14:40).

the church government of the Confession rests on settled and unchanging principles, it is not inflexible.

The *Westminster Confession*, then, is not content merely to assert that the Bible is a sufficient guide to the church's government. In the course of making that claim, it offers reasons why the church must look to the Bible and the Bible alone for her principles of church polity. Chiefly it appeals to the unique crown rights of Jesus Christ over his church. The *Confession* also helps the church understand how the New Testament would have Christians derive from its pages the principles of biblical church government. We must look not only for express statements about the church's government, but also for whatever may be necessarily deduced from Scripture's teaching. But more is needed for the church to have a functioning church government. The *Confession's* doctrine of circumstances ensures that the church has the wherewithal to implement biblical principles of church government in a variety of settings and situations.

What, then, are some of the leading features of biblical polity, according to the *Westminster Confession*?[1] First, the *Confession* articulates the classical distinction between the church invisible and visible. Second, it affirms the biblical teaching that the church's government is altogether distinct from the civil governments of this world. Third, it defines the Christ-assigned mission of the church, and the Christ-supplied means by which the church is to undertake that mission. Fourth, it sketches a biblical church polity in both form and function.

---

[1] Space prevents us from taking up the complex debates within and outside the assembly about the particulars of the church's government. See in particular ed. Chris Coldwell, *The Grand Debate: The Reasons Presented by the Dissenting Brethren Against Certain Propositions Concerning Presbyterian Government ...* , Dallas: Naphtali Press, 2014, and ed. David W. Hall, *Jus Divinum Regiminis Ecclesiastici ...* 1646; Dallas: Naphtali Press, 1995. For a comprehensive listing of the extant texts produced by the assembly in the area of the church's government, see now Chad Van Dixhoorn, ed. *The Minutes and Papers of the Westminster Assembly, 1643–1652, Volume V: Assembly Papers, Supplementary Material, and Indexes,* Oxford: Oxford University Press, 2012, 1–8.

The Church, Invisible and Visible

First, the *Confession* gives considerable attention to the distinction between the church invisible and visible. The opening two paragraphs of the *Westminster Confession of Faith*, 25, 'Of the Church' are dedicated to elucidating this distinction. What is meant by the 'invisible' and 'visible' church? The *Confession* is not referring to two different churches. There is one church of Jesus Christ, considered from two different vantage points. The 'invisible church' is the church as God sees it. The 'visible church' is the church as people see it. There is a great deal of overlap in the composition of each. Even so, they are distinct. How is that so? They differ with respect to membership. The invisible church is 'the whole number of the elect;' the visible church consists of 'all those throughout the world that profess the true religion; and of their children.' Membership in the invisible church is reckoned by the eternal decree of election; in the visible church either by profession of faith or descent from a parent who professes faith in Christ.[1] Membership in the invisible church crosses time and space—'the whole number of the elect, that have been, are, or shall be gathered into one.' Membership in the visible church crosses space but not time—'all those throughout the world that profess the true religion; and of their children.'

Another difference is that the invisible church never changes, while the visible church is subject to change. The invisible church never changes because its membership (the elect) neither increases nor diminishes.[2] The visible church's membership changes when new persons profess Christianity; children of believers are born; or, sadly, people fall away from their profession and leave the church.

---

[1] At this point, an important difference emerges between the *Westminster Confession of Faith* and the *London Baptist Confession* of 1689. The LBC, an influential credobaptist revision of Westminster, not only refrains from using the phrase 'visible church' but also restricts church membership to professing Christians ('visible saints') alone, LBC 26.2.

[2] See *Westminster Confession of Faith*, 3.4.

The visible church is subject to change in another respect. 'Under the law,' that is, the Mosaic Covenant, it was 'confined to one nation.' But now, 'under the Gospel,' it is 'catholic or universal.' The expansion of divine mercy from Israel to the nations that took place after the resurrection of Jesus has resulted in the visible church's transformation. As a people, the visible church is evidence of the outworking of God's purpose to save people *from every tribe and language and people and nation* (Revelation 5:9). It is for this reason that the divines take care to identify the visible church in terms of the biblical images of 'kingdom,' 'house,' and 'family.' Not only do these images help us to understand the dynamism and growth of the visible church, but they also appear in passages of the New Testament that underscore the transformation of the form of God's people that took place at the transition from the Old Covenant to the New Covenant (see Matthew 13:51-52; Ephesians 2:19-22).[1]

What is the biblical basis for this distinction between the church invisible and visible? In his Epistle to the Romans, Paul makes a distinction within Israel. He argues that while the Jews, the people of God under the Old Covenant, had many outward privileges (Romans 9:4-5), those privileges did not suffice to render them true members of God's people. *Not all who are descended from Israel belong to Israel* (Romans 9:6b). That is to say, physical descent from Abraham does not of itself render one a true child of Abraham (Romans 9:7). It is the unchangeable divine decree of election that infallibly secures one's place among the true people of God, that is, the number of those whom God has saved and gives blessing, life, and glory

---

[1] The *Confession* terms the invisible church the 'spouse' and 'body' of Christ. The former biblical image captures the consummate perfection of the church at the return of Christ, the church's Bridegroom (Ephesians 5:27). The latter biblical image addresses the church as the full number of those for whom Christ died and brings into vital relationship with himself, the body's Head (Ephesians 1:22-23; Colossians 1:18), A. A. Hodge, *The Confession of Faith,* 1869; repr. Edinburgh: Banner of Truth, 1958, 312.

through his Son (see Romans 9:11, 15-16, 18).[1] What Paul is describing here is what the *Westminster Confession of Faith* labels the 'invisible church' and 'visible church.' While there is much overlap between the two, the Scripture does not permit us to conceive that overlap to be without remainder. The invisible and visible church may not be strictly identified.

What are some of the practical implications of this teaching? First, the *Westminster Confession* claims that 'out of [the visible Church] there is no ordinary possibility of salvation.'[2] No believer has the liberty of claiming membership in the 'invisible church' while eschewing membership in the 'visible church.' This claim is an entirely biblical one. The Scripture simply assumes that a professing Christian will live his Christian life in the context of the fellowship of other believers.[3] There is neither command nor example to live as a Christian in solitude or isolation from other Christians. Church membership is not an optional extra to the Christian. It is a biblical requirement.[4]

Second, this summary of biblical teaching helps us to understand the sad fact of apostasy in the church. What are we to make of a person who has given every indication of being a strong, vibrant believer, and who has turned his back on the visible church of which he was once part? It may be that he never was a true believer and is now showing his true colours. Even so, his departure need not be positive proof of his reprobation. It may be that his departure will be, in the Lord's hands, the means

---

[1] Compare Paul's similar argument in Romans 2:25-29, where he argues that the Jew who has received 'outward and physical ... circumcision' is not thereby a Jew in the fullest and truest sense of the word (Romans 2:28). The true Jew *is one inwardly, and circumcision is a matter of the heart, by the spirit, not by the letter* (Romans 2:29).

[2] *Westminster Confession of Faith*, 25.2.

[3] The Westminster divines cite in support Acts 2:47, *And the Lord added to their number day by day those who were being saved*. Throughout Acts, we see people who respond to the preaching of the gospel in repentance and faith committing themselves to the life and fellowship of the local assembly of believers. Acts presents no exceptions to this pattern.

[4] For a fuller argument from the New Testament for church membership, see Guy Prentiss Waters, *How Jesus Runs the Church,* Phillipsburg: P&R, 2011, 16-20.

of his conversion. It is also possible that he is a true believer who has come under the powerful influence of some temptation or sin. If he is a true believer then God will, in his time, restore him in the way of repentance and faith in Christ. In any case, the church should be wary of making any ultimate pronouncements about this person's spiritual condition. They should use the means that God has given them (including prayer and the Word of God) in the hope that, through the Lord's blessing, they will be used of God to restore this person to their fellowship.

The Church's Government—Distinct from the Governments of This World

A second leading feature of the *Westminster Confession's* teaching about the church's government appears at *Westminster Confession of Faith*, 30.1, 'The Lord Jesus, as King and Head of His Church, hath therein appointed a government, in the hand of Church officers, distinct from the civil magistrate.' The divines elsewhere affirm that civil government is also of divine appointment, 'God, the supreme Lord and King of all the world, hath ordained civil magistrates, to be, under Him, over the people, for His own glory, and the public good.'[1] Both governments (church and civil) are legitimate, each finding its origin in, and authority from, God himself, and each oriented towards the glory of the God who has appointed them in the world.

And yet these two governments are starkly different. The *Confession* does not only state that they are different ('distinct from the civil magistrate') but proceeds to elaborate their differences. What, then, are these differences? First, they differ as to source. Both proceed from God but in different respects. Civil government proceeds from God as 'the supreme Lord and King of all the world.' Church government proceeds from 'the Lord Jesus, as King and Head of His Church.' Second, they differ as to officers. The officers of civil government are 'civil

---

1 *Westminster Confession of Faith*, 23.1.

magistrates.' The officers of church government are 'Church officers.' Third, they differ as to constituency. Civil government serves 'the public good.' It concerns all men and women, created in the image of God. Church government serves the visible kingdom of Jesus Christ.[1] It principally concerns men and women, not only created in the image of God, but also redeemed from sin by the work of Christ. Fourth, they differ as to means employed. God has 'armed' civil magistrates 'with the power of the sword, for the defence and encouragement of them that are good, and for the punishment of evildoers.'[2] To church officers, Christ has 'committed … the keys of the kingdom.' These keys are used for various spiritual purposes, especially admitting or excluding people from membership in the visible church.[3] Critically, church officers' authority derives directly from Jesus Christ. They are authorized only to declare and to enforce the will of Christ in the Scripture. Their power is exclusively spiritual. Unlike the civil magistrate, church officers have no warrant to exercise physical force or compulsion in the exercise of their office.

These claims were controversial in the seventeenth century. A handful of Westminster divines and an influential segment of Parliament were known as 'Erastians.' Erastians believed that church and civil government were not altogether distinct. The civil magistrate was thought to retain some authority in matters of determining church membership and of administering church discipline.[4] The Westminster Assembly steadfastly excluded Erastianism from its confessional statements, a factor that, we have noted above, contributed to the delay and ultimate demise of the *Westminster Confession* in hands of Parliament.

To what biblical evidence did the *Confession* appeal in

---

[1] See *Westminster Confession of Faith*, 30.2.
[2] *Westminster Confession of Faith*, 23.1).
[3] See *Westminster Confession of Faith*, 30.2).
[4] See further Barker, 'Lord of Lords and King of Commoners,' 412-20; Hetherington, *History,* 266-70; Alexander F. Mitchell, *The Westminster Assembly: Its History and Standards,* 1883; repr. Edmonton, AB: Still Water Revival Books, 1992, 269-324.

support of the independence of church government from civil government? It appealed to the fact that Jesus Christ is the *Prince of Peace, upon [whose] shoulder* would be *the government,* a government that would *increase* without *end,* even *his kingdom, to establish it and to uphold it* (Isaiah 9:6-7). Not only did King Jesus establish a government distinct from the governments of this world, but he personally rules and oversees that government and its flourishing (see also Matthew 28:18-20).

The Westminster Assembly also appealed to passages in the New Testament concerning officers in the church. These officers are expressly appointed by God in his church (1 Corinthians 12:28). They are distinct from the civil magistrate, and are therefore said to be *among you* and *over you* (i.e., the church) (1 Thessalonians 5:12; cf. Hebrews 13:7, 24). They are remunerated by the church for their labors (1 Timothy 5:17-18). They are tasked with keeping *watch over your souls* and will have *to give an account* to Christ, *the great shepherd of the sheep* (Hebrews 13:17, 20).

The divines also appealed to two passages foundational to the New Testament's conception of the church, Matthew 16:18-19 and Matthew 18:15-20.[1] In Matthew 16, Jesus promises Peter that upon Peter Jesus will *build [his] church, and the gates of hell shall not prevail against it* (Matthew 16:19). Jesus is speaking to Peter but he is not speaking only to Peter. Jesus' question that prompted this statement is a question addressed to all the disciples (Matthew 16:15). Peter, then, must be speaking for all the disciples. Jesus' benediction and promise equally apply to Peter and the other disciples (16:17-19). Jesus promises that he will build his church on a single, apostolic foundation.

Jesus, furthermore, entrusts what he calls the *keys of the kingdom of heaven* to the apostles (Matthew 16:19). In context, this promise concerns the authority to administer the affairs of the church, the visible expression of the Kingdom of God. This authority belongs to the apostles, and is in no way entrusted to the civil magistrate. When Jesus later addresses the exercise

---

[1] For fuller consideration, see Waters, *How Jesus Runs the Church*, 36-40.

of the keys in a matter of church discipline (Matthew 18:18), his instructions to the church assume that the church will administer ecclesiastical discipline without the intervention of any outside party, including the civil magistrate.

The church, therefore, has a government all its own. This government, which derives directly from Jesus Christ, is separate from the governments of this world. The functions and activities of this government are to be undertaken by the church's officers, to the exclusion of the participation of the civil magistrate.

The American Presbyterian Church, in adopting the *Westminster Confession of Faith* a little over a century later, proceeded to modify some of the *Confession's* articles pertaining to the church's relationship to the governments of this world. In the judgment of the American Presbyterian Church, the original *Westminster Confession* had not adequately safeguarded the church's independence from the interference of the civil magistrate. To this end, the American church in 1788 amended portions of *Westminster Confession of Faith*, 20.4, 23.3, and 31.1. This effort was complemented by the drafting of eight, prefatory 'Preliminary Principles' to the new church's 'Form of Government,' in which care was taken to reaffirm the independence of the church's government from the interference of the civil magistrate.[1]

When read alongside the original text of the *Westminster Confession*, the American Presbyterians' modifications should not be seen as a repudiation of the original *Confession's* doctrine. On the contrary, the American modifications were advanced in the interest of clarifying and refining the *Confession's* original statements.[2] The amendment of *Westminster Confession of Faith*, 20.4 categorically prohibited any involvement of the

---

1 Lewis S. Mudge, ed., *Digest of the Acts and Deliverance of the General Assembly of the Presbyterian Church in the U.S.A.*, Philadelphia: General Assembly of the PCUSA, 1938, pp. 73-5, as cited at Barker, 'Lord of Lords and King of Commoners,' 425-6.
2 So, rightly, A.A. Hodge, *The Confession of Faith*, 427-9.

civil magistrate in the workings of ecclesiastical discipline.[1] The revision of *Westminster Confession of Faith*, 23.3 clarified that the civil magistrate's obligations and commitments to a particular Christian denomination extended no farther than its obligations and commitments to any other particular Christian denomination.[2] It added the provision that the civil magistrate could not 'in the least interfere in matters of faith,' and omitted lines from the original *Confession* that affirmed the civil magistrate's duty 'that all blasphemies and heresies be suppressed, all corruptions and abuses in worship and discipline prevented or reformed, and all the ordinances of God duly settled, administered and observed.' The revision of *Westminster Confession of Faith*, 31.1 removed from the civil magistrate the right 'lawfully [to] call a synod of ministers, and other fit persons, to consult and advise with about matters of religion,' leaving it to the officers of the church alone to call ecclesiastical synods and councils. In summary, the American revisions served to remove inconsistencies from and to affirm with greater clarity the very biblical principles for which the Westminster divines had so nobly contended and expressed in the *Westminster Confession*.[3]

---

1 For a listing of the original *Westminster Confession* and the American revisions in parallel columns, see A.A. Hodge, *The Confession of Faith,* 22–3.

2 For an influential argument in Colonial America for the civil free exercise of religion and against the establishment of a particular Christian denomination, see the October 24, 1776 Memorial of the Hanover Presbytery. In this Memorial, the Presbytery suggestively argues against even the civil magistrate's preference of Christianity to other religions, '... there is no argument in favor of establishing the Christian religion but what may be pleaded with equal propriety for establishing the tenets of Mohammed by those who believe the Al Koran ...'

3 It is important to stress that, within the seventeenth century, what the *Confession* declared concerning the church and the civil magistrate was a remarkable achievement. As Alexander F. Mitchell has observed, 'Some, I know, will have it, that though the limits of civil obedience are rightly defined in this chapter, too much is allowed to the magistrate in connection with religion. But such should consider that what is here allowed is less than was claimed for him in the old Scotch and other early reformed confessions, and far less than what was conceded in the English and the Irish Articles,' Alexander F. Mitchell and John F. Struthers, eds., *Minutes of the*

What is the practical importance of this teaching for the church today? We may stress, first, that neither the original nor the revised *Westminster Confession* affords immunity to any Christian who has violated the laws of the land. He is subject to those laws and, if he has violated them, must be ready to give an account to the civil magistrate for his actions. What the *Confession* is stressing is that the church's discipline is a process that is conducted apart from civil interference.

Second, the *Confession* reminds the church that she is ultimately accountable to her Head and King, Jesus Christ, for the workings of her government. This fact means that church officers must be sure that the work that they are doing as officers is sanctioned by Jesus in his Word. They must be equally sure that this work is done in a manner that is well-pleasing to Jesus. They are servants, not masters (1 Peter 5:3). They must not be coercive, abusive, or domineering (Luke 22:24-27). They work for the upbuilding, not the destruction of the church (2 Corinthians 13:10).

The Church's Mission—'the Gathering and Perfecting of the Saints'

The *Westminster Confession* states that Jesus supplied the church not only a government all her own, but also a mission all her own. Jesus also supplies his church with the necessary equipment to carry out that mission. An indispensable part of this equipment is the church's government.

In *Westminster Confession of Faith*, 25.3, the Westminster Assembly affirms that to 'this catholic visible Church, Christ hath given the ministry, oracles, and ordinances of God.' The risen Christ, then, has supplied three things to the universal, visible church. First, 'the ministry,' that is, ministers of the Word. Second, 'oracles,' that is, the Scripture. Christ has placed the

---

Sessions of the Westminster Assembly of Divines, 1874; Edmonton, AB: Still Waters Revival Books, 1991, lxix, as cited at Barker, 'Lord of Lords and King of Commoners,' 418-9.

Scriptures of the Old Testament into the hands of his church and, through the apostles, the books of the New Testament as well (see 2 Timothy 3:16; John 14:26; John 16:12-15; 2 Timothy 2:2). Third, the 'ordinances of God,' particularly the reading and preaching of the Word, and the administration of the sacraments of baptism and the Lord's Supper. This threefold provision coalesces in Paul's letter to the Ephesians. The ascended Christ *gave the apostles, the prophets, the evangelists, the pastors and teachers* to the visible church (Ephesians 4:11). These people-gifts bring the Word of God to the visible church, and by their ministry of the Word the church grows to maturity (4:12-16).

Christ furnishes this equipment to his church for the gathering and perfecting of the saints. The ordinary way by which God draws his elect to himself is through the preaching of the Word. This means is certainly the primary way in which the church experiences quantitative growth in the Acts of the Apostles. Christ's ministers engage in the public preaching of the Word. Men and women respond in repentance and faith. They formally associate with the visible church and are thereby recognized as believers, entering into the fellowship and life of the local assembly of Christians.

This equipment not only extends the church but also matures the church (*to mature manhood*, Ephesians 4:13), brings further unity to the church (*until we all attain to the unity of the faith*, 4:13), conforms the church to Christ's image (*to the measure of the fullness of Christ*, 4:13), and stabilizes the church in the face of the destabilizing influences of false teaching (4:14). The church is hardly passive in this enterprise. In receiving the Word from the church's ministry, every true Christian actively participates in the building project that Paul describes here (4:16). No small part of that participation is *speaking the truth* received through the ministry of the Word *in love* to one another (4:15).

In words that echo the Great Commission of Matthew 28:18-20, the *Confession* stresses two further details about this mission. First, it is perpetual. The church's mission of 'gathering and perfecting the saints' continues 'to the end of the world.'[1] Second, it is personal. That is to say, Christ has pledged his presence to the church in order to ensure that her mission will not fail.[2] This presence, pledged in Matthew 28:20,[3] is a presence in the person and ministry of the Holy Spirit. By the Holy Spirit, Jesus will be with his visible church and will make effective the ministry, the Word, and the ordinances until he returns in glory at the end of the age.

This biblical and confessional vision of the church's calling and mission has tremendous implications for the life of the church today. First, we see the importance of well-functioning church government to the effective outworking of this mission. For there to be 'ministry,' the church must be vigilant to follow the biblical injunctions to examine candidates for the ministry, ascertain their qualifications for ministry, and, after a period of testing, set them apart to the ministry. Faithfulness to these commands requires elders who are faithful to the Bible and diligent in their calling. The 'oracles and ordinances,' furthermore, are no small part of the life of the church. The Word is to be purely preached, and the sacraments are to be administered in their biblical integrity. Well-functioning church government helps to ensure that the ministry of Word and sacrament is safeguarded and preserved in the visible church.

Second, we see that the church's mission is both assigned by Christ and set forth in the Scripture. This mission belongs to the church until Christ returns. The church is not free to replace this mission with another, nor to supplement it with other tasks. Her calling is not to political activism, social amelioration, or the merely moral reformation of the world at large. Her mission concerns 'the gathering and perfecting of the saints' with the means and helps that Christ supplies.

Third, we see that Jesus personally equips the church to

---

1 *Westminster Confession*, 25.3; cf. Matthew 28:20, to the end of the age.
2 'and does, by His own presence and Spirit, according to His promise, make them effectual thereunto.' *Westminster Confession*, 25.3.
3 *and behold, I am with you always.*

undertake her work with 'His own presence and Spirit.'[1] The church has all that she needs to undertake the work that Christ has assigned her. We should not rely on money, gifts, influence, or worldly methods of trying to promote and advance Christ's cause in the world. We should prayerfully and humbly ask for fresh supplies of the help that our present Savior is both able and willing to give us.

The Form and Function of the Church's Government

The fourth and final leading feature of biblical church government, according to the *Westminster Confession*, concerns the form and function of the church's government itself. What does biblical church government look like? The *Confession* does not detail a comprehensive, functional polity. Instead it accents leading features of biblical church government. We may observe three that the *Confession* highlights.

First, the *Confession* denies that 'the Pope of Rome' is 'in any sense' the head of the church.[2] The Lord Jesus Christ alone is the church's head.[3] The Confession responds here to claims emanating from the Roman Catholic Church that the Pope is the Vicar of Christ, that is 'Christ's head on earth ... the representative or substitute of the leadership of Jesus.'[4] Christ has not delegated this authority to one man, much less the Roman Pontiff. Christ alone remains head of the church, even

---

[1] *Westminster Confession*, 25.3.
[2] *Westminster Confession*, 25.6)
[3] In the twentieth century, American Presbyterians deleted from its version of the *Westminster Confession* the latter half of the original WCF 25.6, in which the Pope is identified as Antichrist and the Man of Sin—'but is that Antichrist, that man of sin, and son of perdition, that exalteth himself, in the Church, against Christ and all that is called God.' This removal is not so much a repudiation of this proposition as a reticence to bind the church to the affirmation of this proposition, so rightly Chad Van Dixhoorn, *Confessing the Faith: A Reader's Guide to the Westminster Confession of Faith*, Edinburgh: Banner of Truth, 2014, 347-8.
[4] R. C. Sproul, *Are We Together: A Protestant Analyzes Roman Catholicism*, Sanford: Reformation Trust, 2012, 98.

as he has 'committed ... power ... to His Church,' power that is exercised chiefly by the officers of the church.[1]

Second, the officers of the church have biblically defined responsibilities in the church. Individually, ministers are tasked with the preaching of the Word and the administration of the sacraments.[2] Ministers also gather together with other elders to perform certain governmental actions that would not be biblically lawful for individual elders to undertake by themselves.[3]

Third, the governmental actions that the church's elders undertake jointly take place in two levels or layers of the church's government. The first is that of the local congregation. Here, the congregation's elders have the responsibility to admit or to exclude people from the membership of the local church.[4] They also have the authority to inflict and to remove censures.[5] That is to say, the elders of the church are entrusted with the administration of church discipline in the local congregation.

Because church discipline is crucial to the health and well-being of the church, the *Westminster Confession* devotes two paragraphs to sketching its goals and workings. What are the goals of church discipline? One goal is 'the reclaiming and gaining of offending brethren.'[6] Church discipline has in view members of the church who have committed sin. The church's discipline is not punitive but restorative in nature. It seeks to recover a professing Christian from his sin. A second goal is

---

1 The language is that of *The Book of Church Order of the Presbyterian Church in America*, 6th ed, Lawrenceville: Committee on Discipleship Ministries, 2015, 3-1.
2 cf. *Westminster Confession*, 25.3; *Larger Catechism*, 158; *Westminster Confession*, 27.4.
3 *Westminster Confession*, 30-31. Presbyterian churchmen have referred to the distinction expressed in the preceding two sentences as that between the exercise of church power 'severally' and the exercise of church power 'jointly.' Note the recurring plural, 'officers,' in WCF 30—'in the hand of Church officers' (WCF 30.1); 'to these officers ...' (WCF 30.1); "the officers of the Church ..." (WCF 30.4).
4 *Westminster Confession*, 30.2; Matthew 18:17-18.
5 *Westminster Confession*, 30.2, '... and by absolution from censures, as occasion shall require.'
6 *Westminster Confession*, 30.3.

'deterring of others from the like offenses, ... purging out of that leaven which might infect the whole lump.'[1] Discipline has in view the well-being of the church at large. It seeks to discourage other believers from committing sin, and to protect the integrity and holiness of the body from moral contamination. A third goal is 'vindicating the honor of Christ.'[2] Discipline rises above the good of the offender and the well-being of the church to the glory of Jesus Christ, the 'King and Head of His Church.'[3] To tolerate sin in the church is dishonoring to Jesus, who has saved his people from their sins. A fourth goal is 'vindicating ... the holy profession of the Gospel.'[4] Here, the *Confession* stresses that discipline concerns the gospel's reputation before a watching world. In no way may the church ever convey to outsiders that sinful living is appropriate to those who name the name of Christ. Fifth, and finally, the *Confession* states that discipline 'prevent[s] the wrath of God, which might justly fall upon the Church.'[5] In view is Paul's teaching in 1 Corinthians 11:27–34, in which the church's profanation of the Lord's Supper occasioned the Lord's severe mercy of disciplining the church by means of the illness and death of some of its members. This 'wrath' is not the displeasure of an unreconciled Judge, but of a heavenly Father, who, in love and wisdom, will resort to such measures for the spiritual good of his erring church.

What, then, are the censures that the church's officers may inflict within the church? The *Confession* mentions three means of discipline, escalating in severity.[6] The first is 'admonition,' a verbal correction or exhortation.[7] The second is 'suspension

---

[1] *Westminster Confession*, 30.3.
[2] *Westminster Confession*, 30.3.
[3] *Westminster Confession*, 30.1.
[4] *Westminster Confession*, 30.3.
[5] *Westminster Confession*, 30.3.
[6] Note the qualification, 'according to the nature of the crime, and demerit of the person' (WCF 30.4). The elders must exercise biblical wisdom in weighing and inflicting ecclesiastical censures.
[7] *Westminster Confession*, 30.4; see 1 Thessalonians 5:12.

from the sacrament of the Lord's Supper for a season.'[1] (*Westminster Confession*, 30.4). The offender is excluded from this visible expression of the church's communion as a way, in part, to impress upon him the seriousness of his offense (see 2 Thessalonians 3:6, 14-15). The third is 'excommunication from the Church.'[2] The offender is removed from the fellowship of the church and put out into the world. The church does so in the hopes that this removal will stir him to repentance and that he will be restored to the church's fellowship.

The second layer of the church's government in which the elders engage in matters jointly is that of 'synods and councils.'[3] Much of the work described here may and should transpire at the local level, when congregational elders meet together to govern the local church. Primarily in view in the *Westminster Confession*, 31, however, is the work of elders gathered in regional or national assemblies, to undertake matters of common interest and concern to the churches whom they represent.[4]

We have already observed the American Presbyterian church's refining revision of the *Westminster Confession* 30.1-2 to forbid the civil magistrate from calling or participating in the church's synods. How, then, may we characterize the work of ecclesiastical synods and councils so convened? The divines lay down the biblical rule that synods and councils 'are to handle, or conclude nothing, but that which is ecclesiastical.'[5]

---

[1]
[2] *Westminster Confession*, 30.4; see Matthew 18:17; 1 Corinthians 5:4-5, 13.
[3] *Westminster Confession*, 31.
[4] The American revision of WCF 30.1-2 stressed that both ministers *and* elders could call for and participate in these assemblies as representatives of their congregations, 'it belongeth to the overseers and rulers of the particular churches ... to appoint such assemblies; and to convene together in them,' so Van Dixhoorn, *Confessing the Faith*, 413.
[5] *Westminster Confession*, 31.5 [=31.4 US]. Note also, later in this paragraph, the narrow circumstances in which the church may address the civil magistrate in a matter of 'civil affairs which concern the commonwealth,' WCF 31.5 [=31.4 US]—'humble petition in cases extraordinary,' or 'by way of advice, for satisfaction of conscience, if they be thereunto required by the civil magistrate' (ibid.).

The American revision clarified that the work of ecclesiastical assemblies was to be undertaken by 'the power which Christ hath given [the elders] for edification and not for destruction.'[1] The formation, participants, content, and power of the church's synods and councils reflect their exclusively spiritual character.

What kind of business are these synods and councils to take up? Their work falls in three main categories. They have the power of doctrine—'ministerially to determine controversies of faith, and cases of conscience.'[2] They have the power to order details concerning the 'public worship of God, and government of His church.'[3] They also have the power of discipline. These synods and councils may not only receive 'complaints in cases of maladministration' but also 'authoritatively ... determine the same.'[4] Synods and councils sit as courts of appeal, settling complaints against the actions of lower courts, and, we may fairly infer, hearing appeals in judicial matters lawfully brought before them.

The actions of synods and councils are not merely advisory. Their 'decrees and determinations, if consonant to the Word of God, are to be received with reverence and submission.'[5] This is so not only because of 'their agreement with the Word,' but because assemblies' 'decrees and determinations' are an 'ordinance of God appointed thereunto in His Word.'

The biblical example *par excellence* of the *Confession's* formulations is the Council of Jerusalem (Acts 15).[6] An assembly of elders representing local churches, the Jerusalem Council took up purely ecclesiastical matters sent up by the church in Antioch for wider deliberation (Acts 15:1-6). Its decision sought to resolve a controversy concerning the doctrine of justification by faith alone, and a related controversy concerning how Gentile

---

1 *Westminster Confession*, 31.1
2 *Westminster Confession*, 31.3 [=31.2 US].
3 *Westminster Confession*, 31.3 [=31.2 US].
4 *Westminster Confession*, 31.3 [=31.2 US].
5 *Westminster Confession*, 31.3 [=31.2 US].
6 For fuller discussion, see Waters, *How Jesus Runs the Church*, 126-35.

Christians were to relate to Jews both inside and outside the church (Acts 15:23-29). The Council advanced its decision not in its own authority but that of the Holy Spirit (Acts 15:28). As such and as its decisions were 'consonant to the Word of God',[1] the Council's decree was not merely advisory but binding on the churches to whom it was sent (Acts 15:28). God, in turn, blessed his own ordinance to the good of the church, which was strengthened and encouraged as a result of the Council's decrees (Acts 15:31, 41; Acts 16:5).

The *Confession's* foundational observations concerning the form and function of the church's government have wide-ranging implications for the life of the church today. It is tempting to be dismissive of or cynical about the workings and decisions of church courts. While no ecclesiastical assembly today is infallible,[2] we should receive the biblical decisions of elders, lawfully assembled, as from Christ himself. We should also adopt this posture towards the administration of discipline within the church, whether a personal, verbal admonition or a formal excommunication.

Precisely because elders, synods, and councils are fallible, or liable to err, biblical vigilance is required of the Christian church. Every believer must know the teaching of Scripture, particularly what it is that Christ would have him to believe and to do.[3] Unless we are so informed we will be unable properly to assess the decisions of the church's assemblies. If and as we know the teaching of the Bible, we will be prepared to receive the blessings that Christ purposes for his people through the ordinary means of biblical church government.

Conclusions

Although the *Westminster Confession* did not fare well as part of a broader effort to reform the English Church, its influence

---

1 *Westminster Confession*, 31.3 [=31.2 US]
2 So *Westminster Confession*, 31.4; 31.3 [US].
3 *Shorter Catechism*, 3.

over the last three and a half centuries has proven international in scope. No small part of this influence has been in the realm of church government. Although the *Westminster Confession* is a compact and incomplete statement of biblical church polity, it remains a remarkable achievement. In it, the Westminster divines articulated some of the fundamental principles of the church and her government—that the Bible is a sufficient guide to the church's government; that the Scripture speaks of the church in two distinct but inseparable ways—the church invisible and visible; that Christ alone is Head and King of his Church; that the church's government is distinct from the governments of this world; that Christ has assigned to the church a mission all her own; that the church is governed by elders who, according to Christ's authority, undertake the work that Christ has committed to them.

It is on this foundation that Presbyterian churches have been building since the seventeenth century. Dozens of books of order serve as the later church's testimony to the fundamental soundness of the *Confession's* achievement in the area of church government. Neither its work nor that which has been built upon it was an exercise in speculation. It concerned ordering the life of the church according to Scripture in order to display the glorious reign of Jesus Christ over his people. The Christian and the Christian church wants nothing more than to glorify her Savior. It is the kind provision of God that the contemporary church is well furnished in Word and Spirit to magnify Jesus through something as ordinary as church government. It is also the kind provision of God that, in his providence, he has given the contemporary church such helps in that work as the *Westminster Confession*. May he continue to use the *Confession's* testimony to the church's government to stir the church to renewed commitment to her calling in this age.

The Westminster Standards in Modern English Including the Creeds

The Westminster Standards Contents

1. Of the Holy Scripture 171
2. Of God, and of the Holy Trinity 175
3. Of God's Eternal Decree 177
4. Of Creation 179
5. Of Providence 180
6. Of the Fall of Man, of Sin, and the Punishment thereof . . . 182
7. Of God's Covenant with Man 183
8. Of Christ the Mediator 185
9. Of Free Will 188
10. Of Effectual Calling 189
11. Of Justification 191
12. Of Adoption 192
13. Of Sanctification 193
14. Of Saving Faith 194
15. Of Repentance unto Life 195
16. Of Good Works 196
17. Of the Perseverance of the Saints 199
18. Of Assurance of Grace and Salvation 200

19. Of the Law of God.. 201
20. Of Christian Liberty, and Liberty of Conscience 204
21. Of Religious Worship, and the Sabbath Day 206
22. Of Lawful Oaths and Vows 209
23. Of the Civil Magistrate................................ 210
24. Of Marriage and Divorce 212
25. Of the Church 213
26. Of the Communion of Saints 215
27. Of the Sacraments.................................... 216
28. Of Baptism 217
29. Of the Lord's Supper................................. 218
30. Of Church Censures 221
31. Of Synods and Councils.............................. 222
32. Of the State of Men after Death, and of the Resurrection of the Dead... 223
33. Of the Last Judgment 224

The Westminster Larger Catechism 227

The Westminster Shorter Catechism..................... 315

The Creeds... 341

    The Apostles' Creed 343

    The Nicene Creed (AD 381) 345

    The Athanasian Creed 347

    The Definition of the Council of Chalcedon (AD 451).... 351

The Westminster Confession of Faith in Modern English

Chapter 1
Of the Holy Scripture

1. Although the light of nature, and the works of creation and providence do so far manifest the goodness, wisdom, and power of God, as to leave men inexcusable;[1] yet are they not sufficient to give that knowledge of God, and of His will, which is necessary unto salvation.[2] Therefore it pleased the Lord, at sundry [various] times, and in divers manners [different ways], to reveal Himself, and to declare that His will unto His Church;[3] and afterwards for the better preserving and propagating of the truth, and for the more sure establishment and comfort of the Church against the corruption of the flesh, and the malice of Satan and of the world, to commit the same wholly unto writing;[4] which makes the Holy Scripture to be most necessary;[5] those former ways of God's revealing His will unto His people being now ceased.[6]

2. Under the name of Holy Scripture, or the Word of God written, are now contained all the books of the Old and New Testament, which are these:

---

[1] Romans 2:14-15; 1:19, 20; Psalm 19:1-3; Romans 1:32, 2:1.
[2] 1 Corinthians 1:21; 2:13-14
[3] Hebrews 1:1
[4] Proverbs 22:19-21; Luke 1:3-4; Romans 15:4; Matthew 4:4, 7, 10; Isaiah 8:19-20
[5] 2 Timothy 3:15; 2 Peter 1:19
[6] Hebrews 1:1-2

Of the Old Testament:

Genesis, Exodus, Leviticus, Numbers, Deuteronomy, Joshua, Judges, Ruth, I Samuel, II Samuel, I Kings, II Kings, I Chronicles, II Chronicles, Ezra, Nehemiah, Esther, Job, Psalms, Proverbs, Ecclesiastes, The Song of Songs, Isaiah, Jeremiah, Lamentations, Ezekiel, Daniel, Hosea, Joel, Amos, Obadiah, Jonah, Micah, Nahum, Habakkuk, Zephaniah, Haggai, Zechariah, Malachi.

Of the New Testament:

The Gospels according to Matthew, Mark, Luke, John, The Acts of the Apostles, Paul's Epistles to the Romans, Corinthians I, Corinthians II, Galatians, Ephesians, Philippians, Colossians, Thessalonians I, Thessalonians II, To Timothy I, To Timothy II, To Titus, To Philemon, The Epistle to the Hebrews, The Epistle of James, The first and second Epistles of Peter, The first, second, and third Epistles of John, The Epistle of Jude, The Revelation of John. All which are given by inspiration of God to be the rule of faith and life.[1]

3. The books commonly called Apocrypha, not being of divine inspiration, are no part of the canon of the Scripture, and therefore are of no authority in the Church of God, nor to be any otherwise approved, or made use of, than other human writings.[2]

4. The authority of the Holy Scripture, for which it ought to be believed and obeyed, depends not upon the testimony of any man, or Church; but wholly upon God (who is truth itself) the author thereof: and therefore it is to be received because it is the Word of God.[3]

5. We may be moved and induced [persuaded] by the testimony of the Church to a high and reverent esteem of the Holy

---

[1] Luke 16:29, 31; Ephesians 2:20; Revelation 22:18-19; 2 Timothy 3:16
[2] Luke 24:27; Romans 3:2; 2 Peter 1:21
[3] 2 Peter 1:19, 21; 2 Timothy 3:16; 1 John 5:9; 1 Thessalonians 2:13

Scripture.[1] And the heavenliness of the matter, the efficacy of the doctrine, the majesty of the style, the consent of all the parts, the scope of the whole (which is, to give all glory to God), the full discovery it makes of the only way of man's salvation, the many other incomparable excellencies, and the entire perfection thereof, are arguments whereby it does abundantly evidence itself to be the Word of God: yet notwithstanding, our full persuasion and assurance of the infallible truth and divine authority thereof, is from the inward work of the Holy Spirit bearing witness by and with the Word in our hearts.[2]

6. The whole counsel of God concerning all things necessary for His own glory, man's salvation, faith and life, is either expressly set down in Scripture, or by good and necessary consequence may be deduced from Scripture: unto which nothing at any time is to be added, whether by new revelations of the Spirit, or traditions of men.[3] Nevertheless, we acknowledge the inward illumination of the Spirit of God to be necessary for the saving understanding of such things as are revealed in the Word:[4] and that there are some circumstances concerning the worship of God, and government of the Church, common to human actions and societies, which are to be ordered by the light of nature and Christian prudence, according to the general rules of the Word, which are always to be observed.[5]

7. All things in Scripture are not equally plain in themselves, nor equally clear unto all:[6] yet those things which are necessary to be known, believed, and observed for salvation are so clearly propounded, and opened in some place of Scripture or other, that not only the learned, but the unlearned, in a due use of the

---

1   1 Timothy 3:15
2   1 John 2:20, 27; John 16:13- 14; 1 Corinthians 2:10-12; Isaiah 59:21
3   2 Timothy 3:15-17; Galatians 1:8-9; 2 Thessalonians 2:2
4   John 6:45; 1 Corinthians 2:9-12
5   1 Corinthians 11:13-14; 14:26, 40
6   2 Peter 3:16

ordinary means, may attain unto a sufficient understanding of [learn to understand] them.[1]

8. The Old Testament in Hebrew (which was the native language of the people of God of old), and the New Testament in Greek (which, at the time of the writing of it, was most generally known to the nations), being immediately inspired by God, and, by His singular care and providence, kept pure in all ages, are therefore authentic;[2] so as, in all controversies of religion, the Church is finally to appeal unto them.[3] But, because these original tongues are not known to all the people of God, who have right unto, and interest in the Scriptures, and are commanded, in the fear of God, to read and search them,[4] therefore they are to be translated into the common language of every nation unto which they come[5] that, the Word of God dwelling plentifully in all, they may worship Him in an acceptable manner;[6] and, through patience and comfort of the Scriptures, may have hope.[7]

9. The infallible rule of interpretation of Scripture is the Scripture itself: and therefore, when there is a question about the true and full sense of any Scripture (which is not manifold, but one), it must be searched and known by other places that speak more clearly.[8]

10. The supreme judge by which all controversies of religion are to be determined, and all decrees of councils, opinions of ancient writers, doctrines of men, and private spirits, are to be

---

[1] Psalm 119:105, 130
[2] Matthew 5:18
[3] Isaiah 8:20; Acts 15:15; John 5:39, 46
[4] John 5:39
[5] 1 Corinthians 14:6, 9, 11–12, 24, 27–28
[6] Colossians 3:16
[7] Romans 15:4
[8] 2 Peter 1:20–21; Acts 15:15–16

examined, and in whose sentence we are to rest, can be no other but the Holy Spirit speaking in the Scripture.[1]

Chapter 2
Of God, and of the Holy Trinity

1. There is but one only,[2] living, and true God,[3] who is infinite in being and perfection,[4] a most pure spirit,[5] invisible,[6] without body, parts,[7] or passions,[8] immutable,[9] immense,[10] eternal,[11] incomprehensible,[12] almighty,[13] most wise,[14] most holy,[15] most free,[16] most absolute;[17] working all things according to the counsel of His own immutable and most righteous will,[18] for His own glory;[19] most loving,[20] gracious, merciful, long-suffering, abundant in goodness and truth, forgiving iniquity, transgression, and sin;[21] the rewarder of them that diligently seek Him;[22] and in addition, most just, and terrible in His

---

1 Matthew 22:29, 31; Ephesians 2:20; Acts 28:25
2 Deuteronomy 6:4; 1 Corinthians 8:4, 6
3 1 Thessalonians 1:9; Jeremiah 10:10
4 Job 11:7-9; 26:14
5 John 4:24
6 1 Timothy 1:17
7 Deuteronomy 4:15-16; John 4:24; Luke 24:39
8 Acts 14:11, 15
9 James 1:17; Malachi 3:6
10 1 Kings 8:27; Jeremiah 23:23-24
11 Psalm 90:2; 1 Timothy 1:17
12 Psalm 145:3
13 Genesis 17:1; Revelation 4:8
14 Romans 16:27
15 Isaiah 6:3; Revelation 4:8
16 Psalm 115:3
17 Exodus 3:14
18 Ephesians 1:11
19 Proverbs 16:4; Romans 11:36
20 1 John 4:8, 16
21 Exodus 34:6-7
22 Hebrews 11:6

judgments,[1] hating all sin,[2] and who will by no means clear the guilty.[3]

2. God has all life,[4] glory,[5] goodness,[6] blessedness,[7] in and of Himself; and is alone in and unto Himself all-sufficient, not standing in need of any creatures which He has made,[8] nor deriving any glory from them,[9] but only manifesting His own glory in, by, unto, and upon them: He is the alone fountain of all being, of whom, through whom, and to whom are all things;[10] and has most sovereign dominion over them, to do by them, for them, or upon them whatsoever Himself pleases.[11] In His sight all things are open and manifest;[12] His knowledge is infinite, infallible, and independent upon the creature,[13] so as nothing is to Him contingent [conditional], or uncertain.[14] He is most holy in all His counsels, in all His works, and in all His commands.[15] To Him is due from angels and men, and every other creature, whatsoever worship, service, or obedience He is pleased to require of them.[16]

3. In the unity of the Godhead there be three persons, of one substance, power, and eternity; God the Father, God the Son, and God the Holy Spirit.[17] The Father is of none, neither

---

1 Nehemiah 9:32–33
2 Psalm 5:5–6
3 Nahum 1:2–3; Exodus 34:7
4 John 5:26
5 Acts 7:2
6 Psalm 119:68
7 1 Timothy 6:15; Romans 9:5
8 Acts 17:24–25
9 Job 22:2–3
10 Romans 11:36
11 Revelation 4:11; 1 Timothy 6:15; Daniel 4:25, 35
12 Hebrews 4:13
13 Romans 11:33–34; Psalm 147:5
14 Acts 15:18; Ezekiel 11:5
15 Psalm 145:17; Romans 7:12
16 Revelation 5:12–14
17 1 John 5:7; Matthew 3:16–17; Matthew 28:19; 2 Corinthians 13:14

begotten nor proceeding; the Son is eternally begotten of the Father;[1] the Holy Spirit eternally proceeding from the Father and the Son.[2]

Chapter 3
Of God's Eternal Decree

1. God from all eternity, did, by the most wise and holy counsel of His own will, freely, and unchangeably ordain whatsoever comes to pass;[3] yet so, as thereby neither is God the author of sin,[4] nor is violence offered to the will of the creatures; nor is the liberty or contingency [possibility] of second causes taken away, but rather established.[5]

2. Although God knows whatsoever may or can come to pass upon all supposed conditions;[6] yet has He not decreed anything because He foresaw it as future, or as that which would come to pass upon such conditions.[7]

3. By the decree of God, for the manifestation of His glory, some men and angels[8] are predestined unto everlasting life; and others foreordained to everlasting death.[9]

4. These angels and men, thus predestined, and foreordained, are particularly and unchangeably designed, and their number so certain and definite, that it cannot be either increased or diminished.[10]

5. Those of mankind that are predestined unto life, God, before the foundation of the world was laid, according to His

---

1 John 1:14, 18
2 John 15:26; Galatians 4:6
3 Ephesians 1:11; Romans 11:33; Hebrews 6:17; Romans 9:15, 18
4 James 1:13, 17; 1 John 1:5
5 Acts 2:23; Matthew 17:12; Acts 4:27-28; John 19:11; Proverbs 16:33
6 Acts 15:18; 1 Samuel 23:11-12; Matthew 11:21, 23
7 Romans 9:11, 13, 16, 18
8 1 Timothy 5:21; Matthew 25:41
9 Romans 9:22-23; Ephesians 1:5-6; Proverbs 16:4
10 2 Timothy 2:19; John 13:18

eternal and immutable purpose, and the secret counsel and good pleasure of His will, has chosen, in Christ, unto everlasting glory,[1] out of His mere free grace and love, without any foresight of faith, or good works, or perseverance in either of them, or any other thing in the creature, as conditions, or causes moving Him thereunto:[2] and all to the praise of His glorious grace.[3]

6. As God has appointed the elect unto glory, so has He, by the eternal and most free purpose of His will, foreordained all the means thereunto.[4] Wherefore, they who are elected, being fallen in Adam, are redeemed by Christ,[5] are effectually called unto faith in Christ by His Spirit working in due season, are justified, adopted, sanctified,[6] and kept by His power, through faith, unto salvation.[7] Neither are any other redeemed by Christ, effectually called, justified, adopted, sanctified, and saved, but the elect only.[8]

7. The rest of mankind God was pleased, according to the unsearchable counsel of His own will, whereby He extends or withholds mercy, as He pleases, for the glory of His sovereign power over His creatures, to pass by; and to ordain them to dishonour and wrath, for their sin, to the praise of His glorious justice.[9]

8. The doctrine of this high mystery of predestination is to be handled with special prudence and care,[10] that men, attending the will of God revealed in His Word, and yielding obedience thereunto, may, from the certainty of their effectual calling,

1 Ephesians 1:4, 9, 11; Romans 8:30; 2 Timothy 1:9; 1 Thessalonians 5:9
2 Romans 9:11, 13, 16; Ephesians 1:4, 9
3 Ephesians 1:6, 12
4 1 Peter 1:2; Ephesians 1:4–5; 2:10; 2 Thessalonians 2:13
5 1 Thessalonians 5:9–10; Titus 2:14
6 Romans 8:30; Ephesians 1:5; 2 Thessalonians 2:13
7 1 Peter 1:5
8 John 17:9; Romans 8:28–39; John 6:64–65; 10:26; 8:47; 1 John 2:19
9 Matthew 11:25–26; Romans 9:17–18, 21–22; 2 Timothy 2:19–20; Jude 4; 1 Peter 2:8
10 Romans 9:20; 11:33; Deuteronomy 29:29

be assured of their eternal election.[1] So shall this doctrine afford matter of praise, reverence, and admiration of God;[2] and of humility, diligence, and abundant consolation to all that sincerely obey the Gospel.[3]

Chapter 4
Of Creation

1. It pleased God the Father, Son, and Holy Spirit,[4] for the manifestation of the glory of His eternal power, wisdom, and goodness,[5] in the beginning, to create, or make of nothing, the world, and all things therein whether visible or invisible, in the space of six days; and all very good.[6]

2. After God had made all other creatures, He created man, male and female,[7] with reasonable and immortal souls,[8] endued with knowledge, righteousness, and true holiness, after His own image;[9] having the law of God written in their hearts,[10] and power to fulfil it;[11] and yet under a possibility of transgressing, being left to the liberty of their own will, which was subject unto change.[12] Beside this law written in their hearts, they received a command, not to eat of the tree of the knowledge of good and evil;[13] which while they kept, they were happy in their communion with God, and had dominion over the creatures.[14]

---

1 2 Peter 1:10
2 Ephesians 1:6; Romans 11:33
3 Romans 11:5-6, 20; 2 Peter 1:10; Romans 8:33; Luke 10:20
4 Hebrews 1:2; John 1:2-3; Genesis 1:2; Job 26:13; 33:4
5 Romans 1:20; Jeremiah 10:12; Psalm 104:24; 33:5-6
6 Genesis 1; Hebrews 11:3; Colossians 1:16; Acts 17:24
7 Genesis 1:27
8 Genesis 2:7; Ecclesiastes 12:7; Luke 23:43; Matthew 10:28
9 Genesis 1:26; Colossians 3:10; Ephesians 4:24
10 Romans 2:14-15
11 Ecclesiastes 7:29
12 Genesis 3:6; Ecclesiastes 7:29
13 Genesis 2:17, 3:8-11, 23
14 Genesis 1:26, 28

Chapter 5
Of Providence

1. God the great Creator of all things does uphold,[1] direct, dispose, and govern all creatures, actions, and things,[2] from the greatest even to the least,[3] by His most wise and holy providence,[4] according to His infallible foreknowledge,[5] and the free and immutable counsel of His own will,[6] to the praise of the glory of His wisdom, power, justice, goodness, and mercy.[7]

2. Although, in relation to the foreknowledge and decree of God, the first Cause, all things come to pass immutably, and infallibly;[8] yet, by the same providence, He orders them to fall out, according to the nature of second causes, either necessarily, freely, or contingently [circumstantially].[9]

3. God, in His ordinary providence, makes use of means,[10] yet is free to work without,[11] above,[12] and against them,[13] at His pleasure.

4. The almighty power, unsearchable wisdom, and infinite goodness of God so far manifest themselves in His providence, that it extends itself even to the first fall, and all other sins of

---

1 Hebrews 1:3
2 Daniel 4:34–35; Psalm 135:6; Acts 17:25–26, 28; Job 38–41
3 Matthew 10:29–31
4 Proverbs 15:3; Psalm 104:24; 145:17
5 Acts 15:18; Psalm 94:8–11
6 Ephesians 1:11; Psalm 33:10–11
7 Isaiah 63:14; Ephesians 3:10; Romans 9:17; Genesis 45:7; Psalm 145:7
8 Acts 2:23
9 Genesis 8:22; Jeremiah 31:35; Exodus 21:13; Deuteronomy 19:5; 1 Kings 22:28, 34; Isaiah 10:6–7
10 Acts 27:31, 44; Isaiah 55:10–11; Hosea 2:21–22
11 Hosea 1:7; Matthew 4:4; Job 34:10
12 Romans 4:19–21
13 2 Kings 6:6; Daniel 3:27

angels and men;[1] and that not by a bare [mere] permission,[2] but such as has joined with it a most wise and powerful bounding,[3] and otherwise ordering, and governing of them, in a manifold dispensation [varied administration], to His own holy ends;[4] yet so, as the sinfulness thereof proceeds only from the creature, and not from God, who, being most holy and righteous, neither is nor can be the author or approver of sin.[5]

5. The most wise, righteous, and gracious God does often leave, for a season, His own children to manifold temptations, and the corruption of their own hearts, to chastise them for their former sins, or to discover unto them the hidden strength of corruption and deceitfulness of their hearts, that they may be humbled;[6] and, to raise them to a more close and constant dependence for their support upon Himself, and to make them more watchful against all future occasions of sin, and for sundry other just and holy ends.[7]

6. As for those wicked and ungodly men whom God, as a righteous Judge, for former sins, does blind and harden,[8] from them He not only withholds His grace whereby they might have been enlightened in their understandings, and wrought upon in their hearts;[9] but sometimes also withdraws the gifts which they had,[10] and exposes them to such objects as their corruption makes occasions of sin;[11] and, in addition, gives them over to their own lusts, the temptations of the world, and the power of

---

1 Romans 11:32-34; 2 Samuel 24:1; 1 Chronicles 21:1; 1 Kings 22:22-23; 1 Chronicles 10:4, 13-14; 2 Samuel 16:10; Acts 2:23; Acts 4:27-28
2 Acts 14:16
3 Psalm 76:10; 2 Kings 19:28
4 Genesis 50:20; Isaiah 10:6-7, 12
5 James 1:13-14, 17; 1 John 2:16; Psalm 50:21
6 2 Chronicles 32:25-26, 31; 2 Samuel 24:1
7 2 Corinthians 12:7-9; Psalm 73; 77:1-12; Mark 14:66-72; John 21:15-17
8 Romans 1:24, 26, 28; 11:7-8
9 Deuteronomy 29:4
10 Matthew 13:12; 25:29
11 Deuteronomy 2:30; 2 Kings 8:12-13

Satan,[1] whereby it comes to pass that they harden themselves, even under those means which God uses for the softening of others.[2]

7. As the providence of God does, in general, reach to all creatures; so, after a most special manner, it takes care of His Church, and disposes all things to the good thereof.[3]

Chapter 6
Of the Fall of Man, of Sin, and the Punishment thereof

1. Our first parents, being seduced by the subtlety and temptations of Satan, sinned, in eating the forbidden fruit.[4] This their sin, God was pleased, according to His wise and holy counsel, to permit, having purposed to order it to His own glory.[5]

2. By this sin they fell from their original righteousness and communion with God,[6] and so became dead in sin,[7] and wholly defiled in all the faculties and parts of soul and body.[8]

3. They being the root of all mankind, the guilt of this sin was imputed;[9] and the same death in sin, and corrupted nature, conveyed to all their posterity descending from them by ordinary generation.[10]

4. From this original corruption, whereby we are utterly

---

1 Psalm 81:11-12; 2 Thessalonians 2:10-12
2 Exodus 7:3; 8:15, 32; 2 Corinthians 2:15, 16; Isaiah 8:14; 1 Peter 2:7-8; Isaiah 6:9-10; Acts 28:26-27
3 1 Timothy 4:10; Amos 9:8-9; Romans 8:28; Isaiah 43:3-5, 14
4 Genesis 3:13; 2 Corinthians 11:3
5 Romans 11:32
6 Genesis 3:6-8; Ecclesiastes 7:29; Romans 3:23
7 Genesis 2:17; Ephesians 2:1
8 Titus 1:15; Genesis 6:5; Jeremiah 17:9; Romans 3:10-18
9 Genesis 1:27-28; 2:16-17; Acts 17:26; Romans 5:12, 15-19; 1 Corinthians 15:21-22, 49
10 Psalm 51:5; Genesis 5:3; Job 14:4; 15:14

indisposed, disabled, and made opposite to all good,[1] and wholly inclined to all evil,[2] do proceed all actual transgressions.[3]

5. This corruption of nature, during this life, does remain in those that are regenerated;[4] and although it be, through Christ, pardoned, and mortified; yet both itself, and all the motions thereof, are truly and properly sin.[5]

6. Every sin, both original and actual, being a transgression of the righteous law of God, and contrary thereunto,[6] does in its own nature, bring guilt upon the sinner,[7] whereby he is bound over to the wrath of God,[8] and curse of the law,[9] and so made subject to death,[10] with all miseries spiritual,[11] temporal,[12] and eternal.[13]

Chapter 7
Of God's Covenant with Man

1. The distance between God and the creature is so great, that although reasonable creatures do owe obedience unto Him as their Creator, yet they could never have any fruition [enjoyment] of Him as their blessedness and reward, but by some voluntary condescension on God's part, which He has been pleased to express by way of covenant.[14]

---

1 Romans 5:6, 8:7; 7:18; Colossians 1:21
2 Genesis 6:5; 8:21; Romans 3:10-12
3 James 1:14-15; Ephesians 2:2-3; Matthew 15:19
4 1 John 1:8, 10; Romans 7:14, 17-18, 23; James 3:2; Proverbs 20:9; Ecclesiastes 7:20
5 Romans 7:5, 7-8, 25; Galatians 5:17
6 1 John 3:4
7 Romans 2:15, 3:9, 19
8 Ephesians 2:3
9 Galatians 3:10
10 Romans 6:23
11 Ephesians 4:18
12 Romans 8:20; Lamentations 3:39
13 Matthew 25:41; 2 Thessalonians 1:9
14 Isaiah 40:13-17; Job 9:32, 33; 1 Samuel 2:25; Psalm 113:5-6, 100:2-3; Job 22:2-3; 35:7-8; Luke 17:10; Acts 17:24-25

2. The first covenant made with man was a covenant of works,[1] wherein life was promised to Adam, and in him to his posterity,[2] upon condition of perfect and personal obedience.[3]

3. Man, by his fall, having made himself incapable of life by that covenant, the Lord was pleased to make a second,[4] commonly called the covenant of grace; wherein He freely offers unto sinners life and salvation by Jesus Christ; requiring of them faith in Him, that they may be saved,[5] and promising to give unto all those that are ordained unto life His Holy Spirit, to make them willing, and able to believe.[6]

4. This covenant of grace is frequently set forth in Scripture by the name of a Testament, in reference to the death of Jesus Christ the Testator, and to the everlasting inheritance, with all things belonging to it, therein bequeathed.[7]

5. This covenant was differently administered in the time of the law, and in the time of the gospel:[8] under the law, it was administered by promises, prophecies, sacrifices, circumcision, the paschal [Passover] lamb, and other types and ordinances delivered to the people of the Jews, all foreshadowing Christ to come;[9] which were, for that time, sufficient and efficacious, through the operation of the Spirit, to instruct and build up the elect in faith in the promised Messiah,[10] by whom they had full remission of sins, and eternal salvation; and is called the Old Testament.[11]

---

1   Galatians 3:12
2   Romans 10:5; Romans 5:12-20
3   Genesis 2:17; Galatians 3:10
4   Galatians 3:21; Romans 8:3; 3:20-21; Genesis 3:15; Isaiah 42:6
5   Mark 16:15-16; John 3:16; Romans 10:6, 9; Galatians 3:11
6   Ezekiel 36:26-27; John 6:44-45
7   Hebrews 9:15-17; 7:22; Luke 22:20; 1 Corinthians 11:25
8   2 Corinthians 3:6-9
9   Hebrews 8, 9, and 10; Romans 4:11; Colossians 2:11-12; 1 Corinthians 5:7
10 1 Corinthians 10:1-4; Hebrews 11:13; John 8:56
11 Galatians 3:7-9, 14

6. Under the gospel, when Christ, the substance,[1] was exhibited, the ordinances in which this covenant is dispensed are the preaching of the Word, and the administration of the sacraments of Baptism and the Lord's Supper:[2] which, though fewer in number, and administered with more simplicity, and less outward glory; yet, in them, it is held forth in more fullness, evidence, and spiritual efficacy,[3] to all nations, both Jews and Gentiles;[4] and is called the New Testament.[5] There are not therefore two covenants of grace, differing in substance, but one and the same, under various dispensations [administrations].[6]

Chapter 8
Of Christ the Mediator

1. It pleased God, in His eternal purpose, to choose and ordain the Lord Jesus, His only begotten Son, to be the Mediator between God and man,[7] the Prophet,[8] Priest,[9] and King,[10] the Head and Saviour of His Church,[11] the Heir of all things,[12] and Judge of the world:[13] unto whom He did from all eternity give a people, to be His seed,[14] and to be by Him in time redeemed, called, justified, sanctified, and glorified.[15]

2. The Son of God, the second person of the Trinity, being

---

[1] Colossians 2:17
[2] Matthew 28:19-20; 1 Corinthians 11:23-25
[3] Hebrews 12:22-28; Jeremiah 31:33-34
[4] Matthew 28:19; Ephesians 2:15-19
[5] Luke 22:20
[6] Galatians 3:14, 16; Romans 3:21-23, 30; Psalm 32:1 with Romans 4:3, 6, 16-17, 23-24; Hebrews 13:8; Acts 15:11
[7] Isaiah 42:1; 1 Peter 1:19-20; John 3:16; 1 Timothy 2:5
[8] Acts 3:22
[9] Hebrews 5:5-6
[10] Psalm 2:6; Luke 1:33
[11] Ephesians 5:23
[12] Hebrews 1:2
[13] Acts 17:31
[14] John 17:6; Psalm 22:30; Isaiah 53:10
[15] 1 Timothy 2:6; Isaiah 55:4-5; 1 Corinthians 1:30

very and eternal God, of one substance and equal with the Father, did, when the fullness of time was come, take upon Him man's nature,[1] with all the essential properties, and common infirmities thereof, yet without sin;[2] being conceived by the power of the Holy Spirit, in the womb of the virgin Mary, of her substance.[3] So that two whole, perfect, and distinct natures, the Godhead and the manhood, were inseparably joined together in one person, without conversion, composition, or confusion.[4] Which person is very God, and very man, yet one Christ, the only Mediator between God and man.[5]

3. The Lord Jesus, in His human nature thus united to the divine, was sanctified, and anointed with the Holy Spirit, above measure,[6] having in Him all the treasures of wisdom and knowledge;[7] in whom it pleased the Father that all fullness should dwell;[8] to the end that, being holy, harmless, undefiled, and full of grace and truth,[9] He might be thoroughly furnished to execute the office of a Mediator and Surety.[10] Which office He took not unto Himself, but was thereunto called by His Father,[11] who put all power and judgment into His hand, and gave Him commandment to execute the same.[12]

4. This office the Lord Jesus did most willingly undertake;[13] which that He might discharge, He was made under the law,[14]

---

1 John 1:1, 14; 1 John 5:20; Philippians 2:6; Galatians 4:4
2 Hebrews 2:14, 16–17; 4:15
3 Luke 1:27, 31, 35; Galatians 4:4
4 Luke 1:35; Colossians 2:9; Romans 9:5; 1 Peter 3:18; 1 Timothy 3:16
5 Romans 1:3–4; 1 Timothy 2:5
6 Psalm 45:7; John 3:34
7 Colossians 2:3
8 Colossians 1:19
9 Hebrews 7:26; John 1:14
10 Acts 10:38; Hebrews 12:24; 7:22
11 Hebrews 5:4–5
12 John 5:22, 27; Matthew 28:18; Acts 2:36
13 Psalm 40:7–8; Hebrews 10:5–10; John 10:18; Philippians 2:8
14 Galatians 4:4

and did perfectly fulfil it;[1] endured most grievous torments immediately in His soul,[2] and most painful sufferings in His body;[3] was crucified, and died;[4] was buried, and remained under the power of death; yet saw no corruption.[5] On the third day He arose from the dead,[6] with the same body in which He suffered,[7] with which also he ascended into heaven, and there sits at the right hand of His Father,[8] making intercession,[9] and shall return, to judge men and angels, at the end of the world.[10]

5. The Lord Jesus, by His perfect obedience, and sacrifice of Himself, which He through the eternal Spirit, once offered up unto God, has fully satisfied the justice of His Father;[11] and purchased, not only reconciliation, but an everlasting inheritance in the kingdom of heaven, for all those whom the Father has given unto Him.[12]

6. Although the work of redemption was not actually wrought by Christ till after His incarnation, yet the virtue, efficacy, and benefits thereof were communicated unto the elect, in all ages successively from the beginning of the world, in and by those promises, types, and sacrifices, wherein He was revealed, and signified to be the seed of the woman which should bruise the serpent's head; and the Lamb slain from the beginning of the world; being yesterday and today the same, and forever.[13]

7. Christ, in the work of mediation, acts according to both

---

1 Matthew 3:15; 5:17
2 Matthew 26:37-38; Luke 22:44; Matthew 27:46
3 Matthew 26 and 27
4 Philippians 2:8
5 Acts 2:23-24, 27; Acts 13:37; Romans 6:9
6 1 Corinthians 15:3-4
7 John 20:25, 27
8 Mark 16:19
9 Romans 8:34; Hebrews 9:24; 7:25
10 Romans 14:9-10; Acts 1:11; 10:42; Matthew 13:40-42; Jude 6; 2 Peter 2:4
11 Romans 5:19; Hebrews 9:14, 16; 10:14; Ephesians 5:2; Romans 3:25-26
12 Daniel 9:24, 26; Colossians 1:19-20; Ephesians 1:11, 14; John 17:2; Hebrews 9:12, 15
13 Galatians 4:4-5; Genesis 3:15; Revelation 13:8; Hebrews 13:8

natures, by each nature doing that which is proper to itself;[1] yet, by reason of the unity of the person, that which is proper to one nature is sometimes in Scripture attributed to the person denominated by the other nature.[2]

8. To all those for whom Christ has purchased redemption, He does certainly and effectually apply and communicate the same,[3] making intercession for them,[4] and revealing unto them, in and by the Word, the mysteries of salvation;[5] effectually persuading them by His Spirit to believe and obey, and governing their hearts by His Word and Spirit;[6] overcoming all their enemies by His almighty power and wisdom, in such manner, and ways, as are most consonant [agreeable] to His wonderful and unsearchable dispensation [administration].[7]

Chapter 9
Of Free Will

1. God has endued the will of man with that natural liberty, that it is neither forced, nor, by any absolute necessity of nature, determined to good, or evil.[8]

2. Man, in his state of innocence, had freedom, and power to will and to do that which was good and well pleasing to God;[9] but yet, mutably [able to change], so that he might fall from it.[10]

3. Man, by his fall into a state of sin, has wholly lost all ability of will to any spiritual good accompanying salvation:[11] so as, a

---

1 Hebrews 9:14; 1 Peter 3:18
2 Acts 20:28; John 3:13; 1 John 3:16
3 John 6:37, 39; John 10:15-16
4 1 John 2:1-2; Romans 8:34
5 John 15:13, 15; Ephesians 1:7-9; John 17:6
6 John 14:26; Hebrews 12:2; 2 Corinthians 4:13; Romans 8:9, 14; 15:18-19; John 17:17
7 Psalm 110:1; 1 Corinthians 15:25-26; Malachi 4:2-3; Colossians 2:15
8 Matthew 17:12; James 1:14; Deuteronomy 30:19
9 Ecclesiastes 7:29; Genesis 1:26
10 Genesis 2:16-17; 3:6
11 Romans 5:6; 8:7; John 15:5

natural man, being altogether averse from that good,[1] and dead in sin,[2] is not able, by his own strength, to convert himself, or to prepare himself thereunto.[3]

4. When God converts a sinner, and translates him into the state of grace, He frees him from his natural bondage under sin;[4] and, by His grace alone, enables him freely to will and to do that which is spiritually good;[5] yet so, as that by reason of his remaining corruption, he does not perfectly, nor only, will that which is good, but does also will that which is evil.[6]

5. The will of man is made perfectly and immutably free to do good alone in the state of glory only.[7]

Chapter 10
Of Effectual Calling

1. All those whom God has predestined unto life, and those only, He is pleased, in His appointed time, effectually to call,[8] by His Word and Spirit,[9] out of that state of sin and death, in which they are by nature, to grace and salvation, by Jesus Christ;[10] enlightening their minds spiritually and savingly to understand the things of God,[11] taking away their heart of stone, and giving unto them a heart of flesh;[12] renewing their wills, and, by His almighty power, determining them to that which is good,[13] and

---

1 Romans 3:10, 12
2 Ephesians 2:1, 5; Colossians 2:13
3 John 6:44, 65; Ephesians 2:2-5; 1 Corinthians 2:14; Titus 3:3-5
4 Colossians 1:13; John 8:34, 36
5 Philippians 2:13; Romans 6:18, 22
6 Galatians 5:17; Romans 7:15, 18-19, 21, 23
7 Ephesians 4:13; Hebrews 12:23; 1 John 3:2; Jude 24
8 Romans 8:30; 11:7; Ephesians 1:10-11
9 2 Thessalonians 2:13-14; 2 Corinthians 3:3, 6
10 Romans 8:2; Ephesians 2:1-5; 2 Timothy 1:9-10
11 Acts 26:18; 1 Corinthians 2:10, 12; Ephesians 1:17-18
12 Ezekiel 36:26
13 Ezekiel 11:19; Philippians 2:13; Deuteronomy 30:6; Ezekiel 36:27

effectually drawing them to Jesus Christ:[1] yet so, as they come most freely, being made willing by His grace.[2]

2. This effectual call is of God's free and special grace alone, not from anything at all foreseen in man,[3] who is altogether passive therein, until, being quickened and renewed by the Holy Spirit,[4] he is thereby enabled to answer this call, and to embrace the grace offered and conveyed in it.[5]

3. Elect infants, dying in infancy, are regenerated, and saved by Christ, through the Spirit,[6] who works when, and where, and how He pleases:[7] so also are all other elect persons who are incapable of being outwardly called by the ministry of the Word.[8]

4. Others, not elected, although they may be called by the ministry of the Word,[9] and may have some common operations of the Spirit,[10] yet they never truly come unto Christ, and therefore cannot be saved:[11] much less can men, not professing the Christian religion, be saved in any other way whatsoever, be they never so diligent to frame their lives according to the light of nature, and the laws of that religion they do profess.[12] And to assert and maintain that they may, is very pernicious, and to be detested.[13]

---

1 Ephesians 1:19; John 6:44-45
2 Song of Solomon 1:4; Psalm 110:3; John 6:37; Romans 6:16-18
3 2 Timothy 1:9; Titus 3:4-5; Ephesians 2:4-5, 8-9; Romans 9:11
4 1 Corinthians 2:14; Romans 8:7; Ephesians 2:5
5 John 6:37; Ezekiel 36:27; John 5:25
6 Luke 18:15-16 and Acts 2:38-39 and John 3:3, 5 and 1 John 5:12 and Romans 8:9 [compared together]
7 John 3:8
8 1 John 5:12; Acts 4:12
9 Matthew 22:14
10 Matthew 7:22; 13:20-21; Hebrews 6:4-5
11 John 6:64-66; 8:24
12 Acts 4:12; John 14:6; Ephesians 2:12; John 4:22; 17:3
13 2 John 9-11; 1 Corinthians 16:22; Galatians 1:6-8

Chapter 11
Of Justification

1. Those whom God effectually calls, He also freely justifies;[1] not by infusing righteousness into them, but by pardoning their sins, and by accounting and accepting their persons as righteous; not for anything wrought in them, or done by them, but for Christ's sake alone; nor by imputing faith itself, the act of believing, or any other evangelical obedience to them, as their righteousness; but by imputing the obedience and satisfaction of Christ unto them,[2] they receiving and resting on Him and His righteousness, by faith; which faith they have not of themselves, it is the gift of God.[3]

2. Faith, thus receiving and resting on Christ and His righteousness, is the alone instrument of justification:[4] yet is it not alone in the person justified, but is ever accompanied with all other saving graces, and is no dead faith, but works by love.[5]

3. Christ, by His obedience and death, did fully discharge the debt of all those that are thus justified, and did make a proper, real and full satisfaction to His Father's justice in their behalf.[6] Yet, in as much as He was given by the Father for them;[7] and His obedience and satisfaction accepted in their stead;[8] and both, freely, not for anything in them; their justification is only of free grace;[9] that both the exact justice, and rich grace of God might be glorified in the justification of sinners.[10]

---

1 Romans 8:30; 3:24
2 Romans 4:5-8; 2 Corinthians 5:19, 21; Romans 3:22, 24-25, 27-28; Titus 3:5, 7; Ephesians 1:7; Jeremiah 23:6; 1 Corinthians 1:30-31; Romans 5:17-19
3 Acts 10:43; Galatians 2:16; Philippians 3:9; Acts 13:38-39; Ephesians 2:7-8
4 John 1:12; Romans 3:28; 5:1
5 James 2:17, 22, 26; Galatians 5:6
6 Romans 5:8-10, 19; 1 Timothy 2:5-6; Hebrews 10:10, 14; Daniel 9:24, 26; Isaiah 53:4-6, 10-12
7 Romans 8:32
8 2 Corinthians 5:21; Matthew 3:17; Ephesians 5:2
9 Romans 3:24; Ephesians 1:7
10 Romans 3:26; Ephesians 2:7

4. God did, from all eternity, decree to justify all the elect,[1] and Christ did, in the fullness of time, die for their sins, and rise again for their justification:[2] nevertheless, they are not justified, until the Holy Spirit does, in due time, actually apply Christ unto them.[3]

5. God does continue to forgive the sins of those that are justified;[4] and although they can never fall from the state of justification,[5] yet they may, by their sins, fall under God's fatherly displeasure, and not have the light of His countenance restored unto them, until they humble themselves, confess their sins, beg pardon, and renew their faith and repentance.[6]

6. The justification of believers under the Old Testament was, in all these respects, one and the same with the justification of believers under the New Testament.[7]

Chapter 12
Of Adoption

1. All those that are justified, God vouchsafes [promises], in and for His only Son Jesus Christ, to make partakers of the grace of adoption,[8] by which they are taken into the number, and enjoy the liberties and privileges of the children of God,[9] have His name put upon them,[10] receive the spirit of adoption,[11] have access to the throne of grace with boldness,[12] are enabled to

---

1 Galatians 3:8; 1 Peter 1:2, 19–20; Romans 8:30
2 Galatians 4:4; 1 Timothy 2:6; Romans 4:25
3 Colossians 1:21–22; Galatians 2:16; Titus 3:3–7
4 Matthew 6:12; 1 John 1:7, 9; 1 John 2:1–2
5 Luke 22:32; John 10:28; Hebrews 10:14
6 Psalm 89:31–33; 51:7–12; 32:5; Matthew 26:75; 1 Corinthians 11:30; Luke 1:20
7 Galatians 3:9, 13–14; Romans 4:22–24; Hebrews 13:8
8 Ephesians 1:5
9 Galatians 4:4–5; Romans 8:17; John 1:12
10 Jeremiah 14:9; 2 Corinthians 6:18; Revelation 3:12
11 Romans 8:15
12 Ephesians 3:12; Romans 5:2

cry, Abba, Father,[1] are pitied,[2] protected,[3] provided for,[4] and chastened by Him as by a Father:[5] yet never cast off,[6] but sealed to the day of redemption;[7] and inherit the promises,[8] as heirs of everlasting salvation.[9]

Chapter 13
Of Sanctification

1. They, who are once effectually called, and regenerated, having a new heart, and a new spirit created in them, are further sanctified, really and personally, through the virtue of Christ's death and resurrection,[10] by His Word and Spirit dwelling in them:[11] the dominion of the whole body of sin is destroyed,[12] and the several lusts thereof are more and more weakened and mortified;[13] and they more and more quickened and strengthened in all saving graces,[14] to the practice of true holiness, without which no man shall see the Lord.[15]

2. This sanctification is throughout, in the whole man;[16] yet imperfect in this life, there abiding still some remnants of corruption in every part;[17] whence arises a continual and

---

1 Galatians 4:6
2 Psalm 103:13
3 Proverbs 14:26
4 Matthew 6:30, 32; 1 Peter 5:7
5 Hebrews 12:6
6 Lamentations 3:31
7 Ephesians 4:30
8 Hebrews 6:12
9 1 Peter 1:3-4; Hebrews 1:14
10 1 Corinthians 6:11; Acts 20:32; Philippians 3:10; Romans 6:5-6
11 John 17:17; Ephesians 5:26; 2 Thessalonians 2:13
12 Romans 6:6, 14
13 Galatians 5:24; Romans 8:13
14 Colossians 1:11; Ephesians 3:16-19
15 2 Corinthians 7:1; Hebrews 12:14
16 1 Thessalonians 5:23
17 1 John 1:10; Romans 7:18, 23; Philippians 3:12

irreconcilable war, the flesh lusting against the Spirit, and the Spirit against the flesh.[1]

3. In which war, although the remaining corruption, for a time, may much prevail;[2] yet, through the continual supply of strength from the sanctifying Spirit of Christ, the regenerate part does overcome;[3] and so, the saints grow in grace,[4] perfecting holiness in the fear of God.[5]

Chapter 14
Of Saving Faith

1. The grace of faith, whereby the elect are enabled to believe to the saving of their souls,[6] is the work of the Spirit of Christ in their hearts,[7] and is ordinarily wrought by the ministry of the Word:[8] by which also, and by the administration of the sacraments, and prayer, it is increased and strengthened.[9]

2. By this faith, a Christian believes to be true whatsoever is revealed in the Word, for the authority of God Himself speaking therein;[10] and acts differently upon that which each particular passage thereof contains; yielding obedience to the commands,[11] trembling at the threatenings,[12] and embracing the promises of God for this life, and that which is to come.[13] But the principal acts of saving faith are accepting, receiving, and resting upon

---

1 Galatians 5:17; 1 Peter 2:11
2 Romans 7:23
3 Romans 6:14; 1 John 5:4; Ephesians 4:15-16
4 2 Peter 3:18; 2 Corinthians 3:18
5 2 Corinthians 7:1
6 Hebrews 10:39
7 2 Corinthians 4:13; Ephesians 1:17-19; Ephesians 2:8
8 Romans 10:14, 17
9 1 Peter 2:2; Acts 20:32; Romans 4:11; Luke 17:5; Romans 1:16-17
10 John 4:42; 1 Thessalonians 2:13; 1 John 5:10; Acts 24:14
11 Romans 16:26
12 Isaiah 66:2
13 Hebrews 11:13; 1 Timothy 4:8

Christ alone for justification, sanctification, and eternal life, by virtue of the covenant of grace.[1]

3. This faith is different in degrees, weak or strong;[2] may be often and many ways assailed, and weakened, but gets the victory;[3] growing up in many to the attainment of a full assurance, through Christ,[4] who is both the author and finisher of our faith.[5]

Chapter 15
Of Repentance unto Life

1. Repentance unto life is an evangelical grace,[6] the doctrine whereof is to be preached by every minister of the Gospel, as well as that of faith in Christ.[7]

2. By it, a sinner, out of the sight and sense not only of the danger, but also of the filthiness and odiousness of his sins, as contrary to the holy nature, and righteous law of God; and upon the apprehension of His mercy in Christ to such as are penitent, so grieves for, and hates his sins, as to turn from them all unto God,[8] purposing and endeavouring to walk with Him in all the ways of His commandments.[9]

3. Although repentance is not to be rested in, as any satisfaction for sin, or any cause of the pardon thereof,[10] which

---

1 John 1:12; Acts 16:31; Galatians 2:20; Acts 15:11
2 Hebrews 5:13-14; Romans 4:19-20; Matthew 6:30; Matthew 8:10
3 Luke 22:31-32; Ephesians 6:16; 1 John 5:4-5
4 Hebrews 6:11-12; 10:22; Colossians 2:2
5 Hebrews 12:2
6 Zechariah 12:10; Acts 11:18
7 Luke 24:47; Mark 1:15; Acts 20:21
8 Ezekiel 18:30-31; 36:31; Isaiah 30:22; Psalm 51:4; Jeremiah 31:18-19; Joel 2:12-13; Amos 5:15; Psalm 119:128; 2 Corinthians 7:11
9 Psalm 119:6, 59, 106; Luke 1:6; 2 Kings 23:25
10 Ezekiel 36:31-32; 16:61-63

is the act of God's free grace in Christ,[1] yet it is of such necessity to all sinners, that none may expect pardon without it.[2]

4. As there is no sin so small, but it deserves damnation;[3] so there is no sin so great, that it can bring damnation upon those who truly repent.[4]

5. Men ought not to content themselves with a general repentance, but it is every man's duty to endeavour to repent of his particular sins, particularly.[5]

6. As every man is bound to make private confession of his sins to God, praying for the pardon thereof;[6] upon which, and the forsaking of them, he shall find mercy;[7] so he that scandalizes his brother, or the Church of Christ, ought to be willing, by a private or public confession and sorrow for his sin, to declare his repentance to those that are offended,[8] who are thereupon to be reconciled to him, and in love to receive him.[9]

Chapter 16
Of Good Works

1. Good works are only such as God has commanded in His holy Word,[10] and not such as, without the warrant thereof, are devised by men, out of blind zeal, or upon any pretence of good intention.[11]

2. These good works, done in obedience to God's commandments, are the fruits and evidences of a true and lively

---

1 Hosea 14:2, 4; Romans 3:24; Ephesians 1:7
2 Luke 13:3, 5; Acts 17:30-31
3 Romans 6:23; 5:12; Matthew 12:36
4 Isaiah 55:7; Romans 8:1; Isaiah 1:16, 18
5 Psalm 19:13; Luke 19:8; 1 Timothy 1:13, 15
6 Psalm 51:4-5, 7, 9, 14; 32:5-6
7 Proverbs 28:13; 1 John 1:9
8 James 5:16; Luke 17:3-4; Joshua 7:19; Psalm 51
9 2 Corinthians 2:8
10 Micah 6:8; Romans 12:2; Hebrews 13:21
11 Matthew 15:9; Isaiah 29:13; 1 Peter 1:18; Romans 10:2; John 16:2; 1 Samuel 15:21-23

faith:[1] and by them believers manifest their thankfulness,[2] strengthen their assurance,[3] edify their brethren,[4] adorn the profession of the Gospel,[5] stop the mouths of the adversaries,[6] and glorify God,[7] whose workmanship they are, created in Christ Jesus thereunto,[8] that, having their fruit unto holiness, they may have the end, eternal life.[9]

3. Their ability to do good works is not at all of themselves, but wholly from the Spirit of Christ.[10] And that they may be enabled thereunto, beside the graces they have already received, there is required an actual influence of the same Holy Spirit, to work in them to will, and to do, of His good pleasure:[11] yet are they not hereupon to grow negligent, as if they were not bound to perform any duty unless upon a special motion of the Spirit; but they ought to be diligent in stirring up the grace of God that is in them.[12]

4. They who, in their obedience, attain to the greatest height which is possible in this life, are so far from being able to supererogate [go beyond duty], and to do more than God requires, as that they fall short of much which in duty they are bound to do.[13]

5. We cannot by our best works merit pardon of sin, or eternal life at the hand of God, by reason of the great disproportion

---

1 James 2:18, 22
2 Psalm 116:12-13; 1 Peter 2:9
3 1 John 2:3, 5; 2 Peter 1:5-10
4 2 Corinthians 9:2; Matthew 5:16
5 Titus 2:5, 9-12; 1 Timothy 6:1
6 1 Peter 2:15
7 1 Peter 2:12; Philippians 1:11; John 15:8
8 Ephesians 2:10
9 Romans 6:22
10 John 15:4-5; Ezekiel 36:26-27
11 Philippians 2:13; 4:13; 2 Corinthians 3:5
12 Philippians 2:12; Hebrews 6:11-12; 2 Peter 1:3, 5, 10-11; Isaiah 64:7; 2 Timothy 1:6; Acts 26:6-7; Jude 20-21
13 Luke 17:10; Nehemiah 13:22; Job 9:2-3; Galatians 5:17

that is between them and the glory to come; and the infinite distance that is between us and God, whom, by them, we can neither profit, nor satisfy for the debt of our former sins,[1] but when we have done all we can, we have done but our duty, and are unprofitable servants:[2] and because, as they are good, they proceed from His Spirit,[3] and as they are wrought by us, they are defiled, and mixed with so much weakness and imperfection, that they cannot endure the severity of God's judgment.[4]

6. Notwithstanding, the persons of believers being accepted through Christ, their good works also are accepted in Him;[5] not as though they were in this life wholly un-blameable and un-reproveable in God's sight;[6] but that He, looking upon them in His Son, is pleased to accept and reward that which is sincere, although accompanied with many weaknesses and imperfections.[7]

7. Works done by unregenerate men, although for the matter of them they may be things which God commands; and of good use both to themselves and others:[8] yet, because they proceed not from an heart purified by faith;[9] nor are done in a right manner, according to the Word;[10] nor to a right end, the glory of God;[11] they are therefore sinful and cannot please God, or make a man meet to receive grace from God:[12] and yet, their neglect of them is more sinful and displeasing unto God.[13]

---

1 Romans 3:20; 4:2, 4, 6; Ephesians 2:8–9; Titus 3:5–7; Romans 8:18; Psalm 16:2; Job 22:2–3; Job 35:7–8
2 Luke 17:10
3 Galatians 5:22–23
4 Isaiah 64:6; Galatians 5:17; Romans 7:15, 18; Psalm 143:2; 130:3
5 Ephesians 1:6; 1 Peter 2:5; Exodus 28:38; Genesis 4:4; Hebrews 11:4
6 Job 9:20; Psalm 143:2
7 Hebrews 13:20–21; 2 Corinthians 8:12; Hebrews 6:10; Matthew 25:21, 23
8 2 Kings 10:30–31; 1 Kings 21:27, 29; Philippians 1:15–16. 18
9 Genesis 4:5 with Hebrews 11:4; Hebrews 11:6
10 1 Corinthians 13:3; Isaiah 1:12
11 Matthew 6:2, 5, 16
12 Haggai 2:14; Titus 1:15; Amos 5:21–22; Hosea 1:4; Romans 9:16; Titus 3:5
13 Psalm 14:4; 36:3; Job 21:14–15; Matthew 25:41–43, 45; 23:23

Chapter 17
Of the Perseverance of the Saints

1. They, whom God has accepted in His Beloved, effectually called, and sanctified by His Spirit, can neither totally nor finally fall away from the state of grace: but shall certainly persevere therein to the end, and be eternally saved.[1]

2. This perseverance of the saints depends not upon their own free will, but upon the immutability of the decree of election, flowing from the free and unchangeable love of God the Father;[2] upon the efficacy of the merit and intercession of Jesus Christ,[3] the abiding of the Spirit, and of the seed of God within them,[4] and the nature of the covenant of grace:[5] from all which arises also the certainty and infallibility thereof.[6]

3. Nevertheless, they may, through the temptations of Satan and of the world, the prevalence of corruption remaining in them, and the neglect of the means of their preservation, fall into grievous sins;[7] and, for a time, continue therein:[8] whereby they incur God's displeasure,[9] and grieve His Holy Spirit,[10] come to be deprived of some measure of their graces and comforts,[11] have their hearts hardened,[12] and their consciences wounded;[13]

---

1 Philippians 1:6; 2 Peter 1:10; John 10:28–29; 3:9; 1 Peter 1:5, 9
2 2 Timothy 2:18–19; Jeremiah 31:3
3 Hebrews 10:10, 14; 13:20–21; 9:12–15; Romans 8:33–39; John 17:11, 24; Luke 22:32; Hebrews 7:25
4 John 14:16–17; 1 John 2:27; 1 John 3:9
5 Jeremiah 32:40
6 John 10:28; 2 Thessalonians 3:3; 1 John 2:19
7 Matthew 26:70, 72, 74
8 Psalm 51 [title], 14
9 Isaiah 64:5, 7, 9; 2 Samuel 11:27
10 Ephesians 4:30
11 Psalm 51:8, 10, 12; Revelation 2:4; Song of Solomon 5:2–4, 6
12 Isaiah 63:17; Mark 6:52; 16:14
13 Psalm 32:3–4; 51:8

hurt and scandalize others,[1] and bring temporal judgments upon themselves.[2]

Chapter 18
Of Assurance of Grace and Salvation

1. Although hypocrites and other unregenerate men may vainly deceive themselves with false hopes and carnal presumptions of being in the favour of God, and estate of salvation[3] (which hope of theirs shall perish):[4] yet such as truly believe in the Lord Jesus, and love Him in sincerity, endeavouring to walk in all good conscience before Him, may, in this life, be certainly assured that they are in the state of grace,[5] and may rejoice in the hope of the glory of God, which hope shall never make them ashamed.[6]

2. This certainty is not a bare conjectural and probable persuasion grounded upon a fallible hope;[7] but an infallible assurance of faith founded upon the divine truth of the promises of salvation,[8] the inward evidence of those graces unto which these promises are made,[9] the testimony of the Spirit of adoption witnessing with our spirits that we are the children of God:[10] which Spirit is the earnest [the pledge] of our inheritance, whereby we are sealed to the day of redemption.[11]

3. This infallible assurance does not so belong to the essence of faith, but that a true believer may wait long, and conflict with many difficulties, before he be partaker of it:[12] yet, being enabled

---

1 2 Samuel 12:14
2 Psalm 89:31-32; 1 Corinthians 11:32
3 Job 8:13-14; Micah 3:11; Deuteronomy 29:19; John 8:41
4 Matthew 7:22-23
5 1 John 2:3; 3:14, 18-19, 21, 24; 5:13
6 Romans 5:2, 5
7 Hebrews 6:11, 19
8 Hebrews 6:17-18
9 2 Peter 1:4-5, 10-11; 1 John 2:3; 3:14; 2 Corinthians 1:12
10 Romans 8:15-16
11 Ephesians 1:13-14; 4:30; 2 Corinthians 1:21-22
12 1 John 5:13; Isaiah 50:10; Mark 9:24, Psalm 88; 77:1-12

by the Spirit to know the things which are freely given him of God, he may, without extraordinary revelation in the right use of ordinary means, attain thereunto.[1] And therefore it is the duty of every one to give all diligence to make his calling and election sure;[2] that thereby his heart may be enlarged in peace and joy in the Holy Spirit, in love and thankfulness to God, and in strength and cheerfulness in the duties of obedience,[3] the proper fruits of this assurance; so far is it from inclining men to looseness.[4]

4. True believers may have the assurance of their salvation divers [various] ways shaken, diminished, and intermitted [temporarily lost]; as, by negligence in preserving of it, by falling into some special sin which wounds the conscience and grieves the Spirit; by some sudden or vehement temptation, by God's withdrawing the light of His countenance, and suffering even such as fear Him to walk in darkness and to have no light:[5] yet are they never so utterly destitute of that seed of God, and life of faith, that love of Christ and the brethren, that sincerity of heart, and conscience of duty, out of which, by the operation of the Spirit, this assurance may, in due time, be revived;[6] and by the which, in the meantime, they are supported from utter despair.[7]

Chapter 19
Of the Law of God

1. God gave to Adam a law, as a covenant of works, by which He bound him and all his posterity, to personal, entire, exact, and perpetual obedience; promised life upon the fulfilling, and

---

[1] 1 Corinthians 2:12; 1 John 4:13; Hebrews 6:11–12; Ephesians 3:17–19
[2] 2 Peter 1:10
[3] Romans 5:1–2, 5; 14:17; 15:13; Ephesians 1:3–4; Psalm 4:6–7; 119:32
[4] 1 John 2:1–2; Romans 6:1–2; Titus 2:11–12, 14; 2 Corinthians 7:1; Romans 8:1, 12; 1 John 3:2–3; Psalm 130:4; 1 John 1:6–7
[5] Song of Solomon 5:2–3, 6; Psalm 51:8, 12, 14; Ephesians 4:30–31; Psalm 77:1–10; Matthew 26:69–72; Psalm 31:22; Psalm 88; Isaiah 50:10
[6] 1 John 3:9; Luke 22:32; Job 13:15; Psalm 73:15; 51:8, 12; Isaiah 50:10
[7] Micah 7:7–9; Jeremiah 32:40; Isaiah 54:7–10; Psalm 22:1; Psalm 88

threatened death upon the breach of it: and endued him with power and ability to keep it.[1]

2. This law, after his fall, continued to be a perfect rule of righteousness; and, as such, was delivered by God upon Mount Sinai, in ten commandments, and written in two tables:[2] the first four commandments containing our duty towards God; and the other six, our duty to man.[3]

3. Besides this law, commonly called moral, God was pleased to give to the people of Israel, as a church under age, ceremonial laws, containing several typical ordinances, partly of worship, prefiguring Christ, His graces, actions, sufferings, and benefits;[4] and partly, holding forth divers [various] instructions of moral duties.[5] All which ceremonial laws are now abrogated, under the New Testament.[6]

4. To them also, as a body politic, He gave sundry judicial laws, which expired together with the State of that people; not obliging any other now, further than the general equity thereof may require.[7]

5. The moral law does forever bind all, as well justified persons as others, to the obedience thereof;[8] and that, not only in regard of the matter contained in it, but also in respect of the authority of God the Creator, who gave it:[9] neither does Christ, in the Gospel, any way dissolve, but much strengthen this obligation.[10]

---

1 Genesis 1:26-27 with Genesis 2:17; Romans 2:14-15; 10:5; 5:12, 19; Galatians 3:10, 12; Ecclesiastes 7:29; Job 28:28
2 James 1:25; 2:8, 10-12; Romans 13:8-9; Deuteronomy 5:32; 10:4; Exodus 34:1
3 Matthew 22:37-40
4 Hebrews 9; 10:1; Galatians 4:1-3; Colossians 2:17
5 1 Corinthians 5:7; 2 Corinthians 6:17; Jude 23
6 Colossians 2:14, 16-17; Daniel 9:27; Ephesians 2:15-16
7 Exodus 21; 22:1-29; Genesis 49:10 with 1 Peter 2:13-14; Matthew 5:17, 38-39; 1 Corinthians 9:8-10
8 Romans 13:8-10; Ephesians 6:2; 1 John 2:3-4, 7-8
9 James 2:10-11
10 Matthew 5:17-19; James 2:8; Romans 3:31

6. Although true believers be not under the law, as a covenant of works, to be thereby justified, or condemned;[1] yet is it of great use to them, as well as to others; in that, as a rule of life informing them of the will of God, and their duty, it directs and binds them to walk accordingly;[2] discovering also the sinful pollutions of their nature, hearts and lives;[3] so as, examining themselves thereby, they may come to further conviction of, humiliation for, and hatred against sin;[4] together with a clearer sight of the need they have of Christ, and the perfection of His obedience.[5] It is likewise of use to the regenerate, to restrain their corruptions, in that it forbids sin:[6] and the threatenings of it serve to show what even their sins deserve; and what afflictions, in this life, they may expect for them, although freed from the curse thereof threatened in the law.[7] The promises of it, in like manner, show them God's approbation of obedience, and what blessings they may expect upon the performance thereof:[8] although not as due to them by the law as a covenant of works.[9] So as, a man's doing good, and refraining from evil, because the law encourages to the one and deters from the other, is no evidence of his being under the law: and not under grace.[10]

7. Neither are the aforementioned uses of the law contrary to the grace of the Gospel, but do sweetly comply with it;[11] the Spirit of Christ subduing and enabling the will of man to do that

---

1 Romans 6:14; Galatians 2:16; 3:13; 4:4-5; Acts 13:39; Romans 8:1
2 Romans 7:12, 22, 25; Psalm 119:4-6; 1 Corinthians 7:19; Galatians 5:14, 16, 18-23
3 Romans 7:7; 3:20
4 James 1:23-25; Romans 7:9, 14, 24
5 Galatians 3:24; Romans 7:24-25; 8:3-4
6 James 2:11; Psalm 119:101, 104, 128
7 Ezra 9:13-14; Psalm 89:30-34
8 Leviticus 26:1-14; 2 Corinthians 6:16; Ephesians 6:2-3; Psalm 37:11; Matthew 5:5; Psalm 19:11
9 Galatians 2:16; Luke 17:10
10 Romans 6:12, 14; 1 Peter 3:8-12; Psalm 34:12-16; Hebrews 12:28-29
11 Galatians 3:21

freely, and cheerfully, which the will of God, revealed in the law, requires to be done.[1]

Chapter 20
Of Christian Liberty, and Liberty of Conscience

1. The liberty which Christ has purchased for believers under the Gospel consists in their freedom from the guilt of sin, the condemning wrath of God, the curse of the moral law;[2] and, in their being delivered from this present evil world, bondage to Satan, and dominion of sin;[3] from the evil of afflictions, the sting of death, the victory of the grave, and everlasting damnation;[4] as also, in their free access to God,[5] and their yielding obedience unto Him, not out of slavish fear, but a child-like love and willing mind.[6] All which were common also to believers under the law.[7] But, under the New Testament, the liberty of Christians is further enlarged, in their freedom from the yoke of the ceremonial law, to which the Jewish Church was subjected;[8] and in greater boldness of access to the throne of grace,[9] and in fuller communications of the free Spirit of God, than believers under the law did ordinarily partake of.[10]

2. God alone is Lord of the conscience,[11] and has left it free from the doctrines and commandments of men, which are, in anything, contrary to His Word; or beside it, if matters of faith, or worship.[12] So that, to believe such doctrines, or to obey

---

1 Ezekiel 36:27; Hebrews 8:10; Jeremiah 31:33
2 Titus 2:14; 1 Thessalonians 1:10; Galatians 3:13
3 Galatians 1:4; Colossians 1:13; Acts 26:18; Romans 6:14
4 Romans 8:28; Psalm 119:71; 1 Corinthians 15:54-57; Romans 8:1
5 Romans 5:1-2
6 Romans 8:14-15; 1 John 4:18
7 Galatians 3:9, 14
8 Galatians 4:1-3, 6-7; 5:1; Acts 15:10-11
9 Hebrews 4:14, 16; Hebrews 10:19-22
10 John 7:38-39; 2 Corinthians 3:13, 17-18
11 James 4:12; Romans 14:4
12 Acts 4:19; 5:29; 1 Corinthians 7:23; Matthew 23:8-10; 2 Corinthians 1:24; Matthew 15:9

such commands, out of conscience, is to betray true liberty of conscience:[1] and the requiring of an implicit faith, and an absolute and blind obedience, is to destroy liberty of conscience, and reason also.[2]

3. They who, upon pretence of Christian liberty, do practice any sin, or cherish any lust, do thereby destroy the end of Christian liberty, which is, that being delivered out of the hands of our enemies, we might serve the Lord without fear, in holiness and righteousness before Him, all the days of our life.[3]

4. And because the powers which God has ordained, and the liberty which Christ has purchased are not intended by God to destroy, but mutually to uphold and preserve one another; they who, upon pretence of Christian liberty, shall oppose any lawful power, or the lawful exercise of it, whether it be civil or ecclesiastical, resist the ordinance of God.[4] And, for their publishing of such opinions, or maintaining of such practices, as are contrary to the light of nature, or to the known principles of Christianity (whether concerning faith, worship, or conversation), or to the power of godliness; or, such erroneous opinions or practices, as either in their own nature, or in the manner of publishing or maintaining them, are destructive to the external peace and order which Christ has established in the Church, they may lawfully be called to account,[5] and proceeded against, by the censures of the Church, and by the power of the civil magistrate.[6]

---

1 Colossians 2:20, 22-23; Galatians 1:10; 2:4-5; 5:1
2 Romans 10:17; 14:23; Isaiah 8:20; Acts 17:11; John 4:22; Hosea 5:11; Revelation 13:12, 16-17; Jeremiah 8:9
3 Galatians 5:13; 1 Peter 2:16; 2 Peter 2:19; John 8:34; Luke 1:74-75
4 Matthew 12:25; 1 Peter 2:13-14, 16; Romans 13:1-8; Hebrews 13:17
5 Romans 1:32; 1 Corinthians 5:1, 5, 11, 13; 2 John 10-11; 2 Thessalonians 3:14; 1 Timothy 6:3-5; Titus 1:10-11, 13; 3:10; Matthew 18:15-17; 1 Timothy 1:19-20; Revelation 2:2, 14-15, 20; 3:9
6 Deuteronomy 13:6-12; Romans 13:3-4; 2 John 10-11; Ezra 7:23, 25-28; Revelation 17:12, 16-17; Nehemiah 13:15, 17, 21-22, 25, 30; 2 Kings 23:5-6, 9, 20-21; 2 Chronicles 34:33; 15:12-13, 16; Daniel 3:29; 1 Timothy 2:2; Isaiah 49:23; Zechariah 13:2-3

Chapter 21
Of Religious Worship, and the Sabbath Day

1. The light of nature shows that there is a God, who has lordship and sovereignty over all, is good, and does good unto all, and is therefore to be feared, loved, praised, called upon, trusted in, and served, with all the heart, and with all the soul, and with all the might.[1] But the acceptable way of worshipping the true God is instituted by Himself, and so limited by His own revealed will, that He may not be worshipped according to the imaginations and devices of men, or the suggestions of Satan, under any visible representation, or any other way not prescribed in the holy Scripture.[2]

2. Religious worship is to be given to God, the Father, Son, and Holy Spirit; and to Him alone;[3] not to angels, saints, or any other creature:[4] and, since the fall, not without a Mediator; nor in the mediation of any other but of Christ alone.[5]

3. Prayer, with thanksgiving, being one special part of religious worship,[6] is by God required of all men:[7] and, that it may be accepted, it is to be made in the name of the Son,[8] by the help of His Spirit,[9] according to His will,[10] with understanding,

---

1 Romans 1:20; Acts 17:24; Psalm 119:68; Jeremiah 10:7; Psalm 31:23; 18:3; Romans 10:12; Psalm 62:8; Joshua 24:14; Mark 12:33
2 Deuteronomy 12:32; Matthew 15:9; Acts 17:25; Matthew 4:9-10; Deuteronomy 4:15-20; Exodus 20:4-6; Colossians 2:23
3 Matthew 4:10 with John 5:23 and 2 Corinthians 13:14
4 Colossians 2:18; Revelation 19:10; Romans 1:25
5 John 14:6; 1 Timothy 2:5; Ephesians 2:18; Colossians 3:17
6 Philippians 4:6
7 Psalm 65:2
8 John 14:13-14; 1 Peter 2:5
9 Romans 8:26
10 1 John 5:14

reverence, humility, fervency, faith, love and perseverance;[1] and, if vocal, in a known tongue.[2]

4. Prayer is to be made for things lawful;[3] and for all sorts of men living, or that shall live hereafter:[4] but not for the dead,[5] nor for those of whom it may be known that they have sinned the sin unto death.[6]

5. The reading of the Scriptures with godly fear;[7] the sound preaching[8] and conscionable hearing of the Word, in obedience to God, with understanding, faith and reverence;[9] singing of psalms with grace in the heart;[10] as also, the due administration and worthy receiving of the sacraments instituted by Christ; are all parts of the ordinary religious worship of God:[11] beside religious oaths,[12] vows,[13] solemn fastings,[14] and thanksgivings upon special occasions,[15] which are, in their several times and seasons, to be used in a holy and religious manner.[16]

6. Neither prayer, nor any other part of religious worship, is now, under the Gospel, either tied unto, or made more acceptable by any place in which it is performed, or towards

---

1 Psalm 47:7; Ecclesiastes 5:1-2; Hebrews 12:28; Genesis 18:27; James 5:16; 1:6-7; Mark 11:24; Matthew 6:12, 14-15; Colossians 4:2; Ephesians 6:18
2 1 Corinthians 14:14
3 1 John 5:14
4 1 Timothy 2:1-2; John 17:20; 2 Samuel 7:29; Ruth 4:12
5 2 Samuel 12:21-23 with Luke 16:25-26; Revelation 14:13
6 1 John 5:16
7 Acts 15:21; Revelation 1:3
8 2 Timothy 4:2
9 James 1:22; Acts 10:33; Matthew 13:19; Hebrews 4:2; Isaiah 66:2
10 Colossians 3:16; Ephesians 5:19; James 5:13
11 Matthew 28:19; 1 Corinthians 11:23-29; Acts 2:42
12 Deuteronomy 6:13 with Nehemiah 10:29
13 Isaiah 19:21 with Ecclesiastes 5:4-5
14 Joel 2:12; Esther 4:16; Matthew 9:15; 1 Corinthians 7:5
15 Psalm 107; Esther 9:22
16 Hebrews 12:28

which it is directed:[1] but God is to be worshipped everywhere,[2] in spirit and truth;[3] as, in private families[4] daily,[5] and in secret, each one by himself;[6] so, more solemnly in the public assemblies, which are not carelessly or wilfully to be neglected, or forsaken, when God, by His Word or providence, calls thereunto.[7]

7. As it is the law of nature, that, in general, a due proportion of time be set apart for the worship of God; so, in His Word, by a positive, moral, and perpetual commandment, binding all men in all ages, He has particularly appointed one day in seven, for a Sabbath, to be kept holy unto Him:[8] which, from the beginning of the world to the resurrection of Christ, was the last day of the week: and, from the resurrection of Christ, was changed into the first day of the week,[9] which, in Scripture, is called the Lord's Day,[10] and is to be continued to the end of the world, as the Christian Sabbath.[11]

8. This Sabbath is to be kept holy unto the Lord when men, after a due preparing of their hearts, and ordering of their common affairs beforehand, do not only observe a holy rest all the day from their own works, words, and thoughts about their worldly employments and recreations,[12] but also are taken up the whole time in the public and private exercises of His worship, and in the duties of necessity and mercy.[13]

---

1 John 4:21
2 Malachi 1:11; 1 Timothy 2:8
3 John 4:23-24
4 Jeremiah 10:25; Deuteronomy 6:6-7; Job 1:5; 2 Samuel 6:18, 20; 1 Peter 3:7; Acts 10:2
5 Matthew 6:11
6 Matthew 6:6; Ephesians 6:18
7 Isaiah 56:6-7; Hebrews 10:25; Proverbs 1:20-21,-24; 8:34; Acts 13:42; Luke 4:16; Acts 2:42
8 Exodus 20:8, 10-11; Isaiah 56:2, 4, 6-7
9 Genesis 2:2-3; 1 Corinthians 16:1-2; Acts 20:7
10 Revelation 1:10
11 Exodus 20:8, 10 with Matthew 5:17-18
12 Exodus 20:8; 16:23, 25-26, 29-30; 31:15-17; Isaiah 58:13; Nehemiah 13:15-19, 21-22
13 Isaiah 58:13; Matthew 12:1-13

Chapter 22
Of Lawful Oaths and Vows

1. A lawful oath is a part of religious worship,[1] wherein, upon just occasion, the person swearing solemnly calls God to witness what he asserts, or promises, and to judge him according to the truth or falsehood of what he swears.[2]

2. The name of God only is that by which men ought to swear, and therein it is to be used with all holy fear and reverence.[3] Therefore, to swear vainly, or rashly, by that glorious and dreadful Name; or, to swear at all by any other thing, is sinful, and to be abhorred.[4] Yet, as in matters of weight and moment, an oath is warranted by the Word of God, under the New Testament as well as under the Old;[5] so a lawful oath, being imposed by lawful authority, in such matters ought to be taken.[6]

3. Whosoever takes an oath ought duly to consider the weightiness of so solemn an act, and therein to avouch [affirm] nothing but what he is fully persuaded is the truth:[7] neither may any man bind himself by oath to anything but what is good and just, and what he believes so to be, and what he is able and resolved to perform.[8] Yet it is a sin to refuse an oath touching anything that is good and just, being imposed by lawful authority.[9]

4. An oath is to be taken in the plain and common sense of the words, without equivocation, or mental reservation.[10] It cannot oblige to sin; but in anything not sinful, being taken, it binds

---

1 Deuteronomy 10:20
2 Exodus 20:7; Leviticus 19:12; 2 Corinthians 1:23; 2 Chronicles 6:22–23
3 Deuteronomy 6:13
4 Exodus 20:7; Jeremiah 5:7; Matthew 5:34, 37; James 5:12
5 Hebrews 6:16; 2 Corinthians 1:23; Isaiah 65:16
6 1 Kings 8:31; Nehemiah 13:25; Ezra 10:5
7 Exodus 20:7; Jeremiah 4:2
8 Genesis 24:2–3, 5–6, 8–9
9 Numbers 5:19, 21; Nehemiah 5:12; Exodus 22:7–11
10 Jeremiah 4:2; Psalm 24:4

to performance, although to a man's own hurt.[1] Nor is it to be violated, although made to heretics, or infidels.[2]

5. A vow is of the like nature with a promissory oath [promise], and ought to be made with the like religious care, and to be performed with the like faithfulness.[3]

6. It is not to be made to any creature, but to God alone:[4] and that it may be accepted, it is to be made voluntarily, out of faith, and conscience of duty, in way of thankfulness for mercy received, or for the obtaining of what we want; whereby we more strictly bind ourselves to necessary duties; or, to other things, so far and so long as they may fitly conduce [contribute] thereunto.[5]

7. No man may vow to do anything forbidden in the Word of God, or what would hinder any duty therein commanded, or which is not in his own power, and for the performance whereof he has no promise of ability from God.[6] In which respects, Popish monastical vows of perpetual single life, professed poverty, and regular obedience, are so far from being degrees of higher perfection, that they are superstitious and sinful snares, in which no Christian may entangle himself.[7]

Chapter 23
Of the Civil Magistrate

1. God, the supreme Lord and King of all the world, has ordained civil magistrates, to be, under Him, over the people, for His own glory, and the public good: and, to this end, has armed them with the power of the sword, for the defence and

---

[1] 1 Samuel 25:22, 32–34; Psalm 15:4
[2] Ezekiel 17:16, 18–19; Joshua 9:18–19 with 2 Samuel 21:1
[3] Isaiah 19:21; Ecclesiastes 5:4–6; Psalm 61:8; 66:13–14
[4] Psalm 76:11; Jeremiah 44:25–26
[5] Deuteronomy 23:21–23; Psalm 50:14; Genesis 28:20–22; 1 Samuel 1:11; Psalm 66:13–14; 132:2–5
[6] Acts 23:12, 14; Mark 6:26; Numbers 30:5, 8, 12–13
[7] Matthew 19:11–12; 1 Corinthians 7:2, 9; Ephesians 4:28; 1 Peter 4:2; 1 Corinthians 7:23

encouragement of them that are good, and for the punishment of evil doers.[1]

2. It is lawful for Christians to accept and execute the office of a magistrate, when called thereunto;[2] in the managing whereof, as they ought especially to maintain piety, justice, and peace, according to the wholesome laws of each commonwealth;[3] so, for that end, they may lawfully now, under the New Testament, wage war, upon just and necessary occasion.[4]

3. Civil magistrates may not assume to themselves the administration of the Word and sacraments, or the power of the keys of the kingdom of heaven;[5] yet he has authority, and it is his duty, to take order that unity and peace be preserved in the Church, that the truth of God be kept pure and entire, that all blasphemies and heresies be suppressed, all corruptions and abuses in worship and discipline prevented or reformed, and all the ordinances of God duly settled, administered, and observed.[6] For the better effecting whereof, he has power to call synods, to be present at them and to provide that whatsoever is transacted in them be according to the mind of God.[7]

4. It is the duty of people to pray for magistrates,[8] to honour their persons,[9] to pay them tribute and other dues,[10] to obey their lawful commands, and to be subject to their authority, for conscience' sake.[11] Infidelity, or difference in religion, does

---

1   Romans 13:1-4; 1 Peter 2:13-14
2   Proverbs 8:15-16; Romans 13:1-2, 4
3   Psalm 2:10-12; 1 Timothy 2:2; Psalm 82:3-4; 2 Samuel 23:3; 1 Peter 2:13
4   Luke 3:14; Romans 13:4; Matthew 8:9-10; Acts 10:1-2; Revelation 17:14, 16
5   2 Chronicles 26:18 with Matthew 18:17 and Matthew 16:19; 1 Corinthians 12:28-29; Ephesians 4:11-12; 1 Corinthians 4:1-2; Romans 10:15; Hebrews 5:4
6   Isaiah 49:23; Psalm 122:9; Ezra 7:23, 25-28; Leviticus 24:16; Deuteronomy 13:5-6, 12; 2 Kings 18:4; 1 Chronicles 13:1-9; 2 Kings 23:1-26; 2 Chronicles 34:33; 15:12-13
7   2 Chronicles 19:8-11; 2 Chronicles 29 and 30; Matthew 2:4-5
8   1 Timothy 2:1-2
9   1 Peter 2:17
10 Romans 13:6-7
11 Romans 13:5; Titus 3:1

not make void the magistrates' just and legal authority, nor free the people from their due obedience to them:[1] from which ecclesiastical persons are not exempted,[2] much less has the Pope any power and jurisdiction over them in their dominions, or over any of their people; and, least of all, to deprive them of their dominions, or lives, if he shall judge them to be heretics, or upon any other pretence whatsoever.[3]

Chapter 24
Of Marriage and Divorce

1. Marriage is to be between one man and one woman: neither is it lawful for any man to have more than one wife, nor for any woman to have more than one husband, at the same time.[4]

2. Marriage was ordained for the mutual help of husband and wife,[5] for the increase of mankind with a legitimate issue, and of the Church with a holy seed;[6] and for preventing of uncleanness.[7]

3. It is lawful for all sorts of people to marry, who are able with judgment to give their consent.[8] Yet it is the duty of Christians to marry only in the Lord:[9] and therefore such as profess the true reformed religion should not marry with infidels, papists, or other idolaters: neither should such as are godly be unequally yoked, by marrying with such as are notoriously wicked in their life, or maintain damnable heresies.[10]

---

1 1 Peter 2:13-14, 16
2 Romans 13:1; 1 Kings 2:35; Acts 25:9-11; 2 Peter 2:1, 10-11; Jude 8-11
3 2 Thessalonians 2:4; Revelation 13:15-17
4 Genesis 2:24; Matthew 19:5-6; Proverbs 2:17
5 Genesis 2:18
6 Malachi 2:15
7 1 Corinthians 7:2, 9
8 Hebrews 13:4; 1 Timothy 4:3; 1 Corinthians 7:36-38; Genesis 24:57-58
9 1 Corinthians 7:39
10 Genesis 34:14; Exodus 34:16; Deuteronomy 7:3-4; 1 Kings 11:4; Nehemiah 13:25-27; Malachi 2:11-12; 2 Corinthians 6:14

4. Marriage ought not to be within the degrees of consanguinity or affinity forbidden by the Word;[1] nor can such incestuous marriages ever be made lawful by any law of man or consent of parties, so as those persons may live together as man and wife.[2] The man may not marry any of his wife's kindred, nearer in blood then he may of his own; nor the woman of her husband's kindred, nearer in blood than of her own.[3]

5. Adultery or fornication committed after a contract, being detected before marriage, gives just occasion to the innocent party to dissolve that contract.[4] In the case of adultery after marriage, it is lawful for the innocent party to sue out a divorce and, after the divorce,[5] to marry another, as if the offending party were dead.[6]

6. Although the corruption of man be such as is apt to study arguments unduly to put asunder those whom God has joined together in marriage: yet, nothing but adultery, or such wilful desertion as can no way be remedied by the Church, or civil magistrate, is cause sufficient of dissolving the bond of marriage:[7] wherein, a public and orderly course of proceeding is to be observed; and the persons concerned in it not left to their own wills, and discretion, in their own case.[8]

Chapter 25
Of the Church

1. The catholic or universal Church, which is invisible, consists of the whole number of the elect, that have been, are, or shall

---

1 Leviticus 18; 1 Corinthians 5:1; Amos 2:7
2 Mark 6:18; Leviticus 18:24-28
3 Leviticus 20:19-21
4 Matthew 1:18-20
5 Matthew 5:31-32
6 Matthew 19:9; Romans 7:2-3
7 Matthew 19:8-9; 1 Corinthians 7:15; Matthew 19:6
8 Deuteronomy 24:1-4

be gathered into one, under Christ the Head thereof; and is the spouse, the body, the fullness of Him that fills all in all.[1]

2. The visible Church, which is also catholic or universal under the Gospel (not confined to one nation, as before under the law), consists of all those throughout the world that profess the true religion;[2] and of their children:[3] and is the kingdom of the Lord Jesus Christ,[4] the house and family of God,[5] out of which there is no ordinary possibility of salvation.[6]

3. Unto this catholic visible Church Christ has given the ministry, oracles, and ordinances of God, for the gathering and perfecting of the saints, in this life, to the end of the world: and does, by His own presence and Spirit, according to His promise, make them effectual thereunto.[7]

4. This catholic Church has been sometimes more, sometimes less visible.[8] And particular Churches, which are members thereof, are more or less pure, according as the doctrine of the Gospel is taught and embraced, ordinances administered, and public worship performed more or less purely in them.[9]

5. The purest Churches under heaven are subject both to mixture and error;[10] and some have so degenerated, as to become no Churches of Christ, but synagogues of Satan.[11] Nevertheless, there shall be always a Church on earth to worship God according to His will.[12]

---

1 Ephesians 1:10, 22–23; 5:23, 27, 32; Colossians 1:18
2 1 Corinthians 1:2; 12:12–13; Psalm 2:8; Revelation 7:9; Romans 15:9–12
3 1 Corinthians 7:14; Acts 2:39; Ezekiel 16:20–21; Romans 11:16; Genesis 3:15; 17:7
4 Matthew 13:47; Isaiah 9:7
5 Ephesians 2:19; 3:15
6 Acts 2:47
7 1 Corinthians 12:28; Ephesians 4:11–13; Matthew 28:19–20; Isaiah 59:21
8 Romans 11:3–4; Revelation 12:6, 14
9 Revelation 2 and 3; 1 Corinthians 5:6–7
10 1 Corinthians 13:12; Revelation 2 and 3; Matthew 13:24–30, 47
11 Revelation 18:2; Romans 11:18–22
12 Matthew 16:18, Psalm 72:17; 102:28; Matthew 28:19–20

6. There is no other head of the Church but the Lord Jesus Christ;[1] nor can the Pope of Rome, in any sense, be head thereof; but is that Antichrist, that man of sin, and son of perdition, that exalts himself, in the Church, against Christ and all that is called God.[2]

Chapter 26
Of the Communion of Saints

1. All saints, that are united to Jesus Christ their Head, by His Spirit, and by faith, have fellowship with Him in His graces, sufferings, death, resurrection, and glory:[3] and, being united to one another in love, they have communion in each other's gifts and graces,[4] and are obliged to the performance of such duties, public and private, as do conduce to their mutual good, both in the inward and outward man.[5]

2. Saints by profession are bound to maintain a holy fellowship and communion in the worship of God, and in performing such other spiritual services as tend to their mutual edification;[6] as also in relieving each other in outward things, according to their several abilities and necessities. Which communion, as God offers opportunity, is to be extended unto all those who, in every place, call upon the name of the Lord Jesus.[7]

3. This communion which the saints have with Christ, does not make them in any wise partakers of the substance of His Godhead; or to be equal with Christ in any respect: either of which to affirm is impious and blasphemous.[8] Nor does their

---
1 Colossians 1:18; Ephesians 1:22
2 Matthew 23:8-10; 2 Thessalonians 2:3-4, 8-9; Revelation 13:6
3 1 John 1:3; Ephesians 3:16-19; John 1:16; Ephesians 2:5-6; Philippians 3:10; Romans 6:5-6; 2 Timothy 2:12
4 Ephesians 4:15-16; 1 Corinthians 12:7; 3:21-23; Colossians 2:19
5 1 Thessalonians 5:11, 14; Romans 1:11-12, 14; 1 John 3:16-18; Galatians 6:10
6 Hebrews 10:24-25; Acts 2:42, 46; Isaiah 2:3; 1 Corinthians 11:20
7 Acts 2:44-45; 1 John 3:17; 2 Corinthians 8 and 9; Acts 11:29-30
8 Colossians 1:18; 1 Corinthians 8:6; Isaiah 42:8; 1 Timothy 6:15-16; Psalm 45:7 with Hebrews 1:8-9

communion one with another, as saints, take away, or infringe the title or propriety which each man has in his goods and possessions.[1]

Chapter 27
Of the Sacraments

1. Sacraments are holy signs and seals of the covenant of grace,[2] immediately instituted by God,[3] to represent Christ and His benefits; and to confirm our interest in Him;[4] as also, to put a visible difference between those that belong unto the Church and the rest of the world;[5] and solemnly to engage them to the service of God in Christ, according to His Word.[6]

2. There is, in every sacrament, a spiritual relation, or sacramental union, between the sign and the thing signified: whence it comes to pass, that the names and effects of the one are attributed to the other.[7]

3. The grace which is exhibited in or by the sacraments rightly used, is not conferred by any power in them; neither does the efficacy of a sacrament depend upon the piety or intention of him that does administer it:[8] but upon the work of the Spirit,[9] and the word of institution, which contains, together with a precept authorizing the use thereof, a promise of benefit to worthy receivers.[10]

4. There are only two sacraments ordained by Christ our Lord in the Gospel; that is to say, Baptism, and the Supper of

---

1 Exodus 20:15; Ephesians 4:28; Acts 5:4
2 Romans 4:11; Genesis 17:7, 10
3 Matthew 28:19; 1 Corinthians 11:23
4 1 Corinthians 10:16; 11:25-26; Galatians 3:17
5 Romans 15:8; Exodus 12:48; Genesis 34:14
6 Romans 6:3-4; 1 Corinthians 10:16, 21
7 Genesis 17:10; Matthew 26:27-28; Titus 3:5
8 Romans 2:28-29; 1 Peter 3:21
9 Matthew 3:11; 1 Corinthians 12:13
10 Matthew 26:27-28; 28:19-20

the Lord: neither of which may be dispensed by any, but by a minister of the Word lawfully ordained.[1]

5. The sacraments of the Old Testament in regard to the spiritual things thereby signified and exhibited, were, for substance, the same with those of the new.[2]

Chapter 28
Of Baptism

1. Baptism is a sacrament of the New Testament, ordained by Jesus Christ,[3] not only for the solemn admission of the party baptized into the visible Church;[4] but also to be unto him a sign and seal of the covenant of grace,[5] of his ingrafting into Christ,[6] of regeneration,[7] of remission of sins,[8] and of his giving up unto God, through Jesus Christ, to walk in newness of life.[9] Which sacrament is, by Christ's own appointment, to be continued in His Church until the end of the world.[10]

2. The outward element to be used in this sacrament is water, wherewith the party is to be baptized, in the name of the Father, and of the Son, and of the Holy Spirit, by a minister of the Gospel, lawfully called thereunto.[11]

3. Dipping of the person into the water is not necessary; but Baptism is rightly administered by pouring, or sprinkling water upon the person.[12]

---

1 Matthew 28:19; 1 Corinthians 11:20, 23; 4:1; Hebrews 5:4
2 1 Corinthians 10:1–4
3 Matthew 28:19
4 1 Corinthians 12:13
5 Romans 4:11 with Colossians 2:11–12
6 Galatians 3:27; Romans 6:5
7 Titus 3:5
8 Mark 1:14
9 Romans 6:3–4
10 Matthew 28:19–20
11 Matthew 3:11; John 1:33; Matthew 28:19–20
12 Hebrews 9:10, 19–22; Acts 2:41; Acts 16:33; Mark 7:4

4. Not only those that do actually profess faith in and obedience unto Christ,[1] but also the infants of one, or both, believing parents, are to be baptized.[2]

5. Although it is a great sin to contemn [disdain] or neglect this ordinance,[3] yet grace and salvation are not so inseparably annexed unto it, as that no person can be regenerated, or saved, without it:[4] or, that all that are baptized are undoubtedly regenerated.[5]

6. The efficacy of Baptism is not tied to that moment of time wherein it is administered;[6] yet, notwithstanding, by the right use of this ordinance, the grace promised is not only offered, but really exhibited, and conferred, by the Holy Spirit, to such (whether of age or infants) as that grace belongs unto, according to the counsel of God's own will, in His appointed time.[7]

7. The sacrament of Baptism is but once to be administered unto any person.[8]

Chapter 29
Of the Lord's Supper

1. Our Lord Jesus, in the night wherein He was betrayed, instituted the sacrament of His body and blood, called the Lord's Supper, to be observed in His Church, unto the end of the world, for the perpetual remembrance of the sacrifice of Himself in His death; the sealing all benefits thereof unto true believers, their spiritual nourishment and growth in Him, their further engagement in and to all duties which they owe unto Him; and,

---

1 Mark 16:15-16; Acts 8:37-38
2 Genesis 17:7, 9-10 with Galatians 3:9, 14 and Colossians 2:11-12 and Acts 2:38-39 and Romans 4:11-12; 1 Corinthians 7:14; Matthew 28:19; Mark 10:13-16; Luke 18:15
3 Luke 7:30 with Exodus 4:24-26
4 Romans 4:11; Acts 10:2, 4, 22, 31, 45, 47
5 Acts 8:13, 23
6 John 3:5, 8
7 Galatians 3:27; Titus 3:5; Ephesians 5:25-26; Acts 2:38, 41
8 Titus 3:5

to be a bond and pledge of their communion with Him, and with each other, as members of His mystical body.[1]

2. In this sacrament, Christ is not offered up to His Father; nor any real sacrifice made at all, for remission of sins of the quick [living] or dead;[2] but only a commemoration of that one offering up of Himself, by Himself, upon the cross, once for all: and a spiritual oblation [offering] of all possible praise unto God, for the same:[3] so that the Popish sacrifice of the mass (as they call it) is most abominably injurious to Christ's one, only sacrifice, the alone propitiation for all the sins of His elect.[4]

3. The Lord Jesus has, in this ordinance, appointed His ministers to declare His word of institution to the people; to pray, and bless the elements of bread and wine, and thereby to set them apart from a common to an holy use; and to take and break the bread, to take the cup, and (they communicating also themselves) to give both to the communicants;[5] but to none who are not then present in the congregation.[6]

4. Private masses, or receiving this sacrament by a priest, or any other alone;[7] as likewise, the denial of the cup to the people,[8] worshipping the elements, the lifting them up, or carrying them about, for adoration, and the reserving them for any pretended religious use; are all contrary to the nature of this sacrament, and to the institution of Christ.[9]

5. The outward elements in this sacrament, duly set apart to the uses ordained by Christ, have such relation to Him crucified, as that, truly, yet sacramentally only, they are sometimes called

---

1 1 Corinthians 11:23-26; 10:16-17, 21; 12:13
2 Hebrews 9:22, 25-26, 28
3 1 Corinthians 11:24-26; Matthew 26:26-27
4 Hebrews 7:23-24, 27; 10:11-12, 14, 18
5 Matthew 26:26-28 and Mark 14:22-24 and Luke 22:19-20 with 1 Corinthians 11:23-26
6 Acts 20:7; 1 Corinthians 11:20
7 1 Corinthians 10:16
8 Mark 14:23; 1 Corinthians 11:25-29
9 Matthew 15:9

by the name of the things they represent, to wit, the body and blood of Christ;[1] albeit, in substance and nature, they still remain truly and only bread and wine, as they were before.[2]

6. That doctrine which maintains a change of the substance of bread and wine, into the substance of Christ's body and blood (commonly called transubstantiation) by consecration of a priest, or by any other way, is repugnant, not to Scripture alone, but even to common sense, and reason; overthrows the nature of the sacrament, and has been, and is, the cause of manifold superstitions; yes, of gross idolatries.[3]

7. Worthy receivers, outwardly partaking of the visible elements, in this sacrament,[4] do then also, inwardly by faith, really and indeed, yet not carnally and corporally but spiritually, receive and feed upon, Christ crucified, and all benefits of His death: the body and blood of Christ being then, not corporally or carnally, in, with, or under the bread and wine; yet, as really, but spiritually, present to the faith of believers in that ordinance, as the elements themselves are to their outward senses.[5]

8. Although ignorant and wicked men receive the outward elements in this sacrament; yet, they receive not the thing signified thereby; but, by their unworthy coming thereunto, are guilty of the body and blood of the Lord, to their own damnation. Wherefore, all ignorant and ungodly persons, as they are unfit to enjoy communion with Him, so are they unworthy of the Lord's table; and cannot, without great sin against Christ, while they remain such, partake of these holy mysteries,[6] or be admitted thereunto.[7]

---

1 Matthew 26:26–28
2 1 Corinthians 11:26–28; Matthew 26:29
3 Acts 3:21 with 1 Corinthians 11:24–26; Luke 24:6, 39
4 1 Corinthians 11:28
5 1 Corinthians 10:16
6 1 Corinthians 11:27–29; 2 Corinthians 6:14–16
7 1 Corinthians 5:6–7, 13; 2 Thessalonians 3:6, 14–15; Matthew 7:6

Chapter 30
Of Church Censures

1. The Lord Jesus, as king and head of His Church, has therein appointed a government, in the hand of Church officers, distinct from the civil magistrate.[1]

2. To these officers the keys of the kingdom of heaven are committed; by virtue whereof, they have power, respectively, to retain, and remit sins; to shut that kingdom against the impenitent, both by the Word, and censures; and to open it unto penitent sinners, by the ministry of the Gospel; and by absolution from censures, as occasion shall require.[2]

3. Church censures are necessary, for the reclaiming and gaining of offending brethren, for deterring of others from the like offenses, for purging out of that leaven which might infect the whole lump, for vindicating the honour of Christ, and the holy profession of the Gospel, and for preventing the wrath of God, which might justly fall upon the Church, if they should suffer His covenant, and the seals thereof, to be profaned by notorious and obstinate offenders.[3]

4. For the better attaining of these ends, the officers of the Church are to proceed by admonition; suspension from the sacrament of the Lord's Supper for a season; and by excommunication from the Church; according to the nature of the crime, and demerit of the person.[4]

---

1 Isaiah 9:6-7; 1 Timothy 5:17; 1 Thessalonians 5:12; Acts 20:17, 28; Hebrews 13:7, 17, 24; 1 Corinthians 12:28; Matthew 28:18-20
2 Matthew 16:19; 18:17-18; John 20:21-23; 2 Corinthians 2:6-8
3 1 Corinthians 5; 1 Timothy 5:20; Matthew 7:6; 1 Timothy 1:20; 1 Corinthians 11:27-34 with Jude 23
4 1 Thessalonians 5:12; 2 Thessalonians 3:6, 14-15; 1 Corinthians 5:4-5, 13; Matthew 18:17; Titus 3:10

Chapter 31
Of Synods and Councils

1. For the better government, and further edification of the Church, there ought to be such assemblies as are commonly called synods or councils.[1]

2. As magistrates may lawfully call a synod of ministers, and other fit persons, to consult and advise with, about matters of religion;[2] so, if magistrates be open enemies to the Church, the ministers of Christ, of themselves, by virtue of their office, or they, with other fit persons upon delegation from their Churches, may meet together in such assemblies.[3]

3. It belongs to synods and councils, ministerially to determine controversies of faith, and cases of conscience; to set down rules and directions for the better ordering of the public worship of God, and government of His Church; to receive complaints in cases of maladministration, and authoritatively to determine the same: which decrees and determinations, if consonant to the Word of God, are to be received with reverence and submission; not only for their agreement with the Word, but also for the power whereby they are made, as being an ordinance of God appointed thereunto in His Word.[4]

4. All synods or councils, since the Apostles' times, whether general or particular, may err; and many have erred. Therefore they are not to be made the rule of faith, or practice; but to be used as a help in both.[5]

5. Synods and councils are to handle, or conclude, nothing, but that which is ecclesiastical: and are not to intermeddle [interfere] with civil affairs which concern the commonwealth;

---

[1] Acts 15:2, 4, 6
[2] Isaiah 49:23; 1 Timothy 2:1–2; 2 Chronicles 19:8–11; 2 Chronicles 29 and 30; Matthew 2:4–5; Proverbs 11:14
[3] Acts 15:2, 4, 22–23, 25
[4] Acts 15:15, 19, 24, 27–31; 16:4; Matthew 18:17–20
[5] Ephesians 2:20; Acts 17:11; 1 Corinthians 2:5; 2 Corinthians 1:24

unless by way of humble petition in cases extraordinary; or, by way of advice, for satisfaction of conscience, if they be thereunto required by the civil magistrate.[1]

Chapter 32
Of the State of Men after Death, and of the Resurrection of the Dead

1. The bodies of men, after death, return to dust, and see corruption:[2] but their souls, which neither die nor sleep, having an immortal subsistence, immediately return to God who gave them:[3] the souls of the righteous, being then made perfect in holiness, are received into the highest heavens, where they behold the face of God, in light and glory, waiting for the full redemption of their bodies.[4] And the souls of the wicked are cast into hell, where they remain in torments and utter darkness, reserved to the judgment of the great day.[5] Beside these two places, for souls separated from their bodies, the Scripture acknowledges none.

2. At the last day, such as are found alive shall not die, but be changed:[6] and all the dead shall be raised up, with the self-same bodies, and none other (although with different qualities), which shall be united again to their souls forever.[7]

3. The bodies of the unjust shall, by the power of Christ, be raised to dishonour: the bodies of the just, by His Spirit, unto honour; and be made conformable to His own glorious body.[8]

---

1 Luke 12:13-14; John 18:36
2 Genesis 3:19; Acts 13:36
3 Luke 23:43; Ecclesiastes 12:7
4 Hebrews 12:23; 2 Corinthians 5:1, 6, 8; Philippians 1:23 with Acts 3:21 and Ephesians 4:10
5 Luke 16:23-24; Acts 1:25; Jude 6-7; 1 Peter 3:19
6 1 Thessalonians 4:17; 1 Corinthians 15:51-52
7 Job 19:26-27; 1 Corinthians 15:42-44
8 Acts 24:15; John 5:28-29; 1 Corinthians 15:43; Philippians 3:21

Chapter 33
Of the Last Judgment

1. God has appointed a day, wherein He will judge the world, in righteousness, by Jesus Christ,[1] to whom all power and judgment is given of the Father.[2] In which day, not only the apostate angels shall be judged,[3] but likewise all persons that have lived upon earth shall appear before the tribunal of Christ, to give an account of their thoughts, words, and deeds; and to receive according to what they have done in the body, whether good or evil.[4]

2. The end of God's appointing this day is for the manifestation of the glory of His mercy, in the eternal salvation of the elect; and of His justice, in the damnation of the reprobate, who are wicked and disobedient. For then shall the righteous go into everlasting life, and receive that fullness of joy and refreshing, which shall come from the presence of the Lord: but the wicked, who know not God, and obey not the Gospel of Jesus Christ, shall be cast into eternal torments, and be punished with everlasting destruction from the presence of the Lord, and from the glory of His power.[5]

3. As Christ would have us to be certainly persuaded that there shall be a day of judgment, both to deter all men from sin; and for the greater consolation of the godly in their adversity:[6] so will He have that day unknown to men, that they may shake off all carnal security, and be always watchful, because they know

---

[1] Acts 17:31
[2] John 5:22, 27
[3] 1 Corinthians 6:3; Jude 6; 2 Peter 2:4
[4] 2 Corinthians 5:10; Ecclesiastes 12:14; Romans 2:16; 14:10, 12; Matthew 12:36-37
[5] Matthew 25:31-46; Romans 2:5-6; 9:22-23; Matthew 25:21; Acts 3:19; 2 Thessalonians 1:7-10
[6] 2 Peter 3:11, 14; 2 Corinthians 5:10-11; 2 Thessalonians 1:5-7; Luke 21:27-28; Romans 8:23-25

not at what hour the Lord will come; and may be ever prepared to say, Come Lord Jesus, come quickly, Amen.[1]

---

[1] Matthew 24:36, 42-44; Mark 13:35-37; Luke 12:35-36; Revelation 22:20

The Westminster Larger Catechism in Modern English

Q. 1. *What is the chief and highest end of man?*
A. Man's chief and highest end is to glorify God,[1] and fully to enjoy him forever.[2]

Q. 2. *How does it appear that there is a God?*
A. The very light of nature in man, and the works of God, declare plainly that there is a God;[3] but his word and Spirit only do sufficiently and effectually reveal him unto men for their salvation.[4]

Q. 3. *What is the Word of God?*
A. The holy Scriptures of the Old and New Testament are the Word of God,[5] the only rule of faith and obedience.[6]

Q. 4. *How does it appear that the Scriptures are the Word of God?*
A. The Scriptures manifest themselves to be the Word of God, by their majesty[7] and purity;[8] by the consent of all the parts,[9] and the scope of the whole, which is to give all glory to God;[10]

---

1 Romans 11:36; 1 Corinthians 10:31
2 Psalm 73:24-28; John 17:21-23
3 Romans 1:19-20; Psalm 19:1-3; Acts 17:28
4 1 Corinthians 2:9-10; 2 Timothy 3:15-17; Isaiah 59:21
5 2 Timothy 3:16; 2 Peter 1:19-21
6 Ephesians 2:20; Revelation 22:18-19; Isaiah 8:20; Luke 16:29, 31; Galatians 1:8-9; 2 Timothy 3:15-16
7 Hosea 8:12; 1 Corinthians 2:6-7, 13; Psalm 119:18, 129
8 Psalm 12:6; Psalm 119:140
9 Acts 10:43; Acts 26:22
10 Romans 3:19, 27

by their light and power to convince and convert sinners, to comfort and build up believers unto salvation:[1] but the Spirit of God bearing witness by and with the Scriptures in the heart of man, is alone able fully to persuade it that they are the very word of God.[2]

Q. 5. *What do the Scriptures principally teach?*
A. The Scriptures principally teach, what man is to believe concerning God, and what duty God requires of man.[3]

What Man Ought to Believe Concerning God

Q. 6. *What do the Scriptures make known of God?*
A. The Scriptures make known what God is,[4] the persons in the Godhead,[5] his decrees,[6] and the execution of his decrees.[7]

Q. 7. *What is God?*
A. God is a Spirit,[8] in and of himself infinite in being,[9] glory,[10] blessedness,[11] and perfection;[12] all-sufficient,[13] eternal,[14] unchangeable,[15] incomprehensible,[16] everywhere present,[17]

---

1 Acts 18:28; Hebrews 4:12; James 1:18; Psalm 19:7-9; Romans 15:4; Acts 20:32
2 John 16:13-14; 1 John 2:20, 27; John 20:31
3 2 Timothy 1:13
4 Hebrews 11:6
5 1 John 5:17
6 Acts 15:14-15, 18
7 Acts 4:27-28
8 John 4:24
9 Exodus 3:14; Job 11:7-9
10 Acts 7:2
11 1 Timothy 6:15
12 Matthew 5:48
13 Genesis 17:1
14 Psalm 90:2
15 Malachi 3:6; James 1:17
16 1 Kings 8:27
17 Psalm 139:1-13

almighty,[1] knowing all things,[2] most wise,[3] most holy,[4] most just,[5] most merciful and gracious, long-suffering, and abundant in goodness and truth.[6]

Q. 8. *Are there more Gods than one?*
A. There is but one only, the living and true God.[7]

Q. 9. *How many persons are there in the Godhead?*
A. There are three persons in the Godhead, the Father, the Son, and the Holy Spirit; and these three are one true, eternal God, the same in substance, equal in power and glory; although distinguished by their personal properties.[8]

Q. 10. *What are the personal properties of the three persons in the Godhead?*
A. It is proper to the Father to beget the Son,[9] and to the Son to be begotten of the Father,[10] and to the Holy Spirit to proceed from the Father and the Son from all eternity.[11]

Q. 11. *How does it appear that the Son and the Holy Spirit are God equal with the Father?*
A. The Scriptures manifest that the Son and the Holy Spirit are

---

1 Revelation 4:8
2 Hebrews 4:13; Psalm 147:5
3 Romans 16:27
4 Isaiah 6:3; Revelation 15:4
5 Deuteronomy 32:4
6 Exodus 34:6
7 Deuteronomy 6:4; 1 Corinthians 8:4, 6; Jeremiah 10:10
8 1 John 5:7; Matthew 3:16-17; 28:19; 2 Corinthians 13:14; John 10:30
9 Hebrews 1:5-6, 8
10 John 1:14, 18
11 John 15:26; Galatians 4:6

God equal with the Father, ascribing unto them such names,[1] attributes,[2] works,[3] and worship,[4] as are proper to God only.

Q. 12. *What are the decrees of God?*
A. God's decrees are the wise, free, and holy acts of the counsel of his will,[5] whereby, from all eternity, he has, for his own glory, unchangeably foreordained whatsoever comes to pass in time,[6] especially concerning angels and men.

Q. 13. *What has God especially decreed concerning angels and men?*
A. God, by an eternal and immutable decree, out of his mere love, for the praise of his glorious grace, to be manifested in due time, has elected some angels to glory;[7] and in Christ has chosen some men to eternal life, and the means thereof:[8] and also, according to his sovereign power, and the unsearchable counsel of his own will, (whereby he extends or withholds favour as he pleases,) has passed by and foreordained the rest to dishonour and wrath, to be for their sin inflicted, to the praise of the glory of his justice.[9]

Q. 14. *How does God execute his decrees?*
A. God executes his decrees in the works of creation and providence, according to his infallible foreknowledge, and the free and immutable counsel of his own will.[10]

Q. 15. *What is the work of creation?*
A. The work of creation is that wherein God did in the beginning, by the word of his power, make of nothing the

---

1 Isaiah 6:3, 5, 8 compared with John 12:41 and with Acts 28:25; 1 John 5:20; Acts 5:3-4
2 John 1:1; Isaiah 9:6; John 2:24-25; 1 Corinthians 2:10-11
3 Colossians 1:16; Genesis 1:2
4 Matthew 28:19; 2 Corinthians 13:14
5 Ephesians 1:11; Romans 11:33; 9:14-15, 18
6 Ephesians 1:4, 11; Romans 9:22-23; Psalm 33:11
7 1 Timothy 5:21
8 Ephesians 1:4-6; 2 Thessalonians 2:13-14
9 Romans 9:17-18, 21-22; Matthew 11:25-26; 2 Timothy 2:20; Jude 4; 1 Peter 2:8
10 Ephesians 1:11

world, and all things therein, for himself, within the space of six days, and all very good.[1]

Q. 16. *How did God create angels?*
A. God created all the angels[2] spirits,[3] immortal,[4] holy,[5] excelling in knowledge,[6] mighty in power,[7] to execute his commandments, and to praise his name,[8] yet subject to change.[9]

Q. 17. *How did God create man?*
A. After God had made all other creatures, he created man male and female;[10] formed the body of the man of the dust of the ground,[11] and the woman of the rib of the man,[12] endued them with living, reasonable, and immortal souls;[13] made them after his own image,[14] in knowledge,[15] righteousness, and holiness;[16] having the law of God written in their hearts,[17]

---

1 Genesis 1; Hebrews 11:3; Proverbs 16:4
2 Colossians 1:16
3 Psalm 104:4
4 Matthew 22:30
5 Matthew 25:31
6 2 Samuel 14:17; Matthew 24:36
7 2 Thessalonians 1:7
8 Psalm 103:20-21
9 2 Peter 2:4
10 Genesis 1:27
11 Genesis 2:7
12 Genesis 2:22
13 Genesis 2:7 compared with Job 35:11 and with Ecclesiastes 12:7 and with Matthew 10:28 and with Luke 23:43
14 Genesis 1:27
15 Colossians 3:10
16 Ephesians 4:24
17 Romans 2:14-15

and power to fulfil it,[1] and dominion over the creatures;[2] yet subject to fall.[3]

Q. 18. *What are God's works of providence?*
A. God's works of providence are his most holy,[4] wise,[5] and powerful preserving[6] and governing[7] all his creatures; ordering them, and all their actions,[8] to his own glory.[9]

Q. 19. *What is God's providence towards the angels?*
A. God by his providence permitted some of the angels, wilfully and irrecoverably, to fall into sin and damnation,[10] limiting and ordering that, and all their sins, to his own glory;[11] and established the rest in holiness and happiness;[12] employing them all,[13] at his pleasure, in the administrations of his power, mercy, and justice.[14]

Q. 20. *What was the providence of God toward man in the estate in which he was created?*
A. The providence of God toward man in the estate in which he was created, was the placing him in paradise, appointing him to dress it, giving him liberty to eat of the fruit of the earth;[15] putting the creatures under his dominion,[16] and ordaining marriage for his help;[17] affording him communion with

---

1 Ecclesiastes 7:29
2 Genesis 1:28
3 Genesis 3:6; Ecclesiastes 7:29
4 Psalm 145:17
5 Psalm 104:24; Isaiah 28:29
6 Hebrews 1:3
7 Psalm 103:19
8 Matthew 10:29-31; Genesis 45:7
9 Romans 11:36; Isaiah 63:14
10 Jude 6; 2 Peter 2:4; Hebrews 2:16; John 8:44
11 Job 1:12; Matthew 8:31
12 1 Timothy 5:21; Mark 8:38; Hebrews 12:22
13 Psalm 104:4
14 2 Kings 19:35; Hebrews 1:14
15 Genesis 2:8, 15-16
16 Genesis 1:28
17 Genesis 2:18

himself;[1] instituting the Sabbath;[2] entering into a covenant of life with him, upon condition of personal, perfect, and perpetual obedience,[3] of which the tree of life was a pledge;[4] and forbidding to eat of the tree of knowledge of good and evil, upon the pain of death.[5]

Q. 21. *Did man continue in that estate wherein God at first created him?*
A. Our first parents being left to the freedom of their own will, through the temptation of Satan, transgressed the commandment of God in eating the forbidden fruit; and thereby fell from the estate of innocence wherein they were created.[6]

Q. 22. *Did all mankind fall in that first transgression?*
A. The covenant being made with Adam as a public person, not for himself only, but for his posterity, all mankind descending from him by ordinary generation,[7] sinned in him, and fell with him in that first transgression.[8]

Q. 23. *Into what estate did the fall bring mankind?*
A. The fall brought mankind into an estate of sin and misery.[9]

Q. 24. *What is sin?*
A. Sin is any want of conformity unto, or transgression of, any law of God, given as a rule to the reasonable creature.[10]

Q. 25. *Wherein consists the sinfulness of that estate into which man fell?*
A. The sinfulness of that estate into which man fell, consists in

---
1 Genesis 1:26–29; 3:8
2 Genesis 2:3
3 Galatians 3:12; Romans 10:5
4 Genesis 2:9
5 Genesis 2:17
6 Genesis 3:6–8, 13; Ecclesiastes 7:29; 2 Corinthians 11:3
7 Acts 17:26
8 Genesis 2:16–17 compared with Romans 5:12–20 and with 1 Corinthians 15:21–22
9 Romans 5:12; 3:23
10 1 John 3:4; Galatians 3:10, 12

the guilt of Adam's first sin,[1] the want of that righteousness wherein he was created, and the corruption of his nature, whereby he is utterly indisposed, disabled, and made opposite unto all that is spiritually good, and wholly inclined to all evil, and that continually;[2] which is commonly called original sin, and from which do proceed all actual transgressions.[3]

Q. 26. *How is original sin conveyed from our first parents to their posterity?*
A. Original sin is conveyed from our first parents to their posterity by natural generation, so as all that proceed from them in that way are conceived and born in sin.[4]

Q. 27. *What misery did the fall bring upon mankind?*
A. The fall brought upon mankind the loss of communion with God,[5] his displeasure and curse; so as we are by nature children of wrath,[6] bond slaves to Satan,[7] and justly liable to all punishments in this world, and that which is to come.[8]

Q. 28. *What are the punishments of sin in this world?*
A. The punishments of sin in this world are either inward, as blindness of mind,[9] a reprobate sense,[10] strong delusions,[11] hardness of heart,[12] horror of conscience,[13] and vile affections;[14] or outward, as the curse of God upon the

---

1 Romans 5:12, 19
2 Romans 3:10–19; Ephesians 2:1–3; Romans 5:6; 8:7–8; Genesis 6:5
3 James 1:14–15; Matthew 15:19
4 Psalm 51:5; Job 14:4; 15:14; John 3:6
5 Genesis 3:8, 10, 24
6 Ephesians 2:2–3
7 2 Timothy 2:26
8 Genesis 2:17; Lamentations 3:39; Romans 6:23; Matthew 25:41, 46; Jude 7
9 Ephesians 4:18
10 Romans 1:28
11 2 Thessalonians 2:11
12 Romans 2:5
13 Isaiah 33:14; Genesis 4:13; Matthew 27:4
14 Romans 1:26

creatures of our sakes,[1] and all other evils that befall us in our bodies, names, estates, relations, and employments;[2] together with death itself.[3]

Q. 29. *What are the punishments of sin in the world to come?*
A. The punishments of sin in the world to come, are everlasting separation from the comfortable presence of God, and most grievous torments in soul and body, without intermission, in hell-fire forever.[4]

Q. 30. *Does God leave all mankind to perish in the estate of sin and misery?*
A. God does not leave all men to perish in the estate of sin and misery,[5] into which they fell by the breach of the first covenant, commonly called the covenant of works;[6] but of his mere love and mercy delivers his elect out of it, and brings them into an estate of salvation by the second covenant, commonly called the covenant of grace.[7]

Q. 31. *With whom was the covenant of grace made?*
A. The covenant of grace was made with Christ as the second [last] Adam, and in him with all the elect as his seed.[8]

Q. 32. *How is the grace of God manifested in the second covenant?*
A. The grace of God is manifested in the second covenant, in that he freely provides and offers to sinners a Mediator,[9] and life and salvation by him;[10] and requiring faith as the condition to interest them in him,[11] promises and gives his

---

1 Genesis 3:17
2 Deuteronomy 28:15-18
3 Romans 6:21, 23
4 2 Thessalonians 1:9; Mark 9:43, 44, 46, 48; Luke 16:24
5 1 Thessalonians 5:9
6 Galatians 3:10, 12
7 Titus 3:4-7; Galatians 3:21; Romans 3:20-22
8 Galatians 3:16; Romans 5:15-21; Isaiah 53:10-11
9 Genesis 3:15; Isaiah 42:6; John 6:27
10 1 John 5:11-12
11 John 3:16; John 1:12

Holy Spirit[1] to all his elect, to work in them that faith,[2] with all other saving graces;[3] and to enable them unto all holy obedience,[4] as the evidence of the truth of their faith[5] and thankfulness to God,[6] and as the way which he has appointed them to salvation.[7]

Q. 33. *Was the covenant of grace always administered after one and the same manner?*

A. The covenant of grace was not always administered after the same manner, but the administrations of it under the Old Testament were different from those under the New.[8]

Q. 34. *How was the covenant of grace administered under the Old Testament?*

A. The covenant of grace was administered under the Old Testament, by promises,[9] prophecies,[10] sacrifices,[11] circumcision,[12] the Passover,[13] and other types and ordinances, which did all fore-signify Christ then to come, and were for that time sufficient to build up the elect in faith in the

---

1 Proverbs 1:23
2 2 Corinthians 4:13
3 Galatians 5:22–23
4 Ezekiel 36:27
5 James 2:18, 22
6 2 Corinthians 5:14–15
7 Ephesians 2:18
8 2 Corinthians 3:6–9
9 Romans 15:8
10 Acts 3:20, 24
11 Hebrews 10:1
12 Romans 4:11
13 1 Corinthians 5:7

promised Messiah,[1] by whom they then had full remission of sin, and eternal salvation.[2]

Q. 35. *How is the covenant of grace administered under the New Testament?*

A. Under the New Testament, when Christ the substance was exhibited, the same covenant of grace was and still is to be administered in the preaching of the Word,[3] and the administration of the sacraments of Baptism[4] and the Lord's Supper;[5] in which grace and salvation are held forth in more fulness, evidence, and efficacy, to all nations.[6]

Q. 36. *Who is the Mediator of the covenant of grace?*

A. The only Mediator of the covenant of grace is the Lord Jesus Christ,[7] who, being the eternal Son of God, of one substance and equal with the Father,[8] in the fullness of time became man,[9] and so was and continues to be God and man, in two entire distinct natures, and one person, forever.[10]

Q. 37. *How did Christ, being the Son of God, become man?*

A. Christ the Son of God became man, by taking to himself a true body, and a reasonable soul,[11] being conceived by the

---

1 Hebrews 8, 9, 10; 11:13
2 Galatians 3:7-9, 14
3 Mark 16:15
4 Matthew 28:19-20
5 1 Corinthians 11:23-25
6 2 Corinthians 3:6-18; Hebrews 8:6, 10-11; Matthew 28:19
7 1 Timothy 2:5
8 John 1:1, 14; 10:30; Philippians 2:6
9 Galatians 4:4
10 Luke 1:35; Romans 9:5; Colossians 2:9; Hebrews 7:24-25
11 John 1:14; Matthew 26:38

power of the Holy Spirit in the womb of the virgin Mary, of her substance, and born of her,[1] yet without sin.[2]

Q. 38. *Why was it requisite that the Mediator should be God?*

A. It was requisite that the Mediator should be God, that he might sustain and keep the human nature from sinking under the infinite wrath of God, and the power of death;[3] give worth and efficacy to his sufferings, obedience, and intercession;[4] and to satisfy God's justice,[5] procure his favour,[6] purchase a peculiar people,[7] give his Spirit to them,[8] conquer all their enemies,[9] and bring them to everlasting salvation.[10]

Q. 39. *Why was it requisite that the Mediator should be man?*

A. It was requisite that the Mediator should be man, that he might advance our nature,[11] perform obedience to the law,[12] suffer and make intercession for us in our nature,[13] have a fellow-feeling of our infirmities;[14] that we might receive the

---

1 Luke 1:27, 31, 35, 42; Galatians 4:4
2 Hebrews 4:15; Hebrews 7:26
3 Acts 2:24-25; Romans 1:4 compared with Romans 4:25; Hebrews 9:14
4 Acts 20:28; Hebrews 9:14; 7:25-28
5 Romans 3:24-26
6 Ephesians 1:16; Matthew 3:17
7 Titus 2:13-14
8 Galatians 4:6
9 Luke 1:68-69, 71, 74
10 Hebrews 5:8-9; 9:11-15
11 Hebrews 2:16
12 Galatians 4:4
13 Hebrews 2:14; 7:24-25
14 Hebrews 4:15

adoption of sons,[1] and have comfort and access with boldness unto the throne of grace.[2]

Q. 40. *Why was it requisite that the Mediator should be God and man in one person?*
A. It was requisite that the Mediator, who was to reconcile God and man, should himself be both God and man, and this in one person, that the proper works of each nature might be accepted of God for us,[3] and relied on by us as the works of the whole person.[4]

Q. 41. *Why was our Mediator called Jesus?*
A. Our Mediator was called Jesus, because he saves his people from their sins.[5]

Q. 42. *Why was our Mediator called Christ?*
A. Our Mediator was called Christ, because he was anointed with the Holy Spirit above measure;[6] and so set apart, and fully furnished with all authority and ability,[7] to execute the offices of prophet,[8] priest,[9] and king of his church,[10] in the estate both of his humiliation and exaltation.

Q. 43. *How does Christ execute the office of a prophet?*
A. Christ executes the office of a prophet, in his revealing to the church,[11] in all ages, by his Spirit and Word,[12] in divers

---

1 Galatians 4:5
2 Hebrews 4:16
3 Matthew 1:21, 23; 3:17; Hebrews 9:14
4 1 Peter 2:6
5 Matthew 1:21
6 John 3:34; Psalm 45:7
7 John 6:27; Matthew 28:18-20
8 Acts 3:21-22; Luke 4:18, 21
9 Hebrews 5:5-7; Hebrews 4:14-15
10 Psalm 2:6; Matthew 21:5; Isaiah 9:6-7; Philippians 2:8-11
11 John 1:18
12 1 Peter 1:10-12

[various] ways of administration,[1] the whole will of God,[2] in all things concerning their edification and salvation.[3]

Q. 44. *How does Christ execute the office of a priest?*
A. Christ executes the office of a priest, in his once offering himself a sacrifice without spot to God,[4] to be a reconciliation for the sins of his people;[5] and in making continual intercession for them.[6]

Q. 45. *How does Christ execute the office of a king?*
A. Christ executes the office of a king, in calling out of the world a people to himself,[7] and giving them officers,[8] laws,[9] and censures, by which he visibly governs them;[10] in bestowing saving grace upon his elect,[11] rewarding their obedience,[12] and correcting them for their sins,[13] preserving and supporting them under all their temptations and sufferings,[14] restraining and overcoming all their enemies,[15] and powerfully ordering all things for his own glory,[16] and their good;[17] and also in

---

1 Hebrews 1:1-2
2 John 15:15
3 Acts 20:32; Ephesians 4:11-13; John 20:31
4 Hebrews 9:14, 28
5 Hebrews 2:17
6 Hebrews 7:25
7 Acts 15:14-16; Isaiah 55:4-5; Genesis 49:10; Psalm 110:3
8 Ephesians 4:11-12; 1 Corinthians 12:28
9 Isaiah 33:22
10 Matthew 18:17-18; 1 Corinthians 5:4-5
11 Acts 5:31
12 Revelation 22:12; 2:10
13 Revelation 3:19
14 Isaiah 63:9
15 1 Corinthians 15:25; Psalm 110
16 Romans 14:10-11
17 Romans 8:28

taking vengeance on the rest, who know not God, and obey not the gospel.[1]

Q. 46. *What was the estate of Christ's humiliation?*
A. The estate of Christ's humiliation was that low condition, wherein he for our sakes, emptying himself of his glory, took upon him the form of a servant, in his conception and birth, life, death, and after his death, until his resurrection.[2]

Q. 47. *How did Christ humble himself in his conception and birth?*
A. Christ humbled himself in his conception and birth, in that, being from all eternity the Son of God, in the bosom of the Father, he was pleased in the fullness of time to become the son of man, made of a woman of low estate, and to be born of her; with divers [various] circumstances of more than ordinary abasement.[3]

Q. 48. *How did Christ humble himself in his life?*
A. Christ humbled himself in his life, by subjecting himself to the law,[4] which he perfectly fulfilled;[5] and by conflicting with the indignities of the world,[6] temptations of Satan,[7] and infirmities in his flesh, whether common to the nature of man, or particularly accompanying that his low condition.[8]

Q. 49. *How did Christ humble himself in his death?*
A. Christ humbled himself in his death, in that having been betrayed by Judas,[9] forsaken by his disciples,[10] scorned and rejected by the world,[11] condemned by Pilate, and tormented

---
[1] 2 Thessalonians 1:8-9; Psalm 2:8-9
[2] Philippians 2:6-8; Luke 1:31; 2 Corinthians 8:9; Acts 2:24
[3] John 1:14, 18; Galatians 4:4; Luke 2:7
[4] Galatians 4:4
[5] Matthew 5:17; Romans 5:19
[6] Psalm 22:6; Hebrews 12:2-3
[7] Matthew 4:1-12; Luke 4:13
[8] Hebrews 2:17-18; 4:15; Isaiah 52:13-14
[9] Matthew 27:4
[10] Matthew 26:56
[11] Isaiah 53:2-3

by his persecutors;[1] having also conflicted with the terrors of death, and the powers of darkness, felt and borne the weight of God's wrath,[2] he laid down his life an offering for sin,[3] enduring the painful, shameful, and cursed death of the cross.[4]

Q. 50. *Wherein consisted Christ's humiliation after his death?*
A. Christ's humiliation after his death consisted in his being buried,[5] and continuing in the state of the dead, and under the power of death till the third day;[6] which has been otherwise expressed in these words, He descended into hell.

Q. 51. *What was the estate of Christ's exaltation?*
A. The estate of Christ's exaltation comprehends his resurrection,[7] ascension,[8] sitting at the right hand of the Father,[9] and his coming again to judge the world.[10]

Q. 52. *How was Christ exalted in his resurrection?*
A. Christ was exalted in his resurrection, in that, not having seen corruption in death, (of which it was not possible for him to be held,)[11] and having the very same body in which he suffered, with the essential properties thereof,[12] (but without mortality, and other common infirmities belonging to this life,) really united to his soul,[13] he rose again from the dead the third day by his own power;[14] whereby he declared himself

---

1 Matthew 27:26-50; John 19:34
2 Luke 22:44; Matthew 27:46
3 Isaiah 53:10
4 Philippians 2:8; Hebrews 12:2; Galatians 3:13
5 1 Corinthians 15:3-4
6 Psalm 16:10 compared with Acts 2:24-27, 31; Romans 6:9; Matthew 12:40
7 1 Corinthians 15:4
8 Mark 16:19
9 Ephesians 1:20
10 Acts 1:11; 17:31
11 Acts 2:24, 27
12 Luke 24:39
13 Romans 6:9; Revelation 1:18
14 John 10:18

to be the Son of God,[1] to have satisfied divine justice,[2] to have vanquished death, and him that had the power of it,[3] and to be Lord of quick [living] and dead:[4] all which he did as a public person,[5] the head of his church,[6] for their justification,[7] quickening in grace,[8] support against enemies,[9] and to assure them of their resurrection from the dead at the last day.[10]

Q. 53. *How was Christ exalted in his ascension?*
A. Christ was exalted in his ascension, in that having after his resurrection often appeared unto and conversed with his apostles, speaking to them of the things pertaining to the kingdom of God,[11] and giving them commission to preach the gospel to all nations,[12] forty days after his resurrection, he, in our nature, and as our head,[13] triumphing over enemies,[14] visibly went up into the highest heavens, there to receive gifts for men,[15] to raise up our affections thither,[16] and to prepare

---

1 Romans 1:4
2 Romans 8:34
3 Hebrews 2:14
4 Romans 14:9
5 1 Corinthians 15:21-22
6 Ephesians 1:20, 22, 23; Colossians 1:18
7 Romans 4:25
8 Ephesians 2:1, 5-6; Colossians 2:12
9 1 Corinthians 15:25-27
10 1 Corinthians 15:20
11 Acts 1:2-3
12 Matthew 28:19
13 Hebrews 6:20
14 Ephesians 4:8
15 Acts 1:9-11; Ephesians 4:10; Psalm 68:18
16 Colossians 3:1-2

a place for us,[1] where he himself is, and shall continue till his second coming at the end of the world.[2]

Q. 54. *How is Christ exalted in his sitting at the right hand of God?*
A. Christ is exalted in his sitting at the right hand of God, in that as God-man he is advanced to the highest favour with God the Father,[3] with all fullness of joy,[4] glory,[5] and power over all things in heaven and earth;[6] and does gather and defend his church, and subdue their enemies; furnishes his ministers and people with gifts and graces,[7] and makes intercession for them.[8]

Q. 55. *How does Christ make intercession?*
A. Christ makes intercession, by his appearing in our nature continually before the Father in heaven,[9] in the merit of his obedience and sacrifice on earth,[10] declaring his will to have it applied to all believers;[11] answering all accusations against them,[12] and procuring for them quiet of conscience, notwithstanding daily failings,[13] access with boldness to

---

1 John 14:3
2 Acts 3:21
3 Philippians 2:9
4 Acts 2:28 compared with Psalm 16:11
5 John 17:5
6 Ephesians 1:22; 1 Peter 3:22
7 Ephesians 4:10-12; Psalm 110
8 Romans 8:34
9 Hebrews 9:12, 24
10 Hebrews 1:3
11 John 3:16; 17:9, 20, 24
12 Romans 8:33-34
13 Romans 5:1-2; 1 John 2:1-2

the throne of grace,[1] and acceptance of their persons[2] and services.[3]

Q. 56. *How is Christ to be exalted in his coming again to judge the world?*

A. Christ is to be exalted in his coming again to judge the world, in that he, who was unjustly judged and condemned by wicked men,[4] shall come again at the last day in great power,[5] and in the full manifestation of his own glory, and of his Father's, with all his holy angels,[6] with a shout, with the voice of the archangel, and with the trumpet of God,[7] to judge the world in righteousness.[8]

Q. 57. *What benefits has Christ procured by his mediation?*

A. Christ, by his mediation, has procured redemption,[9] with all other benefits of the covenant of grace.[10]

Q. 58. *How do we come to be made partakers of the benefits which Christ has procured?*

A. We are made partakers of the benefits which Christ has procured, by the application of them unto us,[11] which is the work especially of God the Holy Spirit.[12]

Q. 59. *Who are made partakers of redemption through Christ?*

A. Redemption is certainly applied, and effectually communicated, to all those for whom Christ has purchased

---

1 Hebrews 4:16
2 Ephesians 1:6
3 1 Peter 2:5
4 Acts 3:14-15
5 Matthew 24:30
6 Luke 9:26; Matthew 25:31
7 1 Thessalonians 4:16
8 Acts 17:31
9 Hebrews 9:12
10 2 Corinthians 1:20
11 John 1:11-12
12 Titus 3:5-6

it;[1] who are in time by the Holy Spirit enabled to believe in Christ according to the gospel.[2]

Q. 60. *Can they who have never heard the gospel, and so know not Jesus Christ, nor believe in him, be saved by their living according to the light of nature?*

A. They who, having never heard the gospel,[3] know not Jesus Christ,[4] and believe not in him, cannot be saved,[5] be they never so diligent to frame their lives according to the light of nature,[6] or the laws of that religion which they profess;[7] neither is there salvation in any other, but in Christ alone,[8] who is the Saviour only of his body the church.[9]

Q. 61. *Are all they saved who hear the gospel, and live in the church?*

A. All that hear the gospel, and live in the visible church, are not saved; but they only who are true members of the church invisible.[10]

Q. 62. *What is the visible church?*

A. The visible church is a society made up of all such as in all ages and places of the world do profess the true religion,[11] and of their children.[12]

Q. 63. *What are the special privileges of the visible church?*

A. The visible church has the privilege of being under God's special care and government;[13] of being protected and

---

1 Ephesians 1:13-14; John 6:37, 39; 10:15-16
2 Ephesians 2:8; 2 Corinthians 4:13
3 Romans 10:14
4 2 Thessalonians 1:8-9; Ephesians 2:12; John 1:10-12
5 John 8:24; Mark 16:16
6 1 Corinthians 1:20-24
7 John 4:22; Romans 9:31-32; Philippians 3:4-9
8 Acts 4:12
9 Ephesians 5:23
10 John 12:38-40; Romans 9:6; 22:14; Matthew 7:21; Romans 11:7
11 1 Corinthians 1:2; 12:13; Romans 15:9-12; Revelation 7:9; Psalm 2:8; 22:27-31; 45:17; Matthew 28:19-20; Isaiah 59:21
12 1 Corinthians 7:14; Acts 2:39; Romans 11:16; Genesis 17:7
13 Isaiah 9:5-6; 1 Timothy 4:10

preserved in all ages, notwithstanding the opposition of all enemies;[1] and of enjoying the communion of saints, the ordinary means of salvation,[2] and offers of grace by Christ to all the members of it in the ministry of the gospel, testifying, that whosoever believes in him shall be saved,[3] and excluding none that will come unto him.[4]

Q. 64. *What is the invisible church?*
A. The invisible church is the whole number of the elect, that have been, are, or shall be gathered into one under Christ the head.[5]

Q. 65. *What special benefits do the members of the invisible church enjoy by Christ?*
A. The members of the invisible church by Christ enjoy union and communion with him in grace and glory.[6]

Q. 66. *What is that union which the elect have with Christ?*
A. The union which the elect have with Christ is the work of God's grace,[7] whereby they are spiritually and mystically, yet really and inseparably, joined to Christ as their head and husband;[8] which is done in their effectual calling.[9]

Q. 67. *What is effectual calling?*
A. Effectual calling is the work of God's almighty power and grace,[10] whereby (out of his free and special love to his elect, and from nothing in them moving him thereunto)[11] he does, in his accepted time, invite and draw them to Jesus Christ,

---

1 Psalm 115; Isaiah 31:4-5; Zechariah 12:2-4, 8-9
2 Acts 2:39, 42
3 Psalm 147:19-20; Romans 9:4; Ephesians 4:11-12; Mark 16:15-16
4 John 6:37
5 Ephesians 1:10, 22-23; John 10:16; 11:52
6 John 17:21; Ephesians 2:5-6; John 17:24
7 Ephesians 1:22; 2:6-8
8 1 Corinthians 6:17; John 10:28; Ephesians 5:23, 30
9 1 Peter 5:10, 1 Corinthians 1:9
10 John 5:25; Ephesians 1:18-20; 2 Timothy 1:8-9
11 Titus 3:4-5; Ephesians 2:4-5, 7-9; Romans 9:11

by his Word and Spirit;[1] savingly enlightening their minds,[2] renewing and powerfully determining their wills,[3] so as they (although in themselves dead in sin) are hereby made willing and able freely to answer his call, and to accept and embrace the grace offered and conveyed therein.[4]

Q. 68. *Are the elect only effectually called?*
A. All the elect, and they only, are effectually called:[5] although others may be, and often are, outwardly called by the ministry of the Word,[6] and have some common operations of the Spirit;[7] who, for their wilful neglect and contempt of the grace offered to them, being justly left in their unbelief, do never truly come to Jesus Christ.[8]

Q. 69. *What is the communion in grace which the members of the invisible church have with Christ?*
A. The communion in grace which the members of the invisible church have with Christ, is their partaking of the virtue of his mediation, in their justification,[9] adoption,[10] sanctification, and whatever else, in this life, manifests their union with him.[11]

Q. 70. *What is justification?*
A. Justification is an act of God's free grace unto sinners,[12] in which he pardons all their sins, accepts and accounts their

---

1   2 Corinthians 5:20 compared with 2 Corinthians 6:1-2; John 6:44; 2 Thessalonians 2:13-14
2   Acts 26:18; 1 Corinthians 2:10, 12
3   Ezekiel 11:19; 36:26; John 6:45
4   Ephesians 2:5; Philippians 2:13; Deuteronomy 30:6
5   Acts 13:48
6   Matthew 22:14
7   Matthew 7:22; 13:20-21; Hebrews 6:4-6
8   John 12:38-40; Acts 28:25-27; John 6:64-65; Psalm 81:11-12
9   Romans 8:30
10 Ephesians 1:5
11 1 Corinthians 1:30
12 Romans 3:22, 24-25; Romans 4:5

persons righteous in his sight;[1] not for anything wrought in them, or done by them,[2] but only for the perfect obedience and full satisfaction of Christ, by God imputed to them,[3] and received by faith alone.[4]

Q. 71. *How is justification an act of God's free grace?*
A. Although Christ, by his obedience and death, did make a proper, real, and full satisfaction to God's justice in the behalf of them that are justified;[5] yet in as much as God accepts the satisfaction from a surety, which he might have demanded of them, and did provide this surety, his own only Son,[6] imputing his righteousness to them,[7] and requiring nothing of them for their justification but faith,[8] which also is his gift,[9] their justification is to them of free grace.[10]

Q. 72. *What is justifying faith?*
A. Justifying faith is a saving grace,[11] wrought in the heart of a sinner by the Spirit[12] and Word of God,[13] whereby he, being convinced of his sin and misery, and of the disability in himself and all other creatures to recover him out of his lost condition,[14] not only assents to the truth of the promise of the gospel,[15] but receives and rests upon Christ and his

---

1 2 Corinthians 5:19, 21; Romans 3:22, 24–25, 27–28
2 Titus 3:5, 7; Ephesians 1:7
3 Romans 5:17–19; 4:6–8
4 Acts 10:43; Galatians 2:16; Philippians 3:9
5 Romans 5:8–10, 19
6 1 Timothy 2:5–6; Hebrews 10:10; Matthew 20:28; Daniel 9:24, 26; Isaiah 53:4–6, 10–12; Hebrews 7:22; Romans 8:32; 1 Peter 1:18–19
7 2 Corinthians 5:21
8 Romans 3:24–25
9 Ephesians 2:8
10 Ephesians 1:7
11 Hebrews 10:39
12 2 Corinthians 4:13; Ephesians 1:17–19
13 Romans 10:14, 17
14 Acts 2:37; 16:30; John 16:8–9; Romans 6:6; Ephesians 2:1; Acts 4:12
15 Ephesians 1:13

righteousness, therein held forth, for pardon of sin,[1] and for the accepting and accounting of his person righteous in the sight of God for salvation.[2]

Q. 73. *How does faith justify a sinner in the sight of God?*
A. Faith justifies a sinner in the sight of God, not because of those other graces which do always accompany it, or of good works that are the fruits of it,[3] nor as if the grace of faith, or any act thereof, were imputed to him for his justification;[4] but only as it is an instrument by which he receives and applies Christ and his righteousness.[5]

Q. 74. *What is adoption?*
A. Adoption is an act of the free grace of God,[6] in and for his only Son Jesus Christ,[7] whereby all those that are justified are received into the number of his children,[8] have his name put upon them,[9] the Spirit of his Son given to them,[10] are under his fatherly care and dispensations,[11] admitted to all the liberties and privileges of the sons of God, made heirs of all the promises, and fellow-heirs with Christ in glory.[12]

Q. 75. *What is sanctification?*
A. Sanctification is a work of God's grace, whereby they whom God has, before the foundation of the world, chosen to be holy, are in time, through the powerful operation of his Spirit[13] applying the death and resurrection of Christ unto

---

1 John 1:12; Acts 16:31; 10:43
2 Philippians 3:9; Acts 15:11
3 Galatians 3:11; Romans 3:28
4 Romans 4:5 compared with Romans 10:10
5 John 1:12; Philippians 3:9; Galatians 1:16
6 1 John 3:1
7 Ephesians 1:5; Galatians 4:4–5
8 John 1:12
9 2 Corinthians 6:18; Revelation 3:12
10 Galatians 4:6
11 Psalm 103:13; Proverbs 14:26; Matthew 6:32
12 Hebrews 6:12; Romans 8:17
13 Ephesians 1:4; 1 Corinthians 6:11; 2 Thessalonians 2:13

them,[1] renewed in their whole man after the image of God;[2] having the seeds of repentance unto life, and all other saving graces, put into their hearts,[3] and those graces so stirred up, increased, and strengthened,[4] as that they more and more die unto sin, and rise unto newness of life.[5]

Q. 76. *What is repentance unto life?*
A. Repentance unto life is a saving grace,[6] wrought in the heart of a sinner by the Spirit[7] and Word of God,[8] whereby, out of the sight and sense, not only of the danger,[9] but also of the filthiness and odiousness of his sins,[10] and upon the apprehension of God's mercy in Christ to such as are penitent,[11] he so grieves for[12] and hates his sins,[13] as that he turns from them all to God,[14] purposing and endeavouring constantly to walk with him in all the ways of new obedience.[15]

Q. 77. *Wherein do justification and sanctification differ?*
A. Although sanctification be inseparably joined with justification,[16] yet they differ, in that God in justification imputes the righteousness of Christ;[17] in sanctification his

---

1 Romans 6:4-6
2 Ephesians 4:23-24
3 Acts 11:18; 1 John 3:9
4 Jude 20; Hebrews 6:11-12; Ephesians 3:16-19; Colossians 1:10-11
5 Romans 6:4, 6, 14; Galatians 5:24
6 2 Timothy 2:25
7 Zechariah 12:10
8 Acts 11:18, 20-21
9 Ezekiel 18:28.3 0, 32; Luke 15:17-18; Hosea 2:6-7
10 Ezekiel 36:31; Isaiah 30:22
11 Joel 2:12-13
12 Jeremiah 31:18-19
13 2 Corinthians 7:11
14 Acts 26:18; Ezekiel 14:6; 1 Kings 8:47-48
15 Psalm 119:6, 59, 128; Luke 1:6; 2 Kings 23:25
16 1 Corinthians 6:11; 1 Corinthians 1:30
17 Romans 4:6, 8

Spirit infuses grace, and enables to the exercise thereof;[1] in the former, sin is pardoned;[2] in the other, it is subdued:[3] the one does equally free all believers from the revenging wrath of God, and that perfectly in this life, that they never fall into condemnation;[4] the other is neither equal in all,[5] nor in this life perfect in any,[6] but growing up to perfection.[7]

Q. 78. *Whence arises the imperfection of sanctification in believers?*
A. The imperfection of sanctification in believers arises from the remnants of sin abiding in every part of them, and the perpetual lusting of the flesh against the spirit; whereby they are often foiled with temptations, and fall into many sins,[8] are hindered in all their spiritual services,[9] and their best works are imperfect and defiled in the sight of God.[10]

Q. 79. *May not true believers, by reason of their imperfections, and the many temptations and sins they are overtaken with, fall away from the state of grace?*
A. True believers, by reason of the unchangeable love of God,[11] and his decree and covenant to give them perseverance,[12] their inseparable union with Christ,[13] his continual intercession for them,[14] and the Spirit and seed of God abiding in them,[15] can neither totally nor finally fall away from

---

[1] Ezekiel 36:27
[2] Romans 3:24–25
[3] Romans 6:6, 14
[4] Romans 8:33–34
[5] 1 John 2:12–14; Hebrews 5:12–14
[6] 1 John 1:8, 10
[7] 2 Corinthians 7:1; Philippians 3:12–14
[8] Romans 7:18, 23; Mark 14:66–72; Galatians 2:11–12
[9] Hebrew 12:1
[10] Isaiah 64:6; Exodus 28:38
[11] Jeremiah 31:3
[12] 2 Timothy 2:19; Hebrews 13:20–21; 2 Samuel 23:5
[13] 1 Corinthians 1:8–9
[14] Hebrews 7:25; Luke 22:32
[15] 1 John 3:9; 1 John 2:27

the state of grace,[1] but are kept by the power of God through faith unto salvation.[2]

Q. 80. *Can true believers be infallibly assured that they are in the estate of grace, and that they shall persevere therein unto salvation?*
A. Such as truly believe in Christ, and endeavour to walk in all good conscience before him,[3] may, without extraordinary revelation, by faith grounded upon the truth of God's promises, and by the Spirit enabling them to discern in themselves those graces to which the promises of life are made,[4] and bearing witness with their spirits that they are the children of God,[5] be infallibly assured that they are in the estate of grace, and shall persevere therein unto salvation.[6]

Q. 81. *Are all true believers at all times assured of their present being in the estate of grace, and that they shall be saved?*
A. Assurance of grace and salvation not being of the essence of faith,[7] true believers may wait long before they obtain it;[8] and, after the enjoyment thereof, may have it weakened and intermitted, through manifold distempers [afflictions], sins, temptations, and desertions;[9] yet they are never left without such a presence and support of the Spirit of God as keeps them from sinking into utter despair.[10]

Q. 82. *What is the communion in glory which the members of the invisible church have with Christ?*
A. The communion in glory which the members of the invisible

---

1 Jeremiah 32:40; John 10:28
2 1 Peter 1:5
3 1 John 2:3
4 1 Corinthians 2:12; 1 John 3:14, 18–19, 21, 24; 4:13, 16; Hebrews 6:11–12
5 Romans 8:16
6 1 John 5:13
7 Ephesians 1:13
8 Isaiah 50:10; Psalm 88
9 Psalm 77:1–12; Song of Solomon 5:2–3, 6; Psalm 51:8; 31:22; 22:1
10 1 John 3:9; Job 13:15; Psalm 73:15, 23; Isaiah 54:7–10

church have with Christ, is in this life,[1] immediately after death,[2] and at last perfected at the resurrection and day of judgment.[3]

Q. 83. *What is the communion in glory with Christ which the members of the invisible church enjoy in this life?*
A. The members of the invisible church have communicated to them in this life the firstfruits of glory with Christ, as they are members of him their head, and so in him are interested in that glory which he is fully possessed of;[4] and, as an earnest [pledge] thereof, enjoy the sense of God's love,[5] peace of conscience, joy in the Holy Spirit, and hope of glory;[6] as, on the contrary, sense of God's revenging wrath, horror of conscience, and a fearful expectation of judgment, are to the wicked the beginning of their torments which they shall endure after death.[7]

Q. 84. *Shall all men die?*
A. Death being threatened as the wages of sin,[8] it is appointed unto all men once to die;[9] for that all have sinned.[10]

Q. 85. *Death, being the wages of sin, why are not the righteous delivered from death, seeing all their sins are forgiven in Christ?*
A. The righteous shall be delivered from death itself at the last day, and even in death are delivered from the sting and curse of it;[11] so that, although they die, yet it is out of God's love,[12] to

---

1 2 Corinthians 3:18
2 Luke 23:43
3 1 Thessalonians 4:17
4 Ephesians 2:5-6
5 Romans 5:5; 2 Corinthians 1:22
6 Romans 5:1-2; 14:17
7 Genesis 4:13; Matthew 27:4; Hebrews 10:27; Romans 2:9; Mark 9:44
8 Romans 6:23
9 Hebrews 9:27
10 Romans 5:12
11 1 Corinthians 15:26, 55-57; Hebrews 2:15
12 Isaiah 57:1-2; 2 Kings 22:20

free them perfectly from sin and misery,[1] and to make them capable of further communion with Christ in glory, which they then enter upon.[2]

Q. 86. *What is the communion in glory with Christ, which the members of the invisible church enjoy immediately after death?*
A. The communion in glory with Christ, which the members of the invisible church enjoy immediately after death is, in that their souls are then made perfect in holiness,[3] and received into the highest heavens,[4] where they behold the face of God in light and glory,[5] waiting for the full redemption of their bodies,[6] which even in death continue united to Christ,[7] and rest in their graves as in their beds,[8] till at the last day they be again united to their souls.[9] Whereas the souls of the wicked are at their death cast into hell, where they remain in torments and utter darkness, and their bodies kept in their graves, as in their prisons, till the resurrection and judgment of the great day.[10]

Q. 87. *What are we to believe concerning the resurrection?*
A. We are to believe that at the last day there shall be a general resurrection of the dead, both of the just and unjust:[11] when they that are then found alive shall in a moment be changed; and the self-same bodies of the dead which were laid in the grave, being then again united to their souls forever, shall be

---

1 Revelation 14:13; Ephesians 5:27
2 Luke 23:43; Philippians 1:23
3 Hebrews 12:23
4 2 Corinthians 5:1, 6, 8; Philippians 1:23 compared with Acts 3:21 and with Ephesians 4:10
5 1 John 3:2; 1 Corinthians 13:12
6 Romans 8:23; Psalm 16:9
7 1 Thessalonians 4:14
8 Isaiah 57:2
9 Job 19:26–27
10 Luke 16:23–24; Acts 1:25; Jude 6–7
11 Acts 24:15

raised up by the power of Christ.[1] The bodies of the just, by the Spirit of Christ, and by virtue of his resurrection as their head, shall be raised in power, spiritual, incorruptible, and made like to his glorious body;[2] and the bodies of the wicked shall be raised up in dishonour by him, as an offended judge.[3]

Q. 88. *What shall immediately follow after the resurrection?*
A. Immediately after the resurrection shall follow the general and final judgment of angels and men;[4] the day and hour whereof no man knows, that all may watch and pray, and be ever ready for the coming of the Lord.[5]

Q. 89. *What shall be done to the wicked at the day of judgment?*
A. At the day of judgment, the wicked shall be set on Christ's left hand,[6] and, upon clear evidence, and full conviction of their own consciences,[7] shall have the fearful but just sentence of condemnation pronounced against them;[8] and thereupon shall be cast out from the favourable presence of God, and the glorious fellowship with Christ, his saints, and all his holy angels, into hell, to be punished with unspeakable torments, both of body and soul, with the devil and his angels forever.[9]

Q. 90. *What shall be done to the righteous at the day of judgment?*
A. At the day of judgment, the righteous, being caught up to Christ in the clouds,[10] shall be set on his right hand, and there openly acknowledged and acquitted,[11] shall join with him in the judging of reprobate angels and men,[12] and shall be

---

1   1 Corinthians 15:51–53; 1 Thessalonians 4:15–17; John 5:28–29
2   1 Corinthians 15:21–23, 42–44; Philippians 3:21
3   John 5:27–29; Matthew 25:33
4   2 Peter 2:4; Jude 6–7, 14–15; Matthew 25:46
5   Matthew 24–36, 42, 44; Luke 21:35–36
6   Matthew 25:33
7   Romans 2:15–16
8   Matthew 25:41–43
9   Luke 16:26; 2 Thessalonians 1:8–9
10   1 Thessalonians 4:17
11   Matthew 25:33; 10:32
12   1 Corinthians 6:2–3

received into heaven,[1] where they shall be fully and forever freed from all sin and misery;[2] filled with inconceivable joys,[3] made perfectly holy and happy both in body and soul, in the company of innumerable saints and holy angels,[4] but especially in the immediate vision and fruition of God the Father, of our Lord Jesus Christ, and of the Holy Spirit, to all eternity.[5] And this is the perfect and full communion, which the members of the invisible church shall enjoy with Christ in glory, at the resurrection and day of judgment.

Having Seen What the Scriptures Principally Teach Us To Believe Concerning God, It Follows to Consider What They Require as the Duty of Man

Q. 91. *What is the duty which God requires of man?*
A. The duty which God requires of man, is obedience to his revealed will.[6]

Q. 92. *What did God at first reveal unto man as the rule of his obedience?*
A. The rule of obedience revealed to Adam in the estate of innocence, and to all mankind in him, besides a special command not to eat of the fruit of the tree knowledge of good and evil, was the moral law.[7]

Q. 93. *What is the moral law?*
A. The moral law is the declaration of the will of God to mankind, directing and binding everyone to personal, perfect, and perpetual conformity and obedience thereunto,

---

1 Matthew 25:34, 46
2 Ephesians 5:27; Revelation 14:13
3 Psalm 16:11
4 Hebrews 12:22-23
5 1 John 3:2; 1 Corinthians 13:12; 1 Thessalonians 4:17-18
6 Romans 12:1-2; Micah 6:8; 1 Samuel 15:22
7 Genesis 1:26-27; Romans 2:14-15; 10:5; Genesis 2:17

in the frame and disposition of the whole man, soul and body,[1] and in performance of all those duties of holiness and righteousness which he owes to God and man:[2] promising life upon the fulfilling, and threatening death upon the breach of it.[3]

Q. 94. *Is there any use of the moral law to man since the fall?*
A. Although no man, since the fall, can attain to righteousness and life by the moral law:[4] yet there is great use thereof, as well common to all men, as peculiar either to the unregenerate, or the regenerate.[5]

Q. 95. *Of what use is the moral law to all men?*
A. The moral law is of use to all men, to inform them of the holy nature and the will of God,[6] and of their duty, binding them to walk accordingly;[7] to convince them of their disability to keep it, and of the sinful pollution of their nature, hearts, and lives:[8] to humble them in the sense of their sin and misery,[9] and thereby help them to a clearer sight of the need they have of Christ,[10] and of the perfection of his obedience.[11]

Q. 96. *What particular use is there of the moral law to unregenerate men?*
A. The moral law is of use to unregenerate men, to awaken their consciences to flee from wrath to come,[12] and to drive them to

---

[1] Deuteronomy 5:1–3, 31, 33; Luke 10:26–27; 1 Thessalonians 5:23
[2] Luke 1:75; Acts 24:16
[3] Romans 10:5; Galatians 3:10, 12
[4] Romans 8:3; Galatians 2:16
[5] 1 Timothy 1:8
[6] Leviticus 11:44–45; Leviticus 20:7–8; Romans 8:12
[7] Micah 6:8; James 2:10–11
[8] Psalm 19:11–12; Romans 3:20; 7:7
[9] Romans 3:9, 23
[10] Galatians 3:21–22
[11] Romans 10:4
[12] 1 Timothy 1:9–10

Christ;[1] or, upon their continuance in the estate and way of sin, to leave them inexcusable,[2] and under the curse thereof.[3]

Q. 97. *What special use is there of the moral law to the regenerate?*
A. Although they that are regenerate, and believe in Christ, be delivered from the moral law as a covenant of works,[4] so as thereby they are neither justified[5] nor condemned;[6] yet, besides the general uses thereof common to them with all men, it is of special use, to show them how much they are bound to Christ for his fulfilling it, and enduring the curse thereof in their stead, and for their good;[7] and thereby to provoke them to more thankfulness,[8] and to express the same in their greater care to conform themselves thereunto as the rule of their obedience.[9]

Q. 98. *Where is the moral law summarily comprehended?*
A. The moral law is summarily comprehended in the ten commandments, which were delivered by the voice of God upon Mount Sinai, and written by him in two tables of stone;[10] and are recorded in the twentieth chapter of Exodus. The four first commandments containing our duty to God, and the other six our duty to man.[11]

Q. 99. *What rules are to be observed for the right understanding of the Ten Commandments?*
A. For the right understanding of the Ten Commandments, these rules are to be observed:
1. That the law is perfect, and binds everyone to full conformity

---

[1] Galatians 3:24
[2] Romans 1:20 compared with Romans 2:15
[3] Galatians 3:10
[4] Romans 6:14; 7:4, 6; Galatians 4:4-5
[5] Romans 3:20
[6] Galatians 5:23; Romans 8:1
[7] Romans 7:24-25; Galatians 3:13-14; Romans 8:3-4
[8] Luke 1:68-69, 74-75; Colossians 1:12-14
[9] Romans 7:22; 12:2; Titus 2:11-14
[10] Deuteronomy 10:4; Exodus 34:1-4
[11] Matthew 22:37-40

in the whole man unto the righteousness thereof, and unto entire obedience forever; so as to require the utmost perfection of every duty, and to forbid the least degree of every sin.[1]

2. That it is spiritual, and so reaches the understanding, will, affections, and all other powers of the soul; as well as words, works, and gestures.[2]

3. That one and the same thing, in divers [various] respects, is required or forbidden in several commandments.[3]

4. That as, where a duty is commanded, the contrary sin is forbidden;[4] and, where a sin is forbidden, the contrary duty is commanded:[5] so, where a promise is annexed, the contrary threatening is included;[6] and, where a threatening is annexed, the contrary promise is included.[7]

5. That what God forbids, is at no time to be done;[8] what he commands, is always our duty;[9] and yet every particular duty is not to be done at all times.[10]

6. That under one sin or duty, all of the same kind are forbidden or commanded; together with all the causes, means, occasions, and appearances thereof, and provocations thereunto.[11]

7. That what is forbidden or commanded to ourselves, we are bound, according to our places to endeavour that it may be

---

1 Psalm 19:7; James 2:10; Matthew 5:21-22
2 Romans 7:14; Deuteronomy 6:5 compared with Matthew 22:37-39; Matthew 5:21-22, 27-28, 33-34, 37-39, 43-44
3 Colossians 3:5; Amos 8:5; Proverbs 1:19; 1 Timothy 6:10
4 Isaiah 58:13; Deuteronomy 6:13 compared with Matthew 4:9-10; Matthew 15:4-6
5 Matthew 5:21-25; Ephesians 4:28
6 Exodus 20:12 compared with Proverbs 30:17
7 Jeremiah 18:7-8 compared with Psalm 15:1, 4-5 and with Psalm 24:4-5; Exodus 20:7
8 Job 13:7-8; Romans 3:8; Job 36:21
9 Deuteronomy 4:8-9
10 Matthew 12:7
11 Matthew 5:21-22, 27-28; 15:4-6; Hebrews 10:24-25; 1 Thessalonians 5:22; Jude 23; Galatians 5:26; Colossians 3:21

avoided or performed by others, according to the duty of their places.[1]

8. That in what is commanded to others, we are bound, according to our places and callings, to be helpful to them;[2] and to take heed of partaking with others in what is forbidden them.[3]

Q. 100. *What special things are we to consider in the Ten Commandments?*

A. We are to consider in the Ten Commandments, the preface, the substance of the commandments themselves, and several reasons annexed to some of them, the more to enforce them.

Q. 101. *What is the preface to the Ten Commandments?*

A. The preface to the Ten Commandments is contained in these words, I am the Lord your God, who has brought you out of the land of Egypt, out of the house of slavery.[4] Wherein God manifests his sovereignty, as being JEHOVAH [covenant Lord], the eternal, immutable, and almighty God;[5] having his being in and of himself,[6] and giving being to all his words[7] and works:[8] and that he is a God in covenant, as with Israel of old, so with all his people;[9] who, as he brought them out of their bondage in Egypt, so he delivers us from our spiritual thraldom [captivity];[10] and that therefore we are

---

[1] Exodus 20:10; Leviticus 19:17; Genesis 18:19; Joshua 14:15; Deuteronomy 6:6-7
[2] 2 Corinthians 1:24
[3] 1 Timothy 5:22; Ephesians 5:11
[4] Exodus 20:2
[5] Isaiah 44:6
[6] Exodus 3:14
[7] Exodus 6:3
[8] Acts 17:24, 28
[9] Genesis 17:7 compared with Romans 3:29
[10] Luke 1:74-75

bound to take him for our God alone, and to keep all his commandments.[1]

Q. 102. *What is the sum of the four commandments which contain our duty to God?*
A. The sum of the four commandments containing our duty to God is, to love the Lord our God with all our heart, and with all our soul, and with all our strength, and with all our mind.[2]

Q. 103. *Which is the first commandment?*
A. The first commandment is, You shall have no other gods before me.[3]

Q. 104. *What are the duties required in the first commandment?*
A. The duties required in the first commandment are, the knowing and acknowledging of God to be the only true God, and our God;[4] and to worship and glorify him accordingly,[5] by thinking,[6] meditating,[7] remembering,[8] highly esteeming,[9] honouring,[10] adoring,[11] choosing,[12] loving,[13] desiring,[14] fearingof him;[15] believing him;[16] trusting[17] hoping,[18]

---

1 1 Peter 1:15, 17-18; Leviticus 18:30; 19:37
2 Luke 10:27
3 Exodus 20:3
4 1 Chronicles 28:9; Deuteronomy 26:7; Isaiah 43:10; Jeremiah 14:22
5 Psalm 95:6-7; Matthew 4:10; Psalm 29:2
6 Malachi 3:16
7 Psalm 63:6
8 Ecclesiastes 12:1
9 Psalm 71:19
10 Malachi 1:6
11 Isaiah 45:23
12 Joshua 24:15, 22
13 Deuteronomy 6:5
14 Psalm 73:25
15 Isaiah 8:13
16 Exodus 14:31
17 Isaiah 26:4
18 Psalm 130:7

delighting,[1] rejoicing in him;[2] being zealous for him;[3] calling upon him, giving all praise and thanks,[4] and yielding all obedience and submission to him with the whole man;[5] being careful in all things to please him,[6] and sorrowful when in anything he is offended;[7] and walking humbly with him.[8]

Q. 105. *What are the sins forbidden in the first commandment?*
A. The sins forbidden in the first commandment are, atheism, in denying or not having a God;[9] idolatry, in having or worshipping more gods than one, or any with or instead of the true God;[10] the not having and avouching him for God, and our God;[11] the omission or neglect of anything due to him, required in this commandment;[12] ignorance,[13] forgetfullness,[14] misapprehensions,[15] false opinions,[16] unworthy and wicked thoughts of him;[17] bold and curious searching into his secrets;[18] all profaneness,[19] hatred of God;[20] self-love,[21] self-seeking,[22] and all other inordinate and immoderate setting

---

1 Psalm 37:4
2 Psalm 32:11
3 Romans 12:11 compared with Numbers 25:11
4 Philippians 4:6
5 Jeremiah 7:23; James 4:7
6 1 John 3:22
7 Jeremiah 31:18; Psalm 119:136
8 Micah 6:8
9 Psalm 14:1; Ephesians 2:12
10 Jeremiah 2:27, 28 compared with 1 Thessalonians 1:9
11 Psalm 81:11
12 Isaiah 43:2, 23–24
13 Jeremiah 4:22; Hosea 4:1, 6
14 Jeremiah 2:32
15 Acts 17:23, 29
16 Isaiah 40:18
17 Psalm 50:21
18 Deuteronomy 29:29
19 Titus 1:16; Hebrews 12:16
20 Romans 1:30
21 2 Timothy 3:2
22 Philippians 2:21

of our mind, will, or affections upon other things, and taking them off from him in whole or in part;[1] vain credulity,[2] unbelief,[3] heresy,[4] misbelief,[5] distrust,[6] despair,[7] incorrigibleness,[8] and insensibleness under judgments,[9] hardness of heart,[10] pride,[11] presumption,[12] carnal security,[13] tempting of God;[14] using unlawful means,[15] and trusting in lawful means;[16] carnal delights and joys;[17] corrupt, blind, and indiscreet zeal;[18] lukewarmness,[19] and deadness in the things of God;[20] estranging ourselves, and apostatizing from God;[21] praying, or giving any religious worship, to saints, angels, or any other creatures;[22] all compacts and consulting with the devil,[23] and hearkening to his suggestions;[24] making men the lords of our faith and conscience;[25] slighting and

---

1   1 John 2:15-16; 1 Samuel 2:29; Colossians 2:2, 5
2   1 John 4:1
3   Hebrews 3:12
4   Galatians 5:20; Titus 3:10
5   Acts 26:9
6   Psalm 78:22
7   Genesis 4:13
8   Jeremiah 5:3
9   Isaiah 42:25
10 Romans 2:5
11 Jeremiah 13:15
12 Psalm 10:13
13 Zephaniah 1:12
14 Matthew 4:7
15 Romans 3:8
16 Jeremiah 17:5
17 2 Timothy 3:4
18 Galatians 4:17; John 16:2; Romans 10:2; Luke 9:54-55
19 Revelation 3:16
20 Revelation 2:1
21 Ezekiel 14:5; Isaiah 1:4-5
22 Romans 10:13-14; Hosea 4:12; Acts 10:25-26; Revelation 19:10; Matthew 4:10; Colossians 2:18; Romans 1:25
23 Leviticus 20:6; 1 Samuel 28:7, 11 compared with 1 Chronicles 10:13-14
24 Acts 5:3
25 2 Corinthians 1:24; Matthew 23:9

despising God and his commands;[1] resisting and grieving of his Spirit,[2] discontent and impatience at his dispensations, charging him foolishly for the evils he inflicts on us;[3] and ascribing the praise of any good we either are, have or can do, to fortune,[4] idols,[5] ourselves,[6] or any other creature.[7]

Q. 106. *What are we specially taught by these words before me in the first commandment?*
A. These words before me or before my face, in the first commandment, teach us, that God, who sees all things, takes special notice of, and is much displeased with, the sin of having any other God: that so it may be an argument to dissuade from it, and to aggravate it as a most impudent provocation:[8] as also to persuade us to do as in his sight, whatever we do in his service.[9]

Q. 107. *Which is the second commandment?*
A. The second commandment is, You shall not make for yourself a carved image, or any likeness of anything that is in heaven above, or that is in the earth beneath, or that is in the water under the earth. You shall not bow down to them or serve them: for I the Lord your God am a jealous God, visiting the iniquity of the fathers upon the children to the third and fourth generation of those who hate me; and showing steadfast love to thousands of those who love me, and keep my commandments.[10]

Q. 108. *What are the duties required in the second commandment?*
A. The duties required in the second commandment are, the

---

1 Deuteronomy 32:15; 2 Samuel 12:9; Proverbs 13:13
2 Acts 7:51; Ephesians 4:30
3 Psalm 73:2-3, 13-15, 22; Job 1:22
4 1 Samuel 6:7-9
5 Daniel 5:23
6 Deuteronomy 8:17; Daniel 4:30
7 Habakkuk 1:16
8 Ezekiel 8:5-6; Psalm 44:20-21
9 1 Chronicles 28:9
10 Exodus 20:4-6

receiving, observing, and keeping pure and entire, all such religious worship and ordinances as God has instituted in his Word;[1] particularly prayer and thanksgiving in the name of Christ;[2] the reading, preaching, and hearing of the Word;[3] the administration and receiving of the sacraments;[4] church government and discipline;[5] the ministry and maintenance thereof;[6] religious fasting;[7] swearing by the name of God,[8] and vowing unto him:[9] as also the disapproving, detesting, opposing all false worship;[10] and, according to each one's place and calling, removing it, and all monuments of idolatry.[11]

Q. 109. What are the sins forbidden in the second commandment?
A. The sins forbidden in the second commandment are, all devising,[12] counselling,[13] commanding,[14] using,[15] and anywise approving, any religious worship not instituted by God himself;[16] tolerating a false religion; the making any representation of God, of all or of any of the three persons, either inwardly in our mind, or outwardly in any kind of image or likeness of any creature whatsoever;[17] all

---

1 Deuteronomy 32:46–47; Matthew 28:20; Acts 2:42; 1 Timothy 6:13–14
2 Philippians 4:6; Ephesians 5:20
3 Deuteronomy 17:18–19; Acts 15:21; 2 Timothy 4:2; James 1:21–22; Acts 10:33
4 Matthew 28:19; 1 Corinthians 11:23–30
5 Matthew 18:15–17; 16:19; 1 Corinthians 5; 12:28
6 Ephesians 4:11–12; 1 Timothy 5:17–18; 1 Corinthians 9:7–15
7 Joel 2:12–13; 1 Corinthians 7:5
8 Deuteronomy 6:13
9 Psalm 76:11
10 Acts 17:16–17; Psalm 16:4
11 Deuteronomy 7:5; Isaiah 30:22
12 Numbers 15:39
13 Deuteronomy 13:6–8
14 Hosea 5:11; Micah 6:16
15 1 Kings 11:33; 1 Kings 12:33
16 Deuteronomy 12:30–32
17 Deuteronomy 4:15–19; Acts 17:29; Romans 1:21–23, 25

worshipping of it,[1] or God in it or by it;[2] the making of any representation of feigned deities,[3] and all worship of them, or service belonging to them;[4] all superstitious devices,[5] corrupting the worship of God,[6] adding to it, or taking from it,[7] whether invented and taken up of ourselves,[8] or received by tradition from others,[9] though under the title of antiquity,[10] custom,[11] devotion,[12] good intent, or any other pretence whatsoever;[13] simony [selling something spiritual]; [14] sacrilege; [15] all neglect,[16] contempt,[17] hindering,[18] and opposing the worship and ordinances which God has appointed.[19]

Q. 110. *What are the reasons annexed to the second commandment, the more to enforce it?*
A. The reasons annexed to the second commandment, the more to enforce it, contained in these words, For I the Lord your God am a jealous God, visiting the iniquity of the fathers on the children to the third and fourth generation of those who hate me; and showing steadfast love to thousands of those

---

1 Daniel 3:18; Galatians 4:8
2 Exodus 32:5
3 Exodus 32:8
4 1 Kings 18:26, 28; Isaiah 65:11
5 Acts 17:22; Colossians 2:21–23
6 Malachi 1:7–8, 14
7 Deuteronomy 4:2
8 Psalm 106:39
9 Matthew 15:9
10 1 Peter 1:18
11 Jeremiah 44:17
12 Isaiah 65:3–5; Galatians 1:13–14
13 1 Samuel 13:11–12; 15:21
14 Acts 8:18
15 Romans 2:22; Malachi 3:8
16 Exodus 4:24–26
17 Matthew 22:5; Malachi 1:7, 13
18 Matthew 23:13
19 Acts 13:44–45; 1 Thessalonians 2:15–16

who love me, and keep my commandments;[1] are, besides God's sovereignty over us, and propriety in us,[2] his fervent zeal for his own worship,[3] and his revengeful indignation against all false worship, as being a spiritual whoredom;[4] accounting the breakers of this commandment such as hate him, and threatening to punish them unto divers [various] generations;[5] and esteeming the observers of it such as love him and keep his commandments, and promising mercy to them unto many generations.[6]

Q. 111. *Which is the third commandment?*
A. The third commandment is, You shall not take the name of the Lord your God in vain, for the Lord will not hold him guiltless who takes his name in vain.[7]

Q. 112. *What is required in the third commandment?*
A The third commandment requires, that the name of God, his titles, attributes,[8] ordinances,[9] the Word,[10] sacraments,[11] prayer,[12] oaths,[13] vows,[14] lots,[15] his work,[16] and whatsoever else there is whereby he makes himself known, be holily

---

1 Exodus 20:5-6
2 Psalm 45:11; Revelation 15:3-4
3 Exodus 34:13-14
4 1 Corinthians 10:20-22; Deuteronomy 32:16-20
5 Hosea 2:2-4
6 Deuteronomy 5:29
7 Exodus 20:7
8 Matthew 11:9; Deuteronomy 28:58; Psalm 29:2; 68:4; Revelation 15:3-4
9 Malachi 1:14; Ecclesiastes 5:1
10 Psalm 138:2
11 1 Corinthians 11:24-25, 28-29
12 1 Timothy 2:8
13 Jeremiah 4:2
14 Ecclesiastes 5:2, 4-6
15 Acts 1:24, 26
16 Job 36:24

and reverently used in thought,[1] meditation,[2] word,[3] and writing;[4] by a holy profession,[5] and answerable conversation,[6] to the glory of God,[7] and the good of ourselves,[8] and others.[9]

Q. 113. *What are the sins forbidden in the third commandment?*
A. The sins forbidden in the third commandment are, the not using of God's name as is required;[10] and the abuse of it in an ignorant,[11] vain,[12] irreverent, profane,[13] superstitious[14] or wicked mentioning or otherwise using his titles, attributes,[15] ordinances,[16] or works,[17] by blasphemy,[18] perjury;[19] all sinful cursings,[20] oaths,[21] vows,[22] and lots;[23] violating of our oaths and vows, if lawful;[24] and fulfilling them, if of things unlawful;[25] murmuring and quarrelling at,[26] curious prying

---

1 Malachi 3:16
2 Psalm 8:1, 3-4, 9
3 Colossians 3:17; Psalm 105:2, 5
4 Psalm 102:18
5 1 Peter 3:15; Micah 4:5
6 Philippians 1:27
7 1 Corinthians 10:31
8 Jeremiah 32:39
9 1 Peter 2:12
10 Malachi 2:2
11 Acts 17:23
12 Proverbs 30:9
13 Malachi 1:6-7, 12; 3:14
14 1 Samuel 4:3-5; Jeremiah 7:4, 9-10, 14, 31; Colossians 2:20-22
15 2 Kings 18:30, 35; Exodus 5:2; Psalm 139:20
16 Psalm 50:16-17
17 Isaiah 5:12
18 2 Kings 19:22; Leviticus 24:11
19 Zechariah 5:4; 8:17
20 1 Samuel 17:43; 2 Samuel 16:5
21 Jeremiah 5:7; 23:10
22 Deuteronomy 23:18; Acts 23:12, 14
23 Esther 3:7; 9:24; Psalm 22:18
24 Psalm 24:4; Ezekiel 17:16, 18-19
25 Mark 6:26; 1 Samuel 25:22, 32-34
26 Romans 9:14, 19-20

into,[1] and misapplying of God's decrees[2] and providences;[3] misinterpreting,[4] misapplying,[5] or any way perverting the Word, or any part of it;[6] to profane jests,[7] curious or unprofitable questions, vain janglings [discussion], or the maintaining of false doctrines;[8] abusing it, the creatures, or anything contained under the name of God, to charms [witchcraft],[9] or sinful lusts and practices;[10] the maligning,[11] scorning,[12] reviling,[13] or in any way opposing God's truth, grace, and ways;[14] making profession of religion in hypocrisy or for sinister ends;[15] being ashamed of it,[16] or a shame to it, by unconformable,[17] unwise,[18] unfruitful,[19] and offensive walking,[20] or backsliding from it.[21]

Q. 114. *What reasons are annexed to the third commandment?*
A. The reasons annexed to the third commandment, in these words, The Lord your God, and, For the Lord will not hold him guiltless who takes his name in vain,[22] are, because he

---

1 Deuteronomy 29:29
2 Romans 3:5, 7; 6:1
3 Ecclesiastes 8:11; 9:3; Psalm 39
4 Matthew 5:21-22
5 Ezekiel 13:22
6 2 Peter 3:16; Matthew 22:24-31; 25:28-30
7 Isaiah 22:13; Jeremiah 23:34, 36, 38
8 1 Timothy 1:4, 6-7; 6:4-5, 20; 2 Timothy 2:14; Titus 3:9
9 Deuteronomy 18:10-14; Acts 19:13
10 2 Timothy 4:3-4; Romans 13:13-14; 1 Kings 21:9-10; Jude 4
11 Acts 13:45; 1 John 3:12
12 Psalm 1:1; 2 Peter 3:3
13 1 Peter 4:4
14 Acts 13:45-46, 50; Acts 4:18; Acts 19:9; 1 Thessalonians 2:16; Hebrews 10:29
15 2 Timothy 3:5; Matthew 23:14; 6:1-2, 5, 16
16 Mark 8:38
17 Psalm 73:14-15
18 1 Corinthians 6:5-6; Ephesians 5:15-17
19 Isaiah 5:4; 2 Peter 1:8-9
20 Romans 2:23-24
21 Galatians 3:1, 3; Hebrews 6:6
22 Exodus 20:7

is the Lord and our God, therefore his name is not to be profaned, or any way abused by us;[1] especially because he will be so far from acquitting and sparing the transgressors of this commandment, as that he will not suffer them to escape his righteous judgment;[2] albeit many such escape the censures and punishments of men.[3]

Q. 115. *Which is the fourth commandment?*
A. The fourth commandment is, Remember the Sabbath day, to keep it holy. Six days you shall labour, and do all your work; but the seventh day is a Sabbath to the Lord your God: on it you shall not do any work, you, nor your son, nor your daughter, your male-servant, nor your female servant, nor your cattle, nor the sojourner who is within your gates. For in six days the Lord made heaven and earth, the sea, and all that in them is, and rested on the seventh day. Therefore the Lord blessed the Sabbath-day and made it holy.[4]

Q. 116. *What is required in the fourth commandment?*
A. The fourth commandment requires of all men the sanctifying or keeping holy to God such set times as he has appointed in his Word, expressly one whole day in seven; which was the seventh from the beginning of the world to the resurrection of Christ, and the first day of the week ever since, and so to continue to the end of the world; which is the Christian Sabbath,[5] and in the New Testament called The Lord's Day.[6]

Q. 117. *How is the Sabbath or the Lord's Day to be sanctified?*
A. The Sabbath or Lord's Day is to be sanctified by a holy resting all the day,[7] not only from such works as are at all times sinful,

---

1 Leviticus 19:12
2 Ezekiel 36:21–23; Deuteronomy 28:58–59; Zechariah 5:2–4
3 1 Samuel 2:12, 17, 22, 24 compared with 1 Samuel 3:13
4 Exodus 20:8–11
5 Deuteronomy 5:12–14; Genesis 2:2–3; 1 Corinthians 16:1–2; Matthew 5:17–18; Isaiah 56:2, 4, 6–7
6 Revelation 1:10
7 Exodus 20:8, 10

but even from such worldly employments and recreations as are on other days lawful;[1] and making it our delight to spend the whole time (except so much of it as is to be taken up in works of necessity and mercy)[2] in the public and private exercises of God's worship:[3] and, to that end, we are to prepare our hearts, and with such foresight, diligence, and moderation, to dispose and seasonably dispatch our worldly business, that we may be the more free and fit for the duties of that day.[4]

Q. 118. *Why is the charge of keeping the Sabbath more specially directed to governors of families, and other superiors?*
A. The charge of keeping the Sabbath is more specially directed to governors of families, and other superiors, because they are bound not only to keep it themselves, but to see that it be observed by all those that are under their charge; and because they are prone often to hinder them by employments of their own.[5]

Q. 119. *What are the sins forbidden in the fourth commandment?*
A. The sins forbidden in the fourth commandment are, all omissions of the duties required,[6] all careless, negligent, and unprofitable performing of them, and being weary of them;[7] all profaning the day by idleness, and doing that which is in

---

1 Exodus 16:25-28; Nehemiah 13:15-22; Jeremiah 17:21-22
2 Matthew 12:1-13
3 Isaiah 58:13; Luke 4:16; Acts 20:7; 1 Corinthians 16:1-2; Psalm 92 [title]; Isaiah 66:23; Leviticus 23:3
4 Exodus 20:8; Luke 23:54, 56; Exodus 16:22, 25-26, 29; Nehemiah 13:19
5 Exodus 20:10; Joshua 24:15; Nehemiah 13:15, 17; Jeremiah 17:20-22; Exodus 23:12
6 Ezekiel 22:26
7 Acts 20:7, 9; Ezekiel 33:30-32; Amos 8:5; Malachi 1:13

itself sinful;[1] and by all needless works, words, and thoughts, about our worldly employments and recreations.[2]

Q. 120. *What are the reasons annexed to the fourth commandment, the more to enforce it?*

A. The reasons annexed to the fourth commandment, the more to enforce it, are taken from the equity of it, God allowing us six days of seven for our own affairs, and reserving but one for himself in these words, Six days you shall labour, and do all your work:[3] from God's challenging a special propriety in that day, The seventh day is the Sabbath of the Lord your God:[4] from the example of God, who in six days made heaven and earth, the sea, and all that in them is, and rested the seventh day: and from that blessing which God put upon that day, not only in sanctifying it to be a day for his service, but in ordaining it to be a means of blessing to us in our sanctifying it; Therefore the Lord blessed the Sabbath day, and made it holy.[5]

Q. 121. *Why is the word Remember set in the beginning of the fourth commandment?*

A. The word Remember is set in the beginning of the fourth commandment,[6] partly, because of the great benefit of remembering it, we being thereby helped in our preparation to keep it,[7] and, in keeping it, better to keep all the rest of the commandments,[8] and to continue a thankful remembrance of the two great benefits of creation and redemption, which contain a short abridgment of religion;[9] and partly, because

---

1 Ezekiel 23:38
2 Jeremiah 17:24, 27; Isaiah 58:13
3 Exodus 20:9
4 Exodus 20:10
5 Exodus 20:11
6 Exodus 20:8
7 Exodus 16:23; Luke 23:54-56 compared with Mark 15:42; Nehemiah 13:19
8 Psalm 92 [title] compared with verses 13-14; Ezekiel 20:12, 19-20
9 Genesis 2:2-3; Psalm 118:22, 24 compared with Acts 4:10-11; Revelation 1:10

we are very ready to forget it,[1] for that there is less light of nature for it,[2] and yet it restrains our natural liberty in things at other times lawful;[3] that it comes but once in seven days, and many worldly businesses come between, and too often take off our minds from thinking of it, either to prepare for it, or to sanctify it;[4] and that Satan with his instruments labours much to blot out the glory, and even the memory of it, to bring in all irreligion and impiety.[5]

Q. 122. *What is the sum of the six commandments which contain our duty to man?*
A. The sum of the six commandments which contain our duty to man, is, to love our neighbour as ourselves,[6] and to do to others what we would have them to do to us.[7]

Q. 123. *Which is the fifth commandment?*
A. The fifth commandment is, Honour your father and your mother: that your days may be long in the land which the Lord your God is giving you.[8]

Q. 124. *Who are meant by father and mother in the fifth commandment?*
A. By father and mother, in the fifth commandment, are meant, not only natural parents,[9] but all superiors in age[10] and gifts;[11] and especially such as, by God's ordinance, are over

---

1 Ezekiel 22:26
2 Nehemiah 9:14
3 Exodus 34:21
4 Deuteronomy 5:14-15; Amos 8:5
5 Lamentations 1:7; Jeremiah 17:21-23; Nehemiah 13:15-23
6 Matthew 22:39
7 Matthew 7:12
8 Exodus 20:12
9 Proverbs 23:22, 25; Ephesians 6:1-2
10 1 Timothy 5:1-2
11 Genesis 4:20-22; 45:8

us in place of authority, whether in family,[1] church,[2] or commonwealth.[3]

Q. 125. *Why are superiors styled father and mother?*
A. Superiors are styled father and mother, both to teach them in all duties toward their inferiors, like natural parents, to express love and tenderness to them, according to their several relations;[4] and to work inferiors to a greater willingness and cheerfulness in performing their duties to their superiors, as to their parents.[5]

Q. 126. *What is the general scope of the fifth commandment?*
A. The general scope of the fifth commandment is, the performance of those duties which we mutually owe in our several relations, as inferiors [those under authority], superiors [those in authority], or equals.[6]

Q. 127. *What is the honour that inferiors owe to their superiors?*
A. The honour which inferiors owe to their superiors is, all due reverence in heart,[7] word,[8] and behaviour;[9] prayer and thanksgiving for them;[10] imitation of their virtues and graces;[11] willing obedience to their lawful commands and counsels;[12] due submission to their corrections;[13] fidelity to,[14]

---

1 2 Kings 5:13
2 2 Kings 2:12; 13:14; Galatians 4:19
3 Isaiah 49:23
4 Ephesians 6:4; 2 Corinthians 12:14; 1 Thessalonians 2:7-8, 11; Numbers 11:11-12
5 1 Corinthians 4:14-16; 2 Kings 5:13
6 Ephesians 5:21; 1 Peter 2:17; Romans 12:10
7 Malachi 1:6; Leviticus 19:3
8 Proverbs 31:28; 1 Peter 3:6
9 Leviticus 19:32; 1 Kings 2:19
10 1 Timothy 2:1-2
11 Hebrews 13:7; Philippians 3:17
12 Ephesians 6:1-2, 6-7; 1 Peter 2:13-14; Romans 13:1-5; Hebrews 13:17; Proverbs 4:3-4; 23:22; Exodus 18:19, 24
13 Hebrews 12:9; 1 Peter 2:18-20
14 Titus 2:9-10

defence,[1] and maintenance of their persons and authority, according to their several ranks, and the nature of their places;[2] bearing with their infirmities, and covering them in love,[3] that so they may be an honour to them and to their government.[4]

Q. 128. *What are the sins of inferiors against their superiors?*

A. The sins of inferiors against their superiors are, all neglect of the duties required toward them;[5] envying at,[6] contempt of,[7] and rebellion[8] against, their persons[9] and places,[10] in their lawful counsels,[11] commands, and corrections;[12] cursing, mocking[13] and all such refractory and scandalous carriage, as proves a shame and dishonour to them and their government.[14]

Q. 129. *What is required of superiors towards their inferiors?*

A. It is required of superiors, according to that power they receive from God, and that relation wherein they stand, to love,[15] pray for,[16] and bless their inferiors;[17] to instruct,[18]

---

1 1 Samuel 26:15-16; 2 Samuel 18:3; Esther 6:2
2 Matthew 22:21; Romans 13:6-7; 1 Timothy 5:17-18; Galatians 6:6; Genesis 45:11; Genesis 47:12
3 1 Peter 2:18; Proverbs 23:22; Genesis 9:23
4 Psalm 127:3-5; Proverbs 31:23
5 Matthew 15:4-6
6 Numbers 11:28-29
7 1 Samuel 8:7; Isaiah 3:5
8 2 Samuel 15:1-12
9 Exodus 24:15
10 1 Samuel 10:27
11 1 Samuel 2:25
12 Deuteronomy 21:18-21
13 Proverbs 30:11, 17
14 Proverbs 19:26
15 Colossians 3:19; Titus 2:4
16 1 Samuel 12:23; Job 1:5
17 1 Kings 8:55-56; Hebrews 7:7; Genesis 49:28
18 Deuteronomy 6:6-7

counsel, and admonish them;[1] countenancing,[2] commending,[3] and rewarding such as do well;[4] and discountenancing,[5] reproving, and chastising such as do ill;[6] protecting,[7] and providing for them all things necessary for soul[8] and body:[9] and by grave, wise, holy, and exemplary carriage, to procure [obtain] glory to God,[10] honour to themselves,[11] and so to preserve that authority which God has put upon them.[12]

Q. 130. *What are the sins of superiors?*
A. The sins of superiors are, besides the neglect of the duties required of them,[13] and inordinate seeking of themselves,[14] their own glory,[15] ease, profit, or pleasure;[16] commanding things unlawful,[17] or not in the power of inferiors to perform;[18] counselling,[19] encouraging,[20] or favouring them in that which is evil;[21] dissuading, discouraging, or discountenancing them in that which is good;[22] correcting them unduly;[23]

---

1 Ephesians 6:4
2 1 Peter 3:7
3 1 Peter 2:14; Romans 13:3
4 Esther 6:3
5 Romans 13:3-4
6 Proverbs 29:15; 1 Peter 2:14
7 Job 29:12-17; Isaiah 1:10-17
8 Ephesians 6:4
9 1 Timothy 5:8
10 1 Timothy 4:12; Titus 2:3-5
11 1 Kings 3:28
12 Titus 2:15
13 Ezekiel 34:2-4
14 Philippians 2:21
15 John 5:44; 7:18
16 Isaiah 56:10-11; Deuteronomy 17:17
17 Daniel 3:4-6; Acts 4:17-18
18 Exodus 5:10-18; Matthew 23:2, 4
19 Matthew 14:8 compared with Mark 6:24
20 2 Samuel 13:28
21 1 Samuel 3:13
22 John 7:46-49; Colossians 3:21; Exodus 5:17
23 1 Peter 2:18-20; Hebrews 12:10; Deuteronomy 25:3

careless exposing, or leaving them to wrong, temptation, and danger;[1] provoking them to wrath;[2] or any way dishonouring themselves, or lessening their authority, by an unjust, indiscreet, rigorous, or remiss behaviour.[3]

Q. 131. *What are the duties of equals?*
A. The duties of equals are, to regard the dignity and worth of each other,[4] in giving honour to go one before another;[5] and to rejoice in each others' gifts and advancement, as their own.[6]

Q. 132. *What are the sins of equals?*
A. The sins of equals are, besides the neglect of the duties required,[7] the undervaluing of the worth,[8] envying the gifts,[9] grieving at the advancement of prosperity one of another;[10] and usurping pre-eminence one over another.[11]

Q. 133. *What is the reason annexed to the fifth commandment, the more to enforce it?*
A. The reason annexed to the fifth commandment, in these words, That your days may be long in the land which the Lord your God is giving you,[12] is an express promise of long life and

---

1 Genesis 38:11, 26; Acts 18:17
2 Ephesians 6:4
3 Genesis 9:21; 1 Kings 12:13-16; 1:6; 1 Samuel 2:29-31
4 1 Peter 2:17
5 Romans 12:10
6 Romans 12:15-16; Philippians 2:3-4
7 Romans 13:8
8 2 Timothy 3:3
9 Acts 7:9; Galatians 5:26
10 Numbers 12:2; Esther 6:12-13
11 3 John 9; Luke 22:24
12 Exodus 20:12

prosperity, as far as it shall serve for God's glory and their own good, to all such as keep this commandment.[1]

Q. 134. *Which is the sixth commandment?*
A. The sixth commandment is, You shall not kill.[2]

Q. 135. *What are the duties required in the sixth commandment?*
A. The duties required in the sixth commandment are all careful studies, and lawful endeavours, to preserve the life of ourselves[3] and others[4] by resisting all thoughts and purposes,[5] subduing all passions,[6] and avoiding all occasions,[7] temptations,[8] and practices, which tend to the unjust taking away the life of any;[9] by just defence thereof against violence,[10] patient bearing of the hand of God,[11] quietness of mind,[12] cheerfulness of spirit;[13] a sober use of meat,[14] drink,[15] physic [medicine],[16] sleep,[17] labour,[18] and recreations;[19] by charitable thoughts,[20] love,[21] compassion,[22]

---

1 Deuteronomy 5:16; 1 Kings 8:25; Ephesians 6:2-3
2 Exodus 20:13
3 Ephesians 5:28-29
4 1 Kings 18:4
5 Jeremiah 26:15-16; Acts 23:12, 16-17, 21, 27
6 Ephesians 4:26-27
7 2 Samuel 2:22; Deuteronomy 22:8
8 Matthew 4:6-7; Proverbs 1:10-11, 15-16
9 1 Samuel 24:12; 26:9-11; Genesis 37:21-22
10 Psalm 82:4; Proverbs 24:11-12
11 James 5:7-11; Hebrews 12:9
12 1 Thessalonians 4:11; 1 Peter 3:3-4; Psalm 37:8-11
13 Proverbs 17:22
14 Proverbs 25:16, 27
15 1 Timothy 5:23
16 Isaiah 38:21
17 Psalm 127:2
18 Ecclesiastes 5:12; 2 Thessalonians 3:10, 12; Proverbs 16:26
19 Ecclesiastes 3:4, 11
20 1 Samuel 19:4-5; 22:13-14
21 Romans 13:10
22 Luke 10:33-34

meekness, gentleness, kindness;[1] peaceable,[2] mild and courteous speeches and behaviour;[3] forbearance, readiness to be reconciled, patient bearing and forgiving of injuries, and requiting good for evil;[4] comforting and succouring the distressed and protecting and defending the innocent.[5]

Q. 136. *What are the sins forbidden in the sixth commandment?*
A. The sins forbidden in the sixth commandment are, all taking away the life of ourselves,[6] or of others,[7] except in case of public justice,[8] lawful war,[9] or necessary defence;[10] the neglecting or withdrawing the lawful and necessary means of preservation of life;[11] sinful anger,[12] hatred,[13] envy,[14] desire of revenge;[15] all excessive passions,[16] distracting cares;[17] immoderate use of meat, drink,[18] labour,[19] and recreations;[20] provoking words,[21] oppression,[22] quarrelling,[23] striking,

---

1 Colossians 3:12-13
2 James 3:17
3 1 Peter 3:8-11; Proverbs 15:1; Judges 8:1-3
4 Matthew 5:24; Ephesians 5:2, 32; Romans 12:17, 20-21
5 1 Thessalonians 5:14; Job 31:19-20; Matthew 25:35-36; Proverbs 31:8-9
6 Acts 16:28
7 Genesis 9:6
8 Numbers 35:31, 33
9 Jeremiah 48:10; Deuteronomy 20
10 Exodus 22:2-3
11 Matthew 25:42-43; James 2:15-16; Ecclesiastes 6:1-2
12 Matthew 5:22
13 1 John 3:15; Leviticus 19:17
14 Proverbs 14:30
15 Romans 12:19
16 Ephesians 4:31
17 Matthew 6:31, 34
18 Luke 21:34; Romans 13:13
19 Ecclesiastes 12:12; 2:22-23
20 Isaiah 5:12
21 Proverbs 15:1; 12:18
22 Ezekiel 18:18; Exodus 1:14
23 Galatians 5:15; Proverbs 23:29

wounding,[1] and whatsoever else tends to the destruction of the life of any.[2]

Q. 137. *Which is the seventh commandment?*
A. The seventh commandment is, You shall not commit adultery.[3]

Q. 138. *What are the duties required in the seventh commandment?*
A. The duties required in the seventh commandment are, chastity in body, mind, affections,[4] words,[5] and behaviour;[6] and the preservation of it in ourselves and others;[7] watchfulness over the eyes and all the senses;[8] temperance,[9] keeping of chaste company,[10] modesty in apparel;[11] marriage by those that have not the gift of continence,[12] conjugal love,[13] and cohabitation;[14] diligent labour in our callings;[15] shunning all occasions of uncleanness, and resisting temptations thereunto.[16]

Q. 139. *What are the sins forbidden in the seventh commandment?*
A. The sins forbidden in the seventh commandment, besides the neglect of the duties required,[17] are, adultery, fornication,[18]

---

1 Numbers 35:16-18, 21
2 Exodus 21:18-36
3 Exodus 20:14
4 1 Thessalonians 4:4; Job 31:1; 1 Corinthians 7:34
5 Colossians 4:6
6 1 Peter 2:3
7 1 Corinthians 7:2, 35-36
8 Job 31:1
9 Acts 24:24-25
10 Proverbs 2:16-20
11 1 Timothy 2:9
12 1 Corinthians 7:2, 9
13 Proverbs 5:19-20
14 1 Peter 3:7
15 Proverbs 31:11, 27-28
16 Proverbs 5:8; Genesis 39:8-10
17 Proverbs 5:7
18 Hebrews 13:4; Galatians 5:19

rape, incest,[1] sodomy, and all unnatural lusts;[2] all unclean imaginations, thoughts, purposes, and affections;[3] all corrupt or filthy communications, or listening thereunto;[4] wanton looks,[5] impudent or light behaviour, immodest apparel;[6] prohibiting of lawful,[7] and dispensing with unlawful marriages;[8] allowing, tolerating, keeping of stews [brothels], and resorting to them;[9] entangling vows of single life,[10] undue delay of marriage,[11] having more wives or husbands than one at the same time;[12] unjust divorce,[13] or desertion;[14] idleness, gluttony, drunkenness,[15] unchaste company;[16] lascivious songs, books, pictures, dancing, stage plays;[17] and all other provocations to, or acts of uncleanness, either in ourselves or others.[18]

Q. 140. *Which is the eighth commandment?*
A. The eighth commandment is, You shall not steal.[19]

Q. 141. *What are the duties required in the eighth commandment?*
A. The duties required in the eighth commandment are, truth,

---

[1] 2 Samuel 13:14; 1 Corinthians 5:1
[2] Romans 1:24, 26–27; Leviticus 20:15–16
[3] Matthew 5:28; 15:19; Colossians 3:5
[4] Ephesians 5:3–4; Proverbs 7:5, 21–22
[5] Isaiah 3:16; 2 Peter 2:14
[6] Proverbs 7:10, 13
[7] 1 Timothy 4:3
[8] Leviticus 18:1–21; Mark 6:18; Malachi 2:11–12
[9] 1 Kings 15:12; 2 Kings 23:7; Deuteronomy 23:17–18; Leviticus 19:29; Jeremiah 5:7; Proverbs 7:24–27
[10] Matthew 19:10–11
[11] 1 Corinthians 7:7–9; Genesis 38:26
[12] Malachi 2:14–15; Matthew 19:5
[13] Malachi 2:16; Matthew 5:32
[14] 1 Corinthians 7:12–13
[15] Ezekiel 16:49; Proverbs 23:30–33
[16] Genesis 39:10; Proverbs 5:8
[17] Ephesians 5:4; Ezekiel 23:14–16; Isaiah 23:15–17; 3:16; Mark 6:22; Romans 13:13; 1 Peter 4:3
[18] 2 Kings 9:30 compared with Jeremiah 4:30 and with Ezekiel 23:40
[19] Exodus 20:15

faithfulness, and justice in contracts and commerce between man and man;[1] rendering to everyone his due;[2] restitution of goods unlawfully detained from the right owners thereof;[3] giving and lending freely, according to our abilities, and the necessities of others;[4] moderation of our judgments, wills, and affections concerning worldly goods;[5] a provident care and study to get,[6] keep, use, and dispose these things which are necessary and convenient for the sustentation of our nature, and suitable to our condition;[7] a lawful calling,[8] and diligence in it;[9] frugality;[10] avoiding unnecessary lawsuits,[11] and suretyship, or other like engagements;[12] and an endeavour, by all just and lawful means, to procure [obtain], preserve, and further the wealth and outward estate of others, as well as our own.[13]

Q. 142. *What are the sins forbidden in the eighth commandment?*
A. The sins forbidden in the eighth commandment, besides the neglect of the duties required,[14] are, theft,[15] robbery,[16] man-stealing [kidnapping],[17] and receiving any thing that is

---

1 Psalm 15:2, 4; Zechariah 7:4, 10; 8:16-17
2 Romans 13:7
3 Leviticus 6:2-5 compared with Luke 19:8
4 Luke 6:30, 38; 1 John 3:17; Ephesians 4:28; Galatians 6:10
5 1 Timothy 6:6-9; Galatians 6:14
6 1 Timothy 5:8
7 Proverbs 27:23-27; Ecclesiastes 2:2; 3:12-13; 1 Timothy 6:17-18; Isaiah 38:1; Matthew 11:8
8 1 Corinthians 7:20; Genesis 2:15; 3:19
9 Ephesians 4:28; Proverbs 10:4
10 John 6:12; Proverbs 21:20
11 1 Corinthians 6:1-9
12 Proverbs 6:1-6; 11:15
13 Leviticus 25:35; Deuteronomy 22:1-4; Exodus 23:4-5; Genesis 47:14, 20; Philippians 2:4; Matthew 22:39
14 James 2:15-16; 1 John 3:17
15 Ephesians 4:28
16 Psalm 62:10
17 1 Timothy 1:10

stolen;[1] fraudulent dealing,[2] false weights and measures,[3] removing landmarks,[4] injustice and unfaithfulness in contracts between man and man,[5] or in matters of trust;[6] oppression,[7] extortion,[8] usury [unreasonable interest],[9] bribery,[10] vexatious lawsuits,[11] unjust enclosures and depopulations;[12] engrossing commodities to enhance the price;[13] unlawful callings,[14] and all other unjust or sinful ways of taking or withholding from our neighbour what belongs to him, or of enriching ourselves;[15] covetousness;[16] inordinate prizing and affecting worldly goods;[17] distrustful and distracting cares and studies in getting, keeping, and using them;[18] envying at the prosperity of others;[19] as likewise idleness,[20] prodigality, wasteful gaming; and all other ways whereby we do unduly prejudice our own outward estate,[21]

---

1 Proverbs 29:24; Psalm 50:18
2 1 Thessalonians 4:6
3 Proverbs 11:1; 20:10
4 Deuteronomy 19:14; Proverbs 23:10
5 Amos 8:5; Psalm 37:21
6 Luke 16:10–12
7 Ezekiel 22:29; Leviticus 25:17
8 Matthew 23:25; Ezekiel 22:12
9 Psalm 15:5
10 Job 15:34
11 1 Corinthians 6:6–8; Proverbs 3:29–30
12 Isaiah 5:8; Micah 2:2
13 Proverbs 11:26
14 Acts 19:19, 24–25
15 Job 20:19; James 5:4; Proverbs 21:6
16 Luke 12:15
17 1 Timothy 6:5; Colossians 3:2; Proverbs 23:5; Psalm 62:10
18 Matthew 6:25, 31, 34; Ecclesiastes 5:12
19 Psalm 73:3; 37:1, 7
20 2 Thessalonians 3:11; Proverbs 18:9
21 Proverbs 21:7; 23:20–21; 28:19

and defrauding ourselves of the due use and comfort of that estate which God has given us.[1]

Q. 143. *Which is the ninth commandment?*
A. The ninth commandment is, You shall not bear false witness against your neighbour.[2]

Q. 144. *What are the duties required in the ninth commandment?*
A. The duties required in the ninth commandment are, the preserving and promoting of truth between man and man,[3] and the good name of our neighbour, as well as our own;[4] appearing and standing for the truth;[5] and from the heart,[6] sincerely,[7] freely,[8] clearly,[9] and fully,[10] speaking the truth, and only the truth, in matters of judgment and justice,[11] and in all other things whatsoever;[12] a charitable esteem of our neighbours;[13] loving, desiring, and rejoicing in their good name;[14] sorrowing for,[15] and covering of their infirmities;[16] freely acknowledging of their gifts and graces;[17] defending their innocence;[18] a ready receiving of a good report,[19] and unwillingness to admit of an evil report,[20] concerning them;

---

[1] Ecclesiastes 4:8; 6:2; 1 Timothy 5:8
[2] Exodus 20:16
[3] Zechariah 8:16
[4] 3 John 12
[5] Proverbs 31:8-9
[6] Psalm 15:2
[7] 2 Chronicles 19:9
[8] 1 Samuel 19:4-5
[9] Joshua 7:19
[10] 2 Samuel 14:18-20
[11] Leviticus 19:15; Proverbs 14:5, 25
[12] 2 Corinthians 1:17-18; Ephesians 4:25
[13] Hebrews 6:9; 1 Corinthians 13:7
[14] Romans 1:8; 2 John 4; 3 John 3-4
[15] 2 Corinthians 2:4; 12:21
[16] Proverbs 17:9; 1 Peter 4:8
[17] 1 Corinthians 1:4-5, 7; 2 Timothy 1:4-5
[18] 1 Samuel 22:14
[19] 1 Corinthians 13:6-7
[20] Psalm 15:3

discouraging tale-bearers,[1] flatterers,[2] and slanderers;[3] love and care of our own good name, and defending it when need requires;[4] keeping of lawful promises;[5] studying and practicing of whatsoever things are true, honest, lovely, and of good report.[6]

Q. 145. *What are the sins forbidden in the ninth commandment?*
A. The sins forbidden in the ninth commandment are, all prejudicing the truth, and the good name of our neighbours, as well as our own,[7] especially in public judicature;[8] giving false evidence,[9] suborning [bribing] false witnesses,[10] wittingly appearing and pleading for an evil cause, outfacing and overbearing the truth;[11] passing unjust sentence,[12] calling evil good, and good evil; rewarding the wicked according to the work of the righteous, and the righteous according to the work of the wicked;[13] forgery,[14] concealing the truth, undue silence in a just cause,[15] and holding our peace when iniquity calls for either a reproof from ourselves,[16] or complaint to others;[17] speaking the truth unseasonably,[18] or maliciously to a wrong end,[19] or perverting it to a wrong

---

1 Proverbs 25:23
2 Proverbs 26:24-25
3 Psalm 101:5
4 Proverbs 22:1; John 8:49
5 Psalm 15:4
6 Philippians 4:8
7 1 Samuel 17:28; 2 Samuel 16:3; 1:9-10, 15-16
8 Leviticus 19:19; Habakkuk 1:4
9 Proverbs 19:5; Proverbs 6:16, 19
10 Acts 6:13
11 Jeremiah 9:3, 5; Acts 24:2, 5; Psalm 12:3-4; Psalm 52:1-4
12 Proverbs 17:15; 1 Kings 21:9-14
13 Isaiah 5:23
14 Psalm 119:69; Luke 19:8; 16:5-7
15 Leviticus 5:1; Deuteronomy 13:8; Acts 5:3, 8-9; 2 Timothy 4:6
16 1 Kings 1:6; Leviticus 19:17
17 Isaiah 59:4
18 Proverbs 29:11
19 1 Samuel 22:9-10 compared with Psalm 52 [title], verses 1-5

meaning,[1] or in doubtful and equivocal expressions, to the prejudice of truth or justice;[2] speaking untruth,[3] lying,[4] slandering,[5] backbiting,[6] detracting,[7] tale bearing,[8] whispering,[9] scoffing,[10] reviling,[11] rash,[12] harsh,[13] and partial censuring;[14] misconstruing intentions, words, and actions;[15] flattering,[16] vain-glorious boasting;[17] thinking or speaking too highly or too meanly of ourselves or others;[18] denying the gifts and graces of God;[19] aggravating smaller faults;[20] hiding, excusing, or extenuating of sins, when called to a free confession;[21] unnecessary discovering of infirmities;[22] raising false rumours,[23] receiving and countenancing evil reports,[24] and stopping our ears against just defence;[25] evil suspicion;[26] envying or grieving at the deserved credit of

---

1 Psalm 56:5; John 2:19 compared with Matthew 26:60-61
2 Genesis 3:5, 26:7, 9
3 Isaiah 59:13
4 Leviticus 19:11; Colossians 3:9
5 Psalm 50:20
6 Psalm 15:3
7 James 4:11; Jeremiah 38:4
8 Leviticus 19:16
9 Romans 1:29-30
10 Genesis 21:9 compared with Galatians 4:29
11 1 Corinthians 6:10
12 Matthew 7:1
13 Acts 28:4
14 Genesis 38:24; Romans 2:1
15 Nehemiah 6:6-8; Romans 3:8; Psalm 69:10; 1 Samuel 1:13-15; 2 Samuel 10:3
16 Psalm 12:2-3
17 2 Timothy 3:2
18 Luke 18:9, 11; Romans 12:16; 1 Corinthians 4:6; Acts 12:22; Exodus 4:10-14
19 Job 27:5-6; Job 4:6
20 Matthew 7:3-5
21 Proverbs 28:13; 30:20; Genesis 3:12-13; Jeremiah 2:35; 2 Kings 5:25; Genesis 4:9
22 Genesis 9:22; Proverbs 25:9-10
23 Exodus 23:1
24 Proverbs 29:12
25 Acts 7:56-57; Job 31:13-14
26 1 Corinthians 13:5; 1 Timothy 6:4

any,[1] endeavouring or desiring to impair it,[2] rejoicing in their disgrace and infamy;[3] scornful contempt,[4] fond admiration;[5] breach of lawful promises;[6] neglecting such things as are of good report,[7] and practicing, or not avoiding ourselves, or not hindering what we can in others, such things as procure [obtain] an ill name.[8]

Q. 146. *Which is the tenth commandment?*
A. The tenth commandment is, You shall not covet your neighbour's house, you shall not covet your neighbour's wife, nor his male servant, nor his female servant, nor his ox, nor his donkey, nor anything that is your neighbour's.[9]

Q. 147. *What are the duties required in the tenth commandment?*
A. The duties required in the tenth commandment are, such a full contentment with our own condition,[10] and such a charitable frame of the whole soul toward our neighbour, as that all our inward motions and affections touching him, tend unto, and further all that good which is his.[11]

Q. 148. *What are the sins forbidden in the tenth commandment?*
A. The sins forbidden in the tenth commandment are discontentment with our own estate;[12] envying[13] and grieving

---

1 Numbers 11:29; Matthew 21:15
2 Ezra 4:12-13
3 Jeremiah 48:27
4 Psalm 35:15-16, 21; Matthew 27:28-29
5 Jude 16; Acts 12:22
6 Romans 1:31; 2 Timothy 3:3
7 1 Samuel 2:24
8 2 Samuel 13:12-13; Proverbs 5:8-9; 6:33
9 Exodus 20:17
10 Hebrews 13:5; 1 Timothy 6:6
11 Job 31:29; Romans 12:15; Psalm 122:7-9; 1 Timothy 1:5; Esther 10:3; 1 Corinthians 13:4-7
12 1 Kings 21:4; Esther 5:13; 1 Corinthians 10:10
13 Galatians 5:26; James 3:14, 16

at the good of our neighbour,[1] together with all inordinate motions and affections to anything that is his.[2]

Q. 149. *Is any man able perfectly to keep the commandments of God?*

A. No man is able, either of himself,[3] or by any grace received in this life, perfectly to keep the commandments of God;[4] but does daily break them in thought,[5] word, and deed.[6]

Q. 150. *Are all transgressions of the law of God equally heinous in themselves, and in the sight of God?*

A. All transgressions of the law of God are not equally heinous; but some sins in themselves, and by reason of several aggravations, are more heinous in the sight of God than others.[7]

Q. 151. *What are those aggravations that make some sins more heinous than others?*

A. Sins receive their aggravations,

1. From the persons offending[8] if they be of riper age,[9] greater experience or grace,[10] eminent for profession,[11] gifts,[12] place,[13]

1　Psalm 112:9-10; Nehemiah 2:10
2　Romans 7:7-8; 13:9; Deuteronomy 5:21
3　James 3:2; John 15:5; Romans 8:3
4　Ecclesiastes 7:20; 1 John 1:8, 10; Galatians 5:17; Romans 7:18-19
5　Genesis 6:5; 8:21
6　Genesis 3:9-19; James 3:2-13
7　John 19:11; Ezekiel 8:6, 13, 15; 1 John 5:16; Psalm 78:17, 32, 56
8　Jeremiah 2:8
9　Job 32:7, 9; Ecclesiastes 4:13
10　1 Kings 11:4, 9
11　2 Samuel 12:14; 1 Corinthians 5:1
12　James 4:17; Luke 12:47-48
13　Jeremiah 5:4-5

office,[1] guides to others,[2] and whose example is likely to be followed by others.[3]

2. From the parties offended:[4] if immediately against God,[5] his attributes,[6] and worship;[7] against Christ, and his grace;[8] the Holy Spirit,[9] his witness,[10] and workings [actions],[11] against superiors, men of eminency,[12] and such as we stand especially related and engaged unto;[13] against any of the saints,[14] particularly weak brethren,[15] the souls of them, or any other,[16] and the common good of all or many.[17]

3. From the nature and quality of the offense:[18] if it be against the express letter of the law,[19] break many commandments, contain in it many sins:[20] if not only conceived in the heart, but breaks forth in words and actions,[21] scandalize others,[22] and admit of no reparation:[23] if against means,[24] mercies,[25]

---

1 2 Samuel 12:7-9; Ezekiel 8:11-12
2 Romans 2:17-24
3 Galatians 2:11-14
4 Matthew 21:38-39
5 1 Samuel 2:25; Acts 5:4; Psalm 5:4
6 Romans 2:4
7 Malachi 1:8, 14
8 Hebrews 2:2-3; Hebrews 12:25
9 Hebrews 10:29; Matthew 12:31-32
10 Ephesians 4:30
11 Hebrews 6:4-6
12 Jude 8; Numbers 12:8-9; Isaiah 3:5
13 Proverbs 30:17; 2 Corinthians 12:15; Psalm 55:12-15
14 Zephaniah 2:8, 10-11; Matthew 18:6; 1 Corinthians 6:8; Revelation 17:6
15 1 Corinthians 8:11-12; Romans 14:13-15, 21
16 Ezekiel 13:19; 1 Corinthians 8:12; Revelation 18:12-13; Matthew 23:15
17 1 Thessalonians 2:15-16; Joshua 22:20
18 Proverbs 6:30-35
19 Ezra 9:10-12; 1 Kings 11:9-10
20 Colossians 3:5; 1 Timothy 6:10; Proverbs 5:8-12; 6:32-33; Joshua 7:21
21 James 1:14-15; Matthew 5:22; Micah 2:1
22 Matthew 18:7; Romans 2:23-24
23 Deuteronomy 22:22 compared with verses 28-29; Proverbs 6:32-35
24 Matthew 11:21-24; John 15:22
25 Isaiah 1:3; Deuteronomy 32:6

judgments,[1] light of nature,[2] conviction of conscience,[3] public or private admonition,[4] censures of the church,[5] civil punishments;[6] and our prayers, purposes, promises,[7] vows,[8] covenants,[9] and engagements to God or men:[10] if done deliberately,[11] wilfully,[12] presumptuously,[13] impudently,[14] boastingly,[15] maliciously,[16] frequently,[17] obstinately,[18] with delight,[19] continuance,[20] or relapsing after repentance.[21]

4. From circumstances of time[22] and place:[23] if on the Lord's Day,[24] or other times of divine worship;[25] or immediately before[26] or after these,[27] or other helps to prevent or remedy

---

1 Amos 4:8-11; Jeremiah 5:3
2 Romans 1:26-27
3 Romans 1:32; Daniel 5:22; Titus 3:10-11
4 Proverbs 29:1
5 Titus 3:10; Matthew 18:17
6 Proverbs 27:22; Proverbs 23:35
7 Psalm 78:34-37; Jeremiah 2:20; 42:5-6, 20-21
8 Ecclesiastes 5:4-6; Proverbs 20:25
9 Leviticus 26:25
10 Proverbs 2:17; Ezekiel 17:18-19
11 Psalm 36:4
12 Jeremiah 6:16
13 Numbers 15:30; Exodus 21:14
14 Jeremiah 3:3; Proverbs 7:13
15 Psalm 52:1
16 3 John 10
17 Numbers 14:22
18 Zechariah 7:11-12
19 Proverbs 2:14
20 Isaiah 57:17
21 Jeremiah 34:8-11; 2 Peter 2:20-22
22 2 Kings 5:26
23 Jeremiah 7:10; Isaiah 26:10
24 Ezekiel 23:37-29
25 Isaiah 58:3-5; Numbers 25:6-7
26 1 Corinthians 11:20-21
27 Jeremiah 7:8-10; Proverbs 7:14-15; John 13:27, 30

such miscarriages;[1] if in public, or in the presence of others, who are thereby likely to be provoked or defiled.[2]

Q. 152. *What does every sin deserve at the hands of God?*
A. Every sin, even the least, being against the sovereignty,[3] goodness,[4] and holiness of God,[5] and against his righteous law,[6] deserves his wrath and curse,[7] both in this life,[8] and that which is to come;[9] and cannot be expiated but by the blood of Christ.[10]

Q. 153. *What does God require of us, that we may escape his wrath and curse due to us by reason of the transgression of the law?*
A. That we may escape the wrath and curse of God due to us by reason of the transgression of the law, he requires of us repentance toward God, and faith toward our Lord Jesus Christ,[11] and the diligent use of the outward means whereby Christ communicates to us the benefits of his mediation.[12]

Q. 154. *What are the outward means whereby Christ communicates to us the benefits of his mediation?*
A. The outward and ordinary means whereby Christ communicates to his church the benefits of his mediation, are all his ordinances; especially the Word, sacraments, and

---

1 Ezra 9:13-14
2 2 Samuel 16:22; 1 Samuel 2:22-24
3 James 2:10-11
4 Exodus 20:1-2
5 Habakkuk 1:13; Leviticus 10:3; 11:44-45
6 1 John 3:4; Romans 7:12
7 Ephesians 5:6; Galatians 3:10
8 Lamentations 3:39; Deuteronomy 28:15-68
9 Matthew 25:41
10 Hebrews 9:22; 1 Peter 1:18-19
11 Acts 20:21; Matthew 3:7-8; Luke 13:3, 5; Acts 16:30-31; John 3:16, 18
12 Proverbs 2:1-5; 8:33-36

prayer; all which are made effectual to the elect for their salvation.[1]

Q. 155. *How is the Word made effectual to salvation?*
A. The Spirit of God makes the reading, but especially the preaching of the Word, an effectual means of enlightening,[2] convincing, and humbling sinners;[3] of driving them out of themselves, and drawing them unto Christ;[4] of conforming them to his image,[5] and subduing them to his will;[6] of strengthening them against temptations and corruptions;[7] of building them up in grace,[8] and establishing their hearts in holiness and comfort through faith unto salvation.[9]

Q. 156. *Is the Word of God to be read by all?*
A. Although all are not to be permitted to read the Word publicly to the congregation,[10] yet all sorts of people are bound to read it apart by themselves,[11] and with their families:[12] to which end, the Holy Scriptures are to be translated out of the original into vulgar [common] languages.[13]

Q. 157. *How is the Word of God to be read?*
A. The Holy Scriptures are to be read with a high and reverent esteem of them;[14] with a firm persuasion that they are the very Word of God,[15] and that he only can enable us to

---

1 Matthew 28:19-20; Acts 2:42, 46-47
2 Nehemiah 8:8; Acts 26:18; Psalm 19:8
3 1 Corinthians 14:24-25; 2 Chronicles 34:18-19, 26-28
4 Acts 2:37, 41; 8:27-39
5 2 Corinthians 3:18
6 2 Corinthians 10:4-6; Romans 6:17
7 Matthew 4:4, 7, 10; Ephesians 6:16-17; Psalm 19:11; 1 Corinthians 10:11
8 Acts 20:32; 2 Timothy 3:15-17
9 Romans 16:25; 1 Thessalonians 3:2, 10-11, 13; Romans 15:4; 10:13-17; 1:16
10 Deuteronomy 31:9, 11-13; Nehemiah 8:2-3; Nehemiah 9:3-5
11 Deuteronomy 17:19, Revelation 1:3; John 5:39; Isaiah 34:16
12 Deuteronomy 6:6-9; Genesis 18:17, 19; Psalm 78:5-7
13 1 Corinthians 14:6, 9, 11-12, 15-16, 24, 27-28
14 Psalm 19:10; Nehemiah 8:3-10; Exodus 24:7; 2 Chronicles 34:27; Isaiah 66:2
15 2 Peter 1:19-21

understand them;[1] with desire to know, believe, and obey the will of God revealed in them;[2] with diligence,[3] and attention to the matter and scope of them;[4] with meditation,[5] application,[6] self-denial,[7] and prayer.[8]

Q. 158. *By whom is the Word of God to be preached?*
A. The Word of God is to be preached only by such as are sufficiently gifted,[9] and also duly approved and called to that office.[10]

Q. 159. *How is the Word of God to be preached by those that are called thereunto?*
A. They that are called to labour in the ministry of the Word, are to preach sound doctrine,[11] diligently,[12] in season and out of season;[13] plainly,[14] not in the enticing words of man's wisdom, but in demonstration of the Spirit, and of power;[15] faithfully,[16] making known the whole counsel of God;[17] wisely,[18] applying themselves to the necessities and capacities

---

1 Luke 24:45; 2 Corinthians 3:13-16
2 Deuteronomy 17:10, 20
3 Acts 17:11
4 Acts 8:30, 34; Luke 10:26-28
5 Psalm 1:2; 119:97
6 2 Chronicles 34:21
7 Proverbs 3:5; Deuteronomy 33:3
8 Proverbs 2:1-6, Psalm 119:18; Nehemiah 7:6, 8
9 1 Timothy 3:2, 6; Ephesians 4:8-11; Hosea 4:6; Malachi 2:7; 2 Corinthians 3:6
10 Jeremiah 14:15; Romans 10:15; Hebrews 5:4; 1 Corinthians 12:28-29; 1 Timothy 3:10; 4:14; 5:22
11 Titus 2:1, 8
12 Acts 18:25
13 2 Timothy 4:2
14 1 Corinthians 14:19
15 1 Corinthians 2:4
16 Jeremiah 23:28; 1 Corinthians 4:1-2
17 Acts 20:27
18 Colossians 1:28; 2 Timothy 2:15

of the hearers;[1] zealously,[2] with fervent love to God[3] and the souls of his people;[4] sincerely,[5] aiming at his glory,[6] and their conversion,[7] edification,[8] and salvation.[9]

Q. 160. *What is required of those that hear the Word preached?*
A. It is required of those that hear the Word preached, that they attend upon it with diligence,[10] preparation,[11] and prayer;[12] examine what they hear by the Scriptures;[13] receive the truth with faith,[14] love,[15] meekness,[16] and readiness of mind,[17] as the Word of God;[18] meditate,[19] and confer of it;[20] hide it in their hearts,[21] and bring forth the fruit of it in their lives.[22]

Q. 161. *How do the sacraments become effectual means of salvation?*
A. The sacraments become effectual means of salvation, not by any power in themselves, or any virtue derived from the piety or intention of him by whom they are administered, but only

---

1 1 Corinthians 3:2; Hebrews 5:12-14; Luke 12:42
2 Acts 18:25
3 2 Corinthians 5:13-14; Philippians 1:15-17
4 Colossians 4:12; 2 Corinthians 12:15
5 2 Corinthians 2:17; 4:2
6 1 Thessalonians 2:4-6; John 7:18
7 1 Corinthians 9:19-22
8 2 Corinthians 12:19; Ephesians 4:12
9 1 Timothy 4:16; Acts 26:16-18
10 Proverbs 8:34
11 1 Peter 2:1-2; Luke 8:18
12 Psalm 119:18; Ephesians 6:18-19
13 Acts 17:11
14 Hebrews 4:2
15 2 Thessalonians 2:10
16 James 1:21
17 Acts 17:11
18 1 Thessalonians 2:13
19 Luke 9:44; Hebrews 2:1
20 Luke 24:14; Deuteronomy 6:6-7
21 Proverbs 2:1; Psalm 119:11
22 Luke 8:15; James 1:25

by the working of the Holy Spirit, and the blessing of Christ, by whom they are instituted.[1]

Q. 162. *What is a sacrament?*
A. A sacrament is a holy ordinance instituted by Christ in his church,[2] to signify, seal, and exhibit[3] unto those that are within the covenant of grace,[4] the benefits of his mediation;[5] to strengthen and increase their faith, and all other graces;[6] to oblige them to obedience;[7] to testify and cherish their love and communion one with another;[8] and to distinguish them from those that are without.[9]

Q. 163. *What are the parts of a sacrament?*
A. The parts of the sacrament are two; the one an outward and sensible sign, used according to Christ's own appointment; the other an inward and spiritual grace thereby signified.[10]

Q. 164. *How many sacraments has Christ instituted in his church under the New Testament?*
A. Under the New Testament Christ has instituted in his church only two sacraments; baptism and the Lord's supper.[11]

Q. 165. *What is baptism?*
A. Baptism is a sacrament of the New Testament, wherein Christ has ordained the washing with water in the name of the Father, and of the Son, and of the Holy Spirit,[12] to be a sign

---

1 1 Peter 3:21; Acts 8:13 compared with verse 23; 1 Corinthians 3:6-7; 1 Corinthians 12:13
2 Genesis 17:7, 10; Exodus 12; Matthew 28:19; 26:26-28
3 Romans 4:11; 1 Corinthians 11:24-25
4 Romans 15:8; Exodus 12:48
5 Acts 2:38; 1 Corinthians 10:16
6 Romans 4:11; Galatians 3:27
7 Romans 6:3-4; 1 Corinthians 10:21
8 Ephesians 4:2-5; 1 Corinthians 12:13
9 Ephesians 2:11-12; Genesis 34:14
10 Matthew 3:11; 1 Peter 3:21; Romans 2:28-29
11 Matthew 28:19; 1 Corinthians 11:20, 23; Matthew 26:26-28
12 Matthew 28:19

and seal of ingrafting into himself,[1] of remission of sins by his blood,[2] and regeneration by his Spirit;[3] of adoption,[4] and resurrection unto everlasting life;[5] and whereby the parties baptised are solemnly admitted into the visible church,[6] and enter into an open and professed engagement to be wholly and only the Lord's.[7]

Q. 166. *Unto whom is baptism to be administered?*
A. Baptism is not to be administered to any that are out of the visible church, and so strangers from the covenant of promise, till they profess their faith in Christ, and obedience to him,[8] but infants descending from parents, either both, or but one of them, professing faith in Christ, and obedience to him, are in that respect within the covenant, and to be baptised.[9]

Q. 167. *How is our baptism to be improved by us?*
A. The needful but much neglected duty of improving our baptism, is to be performed by us all our life long, especially in the time of temptation, and when we are present at the administration of it to others;[10] by serious and thankful consideration of the nature of it, and of the ends for which Christ instituted it, the privileges and benefits conferred and sealed thereby, and our solemn vow made therein;[11] by being humbled for our sinful defilement, our falling short of, and walking contrary to, the grace of baptism, and our engagements;[12] by growing up to assurance of pardon of

---

1 Galatians 3:27
2 Mark 1:4; Revelation 1:5
3 Titus 3:5; Ephesians 5:26
4 Galatians 3:26-27
5 1 Corinthians 15:29; Romans 6:5
6 1 Corinthians 12:13
7 Romans 6:4
8 Acts 8:36-37; Acts 2:38
9 Genesis 17:7, 9 compared with Galatians 3:9, 14 and with Colossians 2:11-12 and with Acts 2:38-39 and with Romans 4:11-12; 1 Corinthians 7:14; Matthew 28:19; Luke 18:15-16; Romans 11:16
10 Colossians 2:11-12; Romans 6:4, 6, 11
11 Romans 6:3-5
12 1 Corinthians 1:11-13; Romans 6:2-3

sin, and of all other blessings sealed to us in that sacrament;[1] by drawing strength from the death and resurrection of Christ, into whom we are baptised, for the mortifying of sin, and quickening of grace;[2] and by endeavouring to live by faith,[3] to have our conversation in holiness and righteousness,[4] as those that have therein given up their names to Christ;[5] and to walk in brotherly love, as being baptised by the same Spirit into one body.[6]

Q. 168. *What is the Lord's supper?*
A. The Lord's supper is a sacrament of the New Testament,[7] wherein, by giving and receiving bread and wine according to the appointment of Jesus Christ, his death is showed forth; and they that worthily communicate feed upon his body and blood, to their spiritual nourishment and growth in grace;[8] have their union and communion with him confirmed;[9] testify and renew their thankfulness,[10] and engagement to God,[11] and their mutual love and fellowship each with the other, as members of the same mystical body.[12]

Q. 169. *How has Christ appointed bread and wine to be given and received in the sacrament of the Lord's supper?*
A. Christ has appointed the ministers of his Word, in the administration of this sacrament of the Lord's supper, to set apart the bread and wine from common use, by the word of institution, thanksgiving, and prayer; to take and break the bread, and to give both the bread and the wine to

---

1 Romans 4:11–12; 1 Peter 3:21
2 Romans 6:3–5
3 Galatians 3:26–27
4 Romans 6:22
5 Acts 2:38
6 1 Corinthians 12:13, 25–27
7 Luke 22:20
8 Matthew 26:26–28; 1 Corinthians 11:23–26
9 1 Corinthians 10:16
10 1 Corinthians 11:24
11 1 Corinthians 10:14–16, 21
12 1 Corinthians 10:17

the communicants: who are, by the same appointment, to take and eat the bread, and to drink the wine, in thankful remembrance that the body of Christ was broken and given, and his blood shed, for them.[1]

Q. 170. *How do they that worthily communicate in the Lord's supper feed upon the body and blood of Christ therein?*
A. As the body and blood of Christ are not corporally or carnally present in, with, or under the bread and wine in the Lord's supper,[2] and yet are spiritually present to the faith of the receiver, no less truly and really than the elements themselves are to their outward senses;[3] so they that worthily communicate in the sacrament of the Lord's supper, do therein feed upon the body and blood of Christ, not after a corporal and carnal, but in a spiritual manner; yet truly and really,[4] while by faith they receive and apply unto themselves Christ crucified, and all the benefits of his death.[5]

Q. 171. *How are they that receive the sacrament of the Lord's supper to prepare themselves before they come unto it?*
A. They that receive the sacrament of the Lord's supper are, before they come, to prepare themselves thereunto, by examining themselves[6] of their being in Christ,[7] of their sins and wants;[8] of the truth and measure of their knowledge,[9] faith,[10] repentance;[11] love to God and the brethren,[12] charity

---

[1] 1 Corinthians 11:23-24; Matthew 26:26-28; Mark 14:22-24; Luke 22:19-20
[2] Acts 3:21
[3] Matthew 26:26, 28
[4] 1 Corinthians 11:24-29
[5] 1 Corinthians 10:16
[6] 1 Corinthians 11:28
[7] 2 Corinthians 13:5
[8] 1 Corinthians 5:7 compared with Exodus 12:15
[9] 1 Corinthians 11:29
[10] 1 Corinthians 13:5; Matthew 26:28
[11] Zechariah 12:10; 1 Corinthians 11:31
[12] 1 Corinthians 10:16-17; Acts 2:46-47

to all men,[1] forgiving those that have done them wrong;[2] of their desires after Christ,[3] and of their new obedience;[4] and by renewing the exercise of these graces,[5] by serious meditation,[6] and fervent prayer.[7]

Q. 172. *May one who doubts of his being in Christ, or of his due preparation, come to the Lord's supper?*

A. One who doubts of his being in Christ, or of his due preparation to the sacrament of the Lord's supper, may have true interest in Christ, though he be not yet assured thereof;[8] and in God's account has it, if he be duly affected with the apprehension of the want of it,[9] and un-feignedly desires to be found in Christ,[10] and to depart from iniquity:[11] in which case (because promises are made, and this sacrament is appointed, for the relief even of weak and doubting Christians)[12] he is to bewail his unbelief,[13] and labour to have his doubts resolved;[14] and, so doing, he may and ought to come to the Lord's supper, that he may be further strengthened.[15]

Q. 173. *May any who profess the faith, and desire to come to the Lord's supper, be kept from it?*

A. Such as are found to be ignorant or scandalous, notwithstanding their profession of the faith, and desire to come to the Lord's supper, may and ought to be kept from

---

1 1 Corinthians 5:8; 11:18, 20
2 Matthew 5:23-24
3 Isaiah 55:1; John 7:37
4 1 Corinthians 5:7-8
5 1 Corinthians 11:25-26, 28; Hebrews 10:21-22, 24; Psalm 26:6
6 1 Corinthians 11:24-25
7 2 Corinthians 30:18-19; Matthew 26:26
8 Isaiah 50:10; 1 John 5:13; Psalm 88; Psalm 77:1-12; Jonah 2:4, 7
9 Isaiah 54:7-10; Matthew 5:3-4; Psalm 31:22; 73:13, 22-23
10 Philippians 3:8-9; Psalm 10:17; 42:1-2, 5, 11
11 2 Timothy 2:19; Isaiah 50:10; Psalm 66:18-20
12 Isaiah 40:11, 29, 31; Matthew 11:28; 12:20; 26:28
13 Mark 9:24
14 Acts 2:37; 16:30
15 Romans 4:11; 1 Corinthians 11:28

that sacrament, by the power which Christ has left in his church,[1] until they receive instruction, and manifest their reformation.[2]

Q. 174. *What is required of them that receive the sacrament of the Lord's supper in the time of the administration of it?*
A. It is required of them that receive the sacrament of the Lord's supper, that, during the time of the administration of it, with all holy reverence and attention they wait upon God in that ordinance,[3] diligently observe the sacramental elements and actions,[4] heedfully discern the Lord's body,[5] and affectionately meditate on his death and sufferings,[6] and thereby stir up themselves to a vigorous exercise of their graces;[7] in judging themselves,[8] and sorrowing for sin;[9] in earnest hungering and thirsting after Christ,[10] feeding on him by faith,[11] receiving of his fullness,[12] trusting in his merits,[13] rejoicing in his love,[14]

---

1 1 Corinthians 11:27-34 compared with Matthew 7:6 and with 1 Corinthians 5 and with Jude 23 and with 1 Timothy 5:22
2 2 Corinthians 2:7
3 Leviticus 10:3; Hebrews 12:28; Psalm 5:7; 1 Corinthians 11:17, 26-27
4 Exodus 24:8 compared with Matthew 26:28
5 1 Corinthians 11:29
6 Luke 22:19
7 1 Corinthians 11:26; 10:3-5, 11, 14
8 1 Corinthians 11:31
9 Zechariah 12:10
10 Revelation 22:17
11 John 6:35
12 John 1:16
13 Philippians 1:16
14 Psalm 63:4-5; 2 Chronicles 30:21

giving thanks for his grace;[1] in renewing of their covenant with God,[2] and love to all the saints.[3]

Q. 175. *What is the duty of Christians, after they have received the sacrament of the Lord's supper?*
A. The duty of Christians, after they have received the sacrament of the Lord's supper, is seriously to consider how they have behaved themselves therein, and with what success;[4] if they find quickening [restoration] and comfort, to bless God for it,[5] beg the continuance of it,[6] watch against relapses,[7] fulfil their vows,[8] and encourage themselves to a frequent attendance on that ordinance:[9] but if they find no present benefit, more exactly to review their preparation to, and carriage at, the sacrament;[10] in both which, if they can approve themselves to God and their own consciences, they are to wait for the fruit of it in due time:[11] but, if they see they have failed in either, they are to be humbled,[12] and to attend upon it afterwards with more care and diligence.[13]

Q. 176. *Wherein do the sacraments of baptism and the Lord's supper agree?*
A. The sacraments of baptism and the Lord's supper agree, in that the author of both is God;[14] the spiritual part of both is Christ and his benefits;[15] both are seals of the same

---

1 Psalm 22:26
2 Jeremiah 50:5; Psalm 50:5
3 Acts 2:42
4 Psalm 28:7; 85:8; 1 Corinthians 11:17, 3 0-31
5 2 Chronicles 30:21-23, 25-26; Acts 2:42, 46-47
6 Psalm 36:10; Song of Solomon 3:4; 1 Chronicles 29:18
7 1 Corinthians 10:3-5, 12
8 Psalm 50:14
9 1 Corinthians 11:25-26; Acts 2:42, 46
10 Song of Solomon 5:1-6; Ecclesiastes 5:1-6
11 Psalm 123:1-2; 42:5, 8; 43:3-5
12 2 Chronicles 30:18-19; Isaiah 1:16, 18
13 2 Corinthians 7:11; 1 Chronicles 15:12-14
14 Matthew 28:19; 1 Corinthians 11:23
15 Romans 6:3-4; 1 Corinthians 10:16

covenant,[1] are to be dispensed by ministers of the gospel, and by none other;[2] and to be continued in the church of Christ until his second coming.[3]

Q. 177. *Wherein do the sacraments of baptism and the Lord's supper differ?*
A. The sacraments of baptism and the Lord's supper differ, in that baptism is to be administered but once, with water, to be a sign and seal of our regeneration and ingrafting into Christ,[4] and that even to infants;[5] whereas the Lord's supper is to be administered often, in the elements of bread and wine, to represent and exhibit Christ as spiritual nourishment to the soul,[6] and to confirm our continuance and growth in him,[7] and that only to such as are of years and ability to examine themselves.[8]

Q. 178. *What is prayer?*
A. Prayer is an offering up of our desires unto God,[9] in the name of Christ,[10] by the help of his Spirit;[11] with confession of our sins,[12] and thankful acknowledgment of his mercies.[13]

Q. 179. *Are we to pray unto God only?*
A. God only being able to search the hearts,[14] hear the requests,[15]

---

1 Romans 4:11; Colossians 2:12; Matthew 26:27-28
2 John 1:33; Matthew 28:19; 1 Corinthians 11:23; 4:1; Hebrews 5:4
3 Matthew 28:19-20; 1 Corinthians 11:26
4 Matthew 3:11; Titus 3:5; Galatians 3:27
5 Genesis 17:7, 9; Acts 2:38-39; 1 Corinthians 7:14
6 1 Corinthians 11:23-26
7 1 Corinthians 10:16
8 1 Corinthians 11:28-29
9 Psalm 62:8
10 John 16:23
11 Romans 8:26
12 Psalm 32:5-6; Daniel 9:4
13 Philippians 4:6
14 1 Kings 8:39; Acts 1:24; Romans 8:27
15 Psalm 65:2

pardon the sins,[1] and fulfil the desires of all;[2] and only to be believed in,[3] and worshipped with religious worship;[4] prayer, which is a special part thereof,[5] is to be made by all to him alone,[6] and to none other.[7]

Q. 180. *What is it to pray in the name of Christ?*
A. To pray in the name of Christ is, in obedience to his command, and in confidence on his promises, to ask mercy for his sake;[8] not by bare mentioning of his name,[9] but by drawing our encouragement to pray, and our boldness, strength, and hope of acceptance in prayer, from Christ and his mediation.[10]

Q. 181. *Why are we to pray in the name of Christ?*
A. The sinfulness of man, and his distance from God by reason thereof, being so great, as that we can have no access into his presence without a mediator;[11] and there being none in heaven or earth appointed to, or fit for, that glorious work but Christ alone,[12] we are to pray in no other name but his only.[13]

Q. 182. *How does the Spirit help us to pray?*
A. We not knowing what to pray for as we ought, the Spirit helps our infirmities, by enabling us to understand both for whom, and what, and how prayer is to be made; and by working and quickening in our hearts (although not in all persons, nor at all times, in the same measure) those

---

1 Micah 7:18
2 Psalm 145:18-19
3 Romans 10:14
4 Matthew 4:10
5 1 Corinthians 1:2
6 Psalm 50:15
7 Romans 10:14
8 John 14:13-14; John 16:24; Daniel 9:17
9 Matthew 7:21
10 Hebrews 4:14-16; 1 John 5:13-15
11 John 14:6; Isaiah 59:2; Ephesians 3:12
12 John 6:27; Hebrews 7:25-27; 1 Timothy 2:5
13 Colossians 3:17; Hebrews 13:15

apprehensions, affections, and graces which are requisite for the right performance of that duty.[1]

Q. 183. *For whom are we to pray?*
A. We are to pray for the whole church of Christ upon earth;[2] for magistrates,[3] and ministers;[4] for ourselves,[5] our brethren,[6] yea, our enemies;[7] and for all sorts of men living,[8] or that shall live hereafter;[9] but not for the dead,[10] nor for those that are known to have sinned the sin unto death.[11]

Q. 184. *For what things are we to pray?*
A. We are to pray for all things tending to the glory of God,[12] the welfare of the church,[13] our own[14] or others', good;[15] but not for anything that is unlawful.[16]

Q. 185. *How are we to pray?*
A. We are to pray with an awful apprehension of the majesty of God,[17] and deep sense of our own unworthiness,[18]

---

1 Romans 8:26–27; Psalm 10:17; Zechariah 12:10
2 Ephesians 6:18; Psalm 28:9
3 1 Timothy 2:1–2
4 Colossians 4:3
5 Genesis 32:11
6 James 5:16
7 Matthew 5:44
8 1 Timothy 2:1–2
9 John 17:20; 2 Samuel 7:29
10 2 Samuel 12:21–23
11 1 John 5:16
12 Matthew 6:9
13 Psalm 51:18; 122:6
14 Matthew 7:11
15 Psalm 125:4
16 1 John 5:14
17 Ecclesiastes 5:1
18 Genesis 18:27; 32:10

necessities,[1] and sins;[2] with penitent,[3] thankful,[4] and enlarged hearts;[5] with understanding,[6] faith,[7] sincerity,[8] fervency,[9] love,[10] and perseverance,[11] waiting upon him,[12] with humble submission to his will.[13]

Q. 186. *What rule has God given for our direction in the duty of prayer?*
A. The whole Word of God is of use to direct us in the duty of prayer;[14] but the special rule of direction is that form of prayer which our Saviour Christ taught his disciples, commonly called The Lord's Prayer.[15]

Q. 187. *How is the Lord's Prayer to be used?*
A. The Lord's Prayer is not only for direction, as a pattern, according to which we are to make other prayers; but may also be used as a prayer, so that it be done with

---

1 Luke 15:17-19
2 Luke 18:13-14
3 Psalm 51:17
4 Philippians 4:6
5 1 Samuel 1:15; 2:1
6 1 Corinthians 14:15
7 Mark 11:24; James 1:6
8 Psalm 145:18; Psalm 17:1
9 James 5:16
10 1 Timothy 2:8
11 Ephesians 6:18
12 Micah 7:7
13 Matthew 26:39
14 1 John 5:14
15 Matthew 6:9-13; Luke 11:2-4

understanding, faith, reverence, and other graces necessary to the right performance of the duty of prayer.[1]

Q. 188. *Of how many parts does the Lord's Prayer consist?*
A. The Lord's Prayer consists of three parts; a preface, petitions, and a conclusion.

Q. 189. *What does the preface of the Lord's Prayer teach us?*
A. The preface of the Lord's Prayer (contained in these words, Our Father in heaven,)[2] teaches us, when we pray, to draw near to God with confidence of his fatherly goodness, and our interest therein;[3] with reverence, and all other childlike dispositions,[4] heavenly affections,[5] and due apprehensions of his sovereign power, majesty, and gracious condescension:[6] as also, to pray with and for others.[7]

Q. 190. *What do we pray for in the first petition?*
A. In the first petition, (which is, Hallowed be your name,)[8] acknowledging the utter inability and indisposition that is in ourselves and all men to honour God aright,[9] we pray, that God would by his grace enable and incline us and others to know, to acknowledge, and highly to esteem him,[10] his titles,[11] attributes,[12] ordinances, Word,[13] works, and whatsoever he is pleased to make himself known by;[14] and to glorify him

---

[1] Matthew 6:9 compared with Luke 11:2
[2] Matthew 6:9
[3] Luke 11:13; Romans 8:15
[4] Isaiah 64:9
[5] Psalm 123:1; Lamentations 3:41
[6] Isaiah 63:15-16; Nehemiah 1:4-6
[7] Acts 12:5
[8] Matthew 6:9
[9] 2 Corinthians 3:5; Psalm 51:15
[10] Psalm 67:2-3
[11] Psalm 83:18
[12] Psalm 86:10-13, 15
[13] 2 Thessalonians 3:1; Psalm 147:19-20; 138:1-3; 2 Corinthians 2:14-15
[14] Psalm 145; 8

in thought, word,[1] and deed:[2] that he would prevent and remove atheism,[3] ignorance,[4] idolatry,[5] profaneness,[6] and whatsoever is dishonourable to him;[7] and, by his over-ruling providence, direct and dispose of all things to his own glory.[8]

Q. 191. *What do we pray for in the second petition?*
A. In the second petition, (which is, Your kingdom come,)[9] acknowledging ourselves and all mankind to be by nature under the dominion of sin and Satan,[10] we pray, that the kingdom of sin and Satan may be destroyed,[11] the gospel propagated throughout the world,[12] the Jews called,[13] the fullness of the Gentiles brought in;[14] the church furnished with all gospel-officers and ordinances,[15] purged from corruption,[16] countenanced and maintained by the civil magistrate:[17] that the ordinances of Christ may be purely dispensed, and made effectual to the converting of those that are yet in their sins, and the confirming, comforting, and building up of those that are already converted:[18] that Christ would rule in our hearts here,[19] and hasten the time of his

---

1 Psalm 103:1; 19:14
2 Philippians 1:9, 11
3 Psalm 67:1-4
4 Ephesians 1:17-18
5 Psalm 97:7
6 Psalm 74:18, 22-23
7 2 Kings 19:15-16
8 2 Chronicles 20:6, 10-12; Psalm 83; 140:4, 8
9 Matthew 6:10
10 Ephesians 2:2-3
11 Psalm 68:1, 18; Revelation 12:10-11
12 2 Thessalonians 3:1
13 Romans 10:1
14 John 17:9, 20; Romans 11:25-26; Psalm 67
15 Matthew 9:38; 2 Thessalonians 3:1
16 Malachi 1:11; Zephaniah 3:9
17 1 Timothy 2:1-2
18 Acts 4:29-30; Ephesians 6:18-20; Romans 15:29-30, 32; 2 Thessalonians 1:11; 2:16-17
19 Ephesians 3:14-20

second coming, and our reigning with him forever:[1] and that he would be pleased so to exercise the kingdom of his power in all the world, as may best conduce to these ends.[2]

Q. 192. *What do we pray for in the third petition?*
A. In the third petition, (which is, Your will be done, on earth as it is in heaven,)[3] acknowledging, that by nature we and all men are not only utterly unable and unwilling to know and do the will of God,[4] but prone to rebel against his Word,[5] to repine [fret] and murmur against his providence,[6] and wholly inclined to do the will of the flesh, and of the devil:[7] we pray, that God would by his Spirit take away from ourselves and others all blindness,[8] weakness,[9] indisposedness,[10] and perverseness of heart;[11] and by his grace make us able and willing to know, do, and submit to his will in all things,[12] with humility,[13] cheerfulness,[14] faithfulness,[15] diligence,[16] zeal,[17] sincerity,[18] and constancy,[19] as the angels do in heaven.[20]

Q. 193. *What do we pray for in the fourth petition?*
A. In the fourth petition,(which is, Give us this day our daily

---

1 Revelation 22:20
2 Isaiah 64:1-2; Revelation 4:8-11
3 Matthew 6:10
4 Romans 7:18; Job 21:14; 1 Corinthians 2:14
5 Romans 8:7
6 Exodus 17:7; Numbers 14:2
7 Ephesians 2:2
8 Ephesians 1:17-18
9 Ephesians 3:16
10 Matthew 26:40-41
11 Jeremiah 31:18-19
12 Psalm 119:1, 8, 35-36; Acts 21:14
13 Micah 6:8
14 Psalm 100:2; Job 1:21; 2 Samuel 15:25-26
15 Isaiah 38:3
16 Psalm 119:4-5
17 Romans 12:11
18 Psalm 119:80
19 Psalm 119:112
20 Isaiah 6:2-3; Psalm 103:20-21; Matthew 18:10

bread,)[1] acknowledging, that in Adam, and by our own sin, we have forfeited our right to all the outward blessings of this life, and deserve to be wholly deprived of them by God, and to have them cursed to us in the use of them;[2] and that neither they of themselves are able to sustain us,[3] nor we to merit,[4] or by our own industry to procure [obtain] them;[5] but prone to desire,[6] get,[7] and use them unlawfully:[8] we pray for ourselves and others, that both they and we, waiting upon the providence of God from day to day in the use of lawful means, may, of his free gift, and as to his fatherly wisdom shall seem best, enjoy a competent portion of them;[9] and have the same continued and blessed unto us in our holy and comfortable use of them,[10] and contentment in them;[11] and be kept from all things that are contrary to our temporal support and comfort.[12]

Q. 194. *What do we pray for in the fifth petition?*
A. In the fifth petition, (which is, Forgive us our debts, as we also have forgiven our debtors,)[13] acknowledging, that we and all others are guilty both of original and actual sin, and thereby become debtors to the justice of God; and that neither we, nor any other creature, can make the least satisfaction for that debt:[14] we pray for ourselves and others, that God of his free grace would, through the obedience and satisfaction

---

1 Matthew 6:11
2 Genesis 2:17; 3:17; Romans 8:20-22; Jeremiah 5:25; Deuteronomy 28:15-68
3 Deuteronomy 8:3
4 Genesis 32:10
5 Deuteronomy 8:17-18
6 Jeremiah 6:13; Mark 7:21-22
7 Hosea 12:7
8 James 4:3
9 Genesis 43:12-14; 28:20; Ephesians 4:28; 2 Thessalonians 3:11-12; Philippians 4:6
10 1 Timothy 4:3-5
11 1 Timothy 6:6-8
12 Proverbs 30:8-9
13 Matthew 6:12
14 Romans 3:9-22; Matthew 18:24-25; Psalm 130:3-4

of Christ, apprehended and applied by faith, acquit us both from the guilt and punishment of sin,[1] accept us in his Beloved;[2] continue his favour and grace to us,[3] pardon our daily failings,[4] and fill us with peace and joy, in giving us daily more and more assurance of forgiveness;[5] which we are the rather emboldened to ask, and encouraged to expect, when we have this testimony in ourselves, that we from the heart forgive others their offenses.[6]

Q. 195. *What do we pray for in the sixth petition?*
A. In the sixth petition, (which is, And lead us not into temptation, but deliver us from evil,)[7] acknowledging, that the most wise, righteous, and gracious God, for divers [various] holy and just ends, may so order things, that we may be assaulted, foiled, and for a time led captive by temptations;[8] that Satan,[9] the world,[10] and the flesh, are ready powerfully to draw us aside, and ensnare us;[11] and that we, even after the pardon of our sins, by reason of our corruption,[12] weakness, and want of watchfulness,[13] are not only subject to be tempted, and forward to expose ourselves unto temptations,[14] but also of ourselves unable and unwilling to resist them, to recover out of them, and to improve them;[15] and worthy to

---

1 Romans 3:24-26; Hebrews 9:22
2 Ephesians 1:6-7
3 2 Peter 1:2
4 Hosea 14:2; Jeremiah 14:7
5 Romans 15:13; Psalm 51:7-10, 12
6 Luke 11:4; Matthew 6:14-15; 18:35
7 Matthew 6:13
8 2 Chronicles 32:31
9 1 Chronicles 21:1
10 Luke 21:34; Mark 4:19
11 James 1:14
12 Galatians 5:17
13 Matthew 26:41
14 Matthew 26:69-72; Galatians 2:11-14; 2 Chronicles 18:3 compared with 2 Chronicles 19:2
15 Romans 7:23-24; 1 Chronicles 21:1-4; 2 Chronicles 16:7-10

be left under the power of them:[1] we pray, that God would so overrule the world and all in it,[2] subdue the flesh,[3] and restrain Satan,[4] order all things,[5] bestow and bless all means of grace,[6] and quicken [awaken] us to watchfulness in the use of them, that we and all his people may by his providence be kept from being tempted to sin;[7] or, if tempted, that by his Spirit we may be powerfully supported and enabled to stand in the hour of temptation;[8] or when fallen, raised again and recovered out of it,[9] and have a sanctified use and improvement thereof:[10] that our sanctification and salvation may be perfected,[11] Satan trodden under our feet,[12] and we fully freed from sin, temptation, and all evil, forever.[13]

Q. 196. *What does the conclusion of the Lord's Prayer teach us?*
A. The conclusion of the Lord's Prayer, (which is, For yours is the kingdom, and the power, and the glory, for ever. Amen.)[14] teaches us to enforce our petitions with arguments,[15] which are to be taken, not from any worthiness in ourselves, or in any other creature, but from God;[16] and with our prayers to join praises,[17] ascribing to God alone eternal sovereignty, omnipotence, and glorious excellency;[18] in regard whereof,

---

[1] Psalm 81:11-12
[2] John 17:15
[3] Psalm 51:10; 119:133
[4] 2 Corinthians 12:7-8
[5] 1 Corinthians 10:12-13
[6] Hebrews 13:20-21
[7] Matthew 26:41; Psalm 19:13
[8] Ephesians 3:14-17; 1 Thessalonians 3:13; Jude 24
[9] Psalm 51:12
[10] 1 Peter 5:8-10
[11] 2 Corinthians 13:7, 9
[12] Romans 16:20; Zechariah 3:2; Luke 22:31-32
[13] John 17:15; 1 Thessalonians 5:23
[14] Matthew 6:13
[15] Romans 15:30
[16] Daniel 9:4, 7-9, 16-19
[17] Philippians 4:6
[18] 1 Chronicles 29:10-13

as he is able and willing to help us,[1] so we by faith are emboldened to plead with him that he would,[2] and quietly to rely upon him, that he will fulfil our requests.[3] And, to testify this our desire and assurance, we say, Amen.[4]

---

1 Ephesians 3:20-21; Luke 11:13
2 2 Chronicles 20:6, 11
3 2 Chronicles 14:11
4 1 Corinthians 14:16; Revelation 22:20-21

The Westminster Shorter Catechism in Modern English

Q. 1. *What is the chief end of man?*
A. Man's chief end is to glorify God,[1] and to enjoy him forever.[2]

Q. 2. *What rule has God given to direct us how we may glorify and enjoy him?*
A. The Word of God, which is contained in the Scriptures of the Old and New Testaments,[3] is the only rule to direct us how we may glorify and enjoy him.[4]

Q. 3. *What do the Scriptures principally teach?*
A. The Scriptures principally teach, what man is to believe concerning God, and what duty God requires of man.[5]

Q. 4. *What is God?*
A. God is a Spirit,[6] infinite,[7] eternal,[8] and unchangeable,[9] in his

---

[1] 1 Corinthians 10:31
[2] Psalms 73:25-26
[3] Ephesians 2:20; 2 Timothy 3:16
[4] 1 John 1:3
[5] 2 Timothy 1:13
[6] John 4:24
[7] Job 11:7
[8] Psalms 90:2
[9] James 1:17

being,[1] wisdom,[2] power,[3] holiness,[4] justice, goodness, and truth.[5]

Q. 5. *Are there more Gods than one?*
A. There is only one,[6] the living and true God.[7]

Q. 6. *How many persons are there in the Godhead?*
A. There are three persons in the Godhead: the Father, the Son, and the Holy Spirit;[8] and these three are one God, the same in substance, equal in power and glory.[9]

Q. 7. *What are the decrees of God?*
A. The decrees of God are, his eternal purpose, according to the counsel of his will, whereby, for his own glory, he has foreordained whatsoever comes to pass.[10]

Q. 8. *How does God execute his decrees?*
A. God executes his decrees in the works of creation[11] and providence.[12]

Q. 9. *What is the work of creation?*
A. The work of creation is, God's making all things out of

---

1 Exodus 3:14
2 Psalms 147:5
3 Revelation 4:8
4 Revelation 15:4
5 Exodus 34:6-7
6 Deuteronomy 6:4
7 Jeremiah 10:10
8 Matthew 28:19
9 1 John 5:7
10 Ephesians 1:11-12
11 Revelation 4:11
12 Daniel 4:35

nothing,[1] by the word of his power,[2] in the space of six days, and all very good.[3]

Q. 10. *How did God create man?*
A. God created man male and female, after his own image,[4] in knowledge, righteousness, and holiness,[5] with dominion over the creatures.[6]

Q. 11. *What are God's works of providence?*
A. God's works of providence are, his most holy,[7] wise,[8] and powerful preserving[9] and governing all his creatures, and all their actions.[10]

Q. 12. *What special act of providence did God exercise towards man in the estate in which he was created?*
A. When God had created man, he entered into a covenant of life with him, upon condition of perfect obedience;[11] forbidding him to eat of the tree of the knowledge of good and evil, upon the pain of death.[12]

Q. 13. *Did our first parents continue in the estate in which they were created?*
A. Our first parents, being left to the freedom of their own will,

---

1 Genesis 1:1
2 Hebrews 11:3
3 Genesis 1:31
4 Genesis 1:27
5 Colossians 3:10; Ephesians 4:24
6 Genesis 1:28
7 Psalms 145:17
8 Isaiah 28:29
9 Hebrews 1:3
10 Psalm 103:19; Matthew 10:29
11 Galatians 3:12
12 Genesis 2:17

fell from the estate in which they were created, by sinning against God.[1]

Q. 14. *What is sin?*
A. Sin is any lack of conformity unto, or transgression of, the law of God.[2]

Q. 15. *What was the sin whereby our first parents fell from the estate wherein they were created?*
A. The sin whereby our first parents fell from the estate wherein they were created, was their eating the forbidden fruit.[3]

Q. 16. *Did all mankind fall in Adam's first transgression?*
A. The covenant being made with Adam, not only for himself, but for his posterity;[4] all mankind, descending from him by natural birth, sinned in him, and fell with him, in his first transgression.[5]

Q. 17. *Into what estate did the fall bring mankind?*
A. The fall brought mankind into an estate of sin and misery.[6]

Q. 18. *Wherein consists the sinfulness of that estate into which man fell?*
A. The sinfulness of that estate into which man fell, consists in the guilt of Adam's first sin,[7] the lack of original righteousness,[8] and the corruption of his whole nature, which

---

1 Ecclesiastes 7:29
2 1 John 3:4
3 Genesis 3:6-8
4 Genesis 1:28; 2:16-17
5 Romans 5:18
6 Romans 5:12
7 Romans 5:19
8 Romans 3:10

is commonly called Original Sin;[1] together with all actual transgressions which proceed from it.[2]

Q. 19. *What is the misery of that estate into which man fell?*
A. All mankind by their fall lost communion with God,[3] are under his wrath and curse,[4] and so made liable to all the miseries of this life, to death itself, and to the pains of hell forever.[5]

Q. 20. *Did God leave all mankind to perish in the estate of sin and misery?*
A. God, having out of his mere good pleasure, from all eternity, elected some to everlasting life,[6] did enter into a covenant of grace to deliver them out of the estate of sin and misery, and to bring them into an estate of salvation by a Redeemer.[7]

Q. 21. *Who is the Redeemer of God's elect?*
A. The only Redeemer of God's elect is the Lord Jesus Christ,[8] who, being the eternal Son of God, became man,[9] and so was, and continues to be, God and man in two distinct natures, and one person,[10] forever.[11]

Q. 22. *How did Christ, being the Son of God, become man?*
A. Christ, the Son of God, became man, by taking to himself a true body,[12] and a reasonable soul,[13] being conceived by the

---

1 Ephesians 2:1; Psalms 51:5
2 Matthew 15:19-20
3 Genesis 3:8, 24
4 Ephesians 2:3; Galatians 3:10
5 Romans 6:23; Matthew 25:41
6 Ephesians 1:4
7 Romans 3:21-22
8 1 Timothy 2:5
9 John 1:14
10 Romans 9:5
11 Hebrews 7:24
12 Hebrews 2:14
13 Matthew 26:38

power of the Holy Spirit, in the womb of the Virgin Mary, and born of her,[1] yet without sin.[2]

Q. 23. *What offices does Christ execute as our Redeemer?*
A. Christ, as our Redeemer, executes the offices of a prophet,[3] of a priest,[4] and of a king,[5] both in his estate of humiliation and exaltation.

Q. 24. *How does Christ execute the office of a prophet?*
A. Christ executes the office of a prophet, in revealing to us,[6] by his Word[7] and Spirit,[8] the will of God for our salvation.

Q. 25. *How does Christ execute the office of a priest?*
A. Christ executes the office of a priest, in his once offering up of himself a sacrifice to satisfy divine justice,[9] and reconcile us to God,[10] and in making continual intercession for us.[11]

Q. 26. *How does Christ execute the office of a king?*
A. Christ executes the office of a king, in subduing us to himself,[12] in ruling and defending us,[13] and in restraining and conquering all his and our enemies.[14]

Q. 27. *Wherein did Christ's humiliation consist?*
A. Christ's humiliation consisted in his being born, and that

---

1 Luke 1:31, 35
2 Hebrews 7:26
3 Acts 3:22
4 Hebrews 5:6
5 Psalm 2:6
6 John 1:18
7 John 20:31
8 John 14:26
9 Hebrews 9:28
10 Hebrews 2:17
11 Hebrews 7:25
12 Psalms 110:3
13 Isaiah 33:22
14 1 Corinthians 15:25

in a low condition,[1] made under the law,[2] undergoing the miseries of this life,[3] the wrath of God,[4] and the cursed death of the cross;[5] in being buried, and continuing under the power of death for a time.[6]

Q. 28. *Wherein consists Christ's exaltation?*
A. Christ's exaltation consists in his rising again from the dead on the third day,[7] in ascending up into heaven, in sitting at the right hand of God the Father,[8] and in coming to judge the world at the last day.[9]

Q. 29. *How are we made partakers of the redemption purchased by Christ?*
A. We are made partakers of the redemption purchased by Christ, by the effectual application of it to us[10] by his Holy Spirit.[11]

Q. 30. *How does the Spirit apply to us the redemption purchased by Christ?*
A. The Spirit applies to us the redemption purchased by Christ, by working faith in us,[12] and thereby uniting us to Christ in our effectual calling.[13]

Q. 31. *What is effectual calling?*
A. Effectual calling is the work of God's Spirit,[14] whereby,

---

[1] Luke 2:7
[2] Galatians 4:4
[3] Isaiah 53:3
[4] Matthew 27:46
[5] Philippians 2:8
[6] Matthew 12:40
[7] 1 Corinthians 15:4
[8] Mark 16:19
[9] Acts 17:31
[10] John 1:12
[11] Titus 3:5-6
[12] Ephesians 2:8
[13] 1 Corinthians 1:9; Ephesians 3:17
[14] 2 Timothy 1:9

convincing us of our sin and misery,[1] enlightening our minds in the knowledge of Christ,[2] and renewing our wills,[3] he does persuade and enable us to embrace Jesus Christ, freely offered to us in the gospel.[4]

Q. 32. *What benefits do they that are effectually called partake of in this life?*
A. They that are effectually called do in this life partake of justification,[5] adoption,[6] and sanctification, and the several benefits which in this life do either accompany or flow from them.[7]

Q. 33. *What is justification?*
A. Justification is an act of God's free grace, wherein he pardons all our sins,[8] and accepts us as righteous in His sight,[9] only for the righteousness of Christ imputed to us,[10] and received by faith alone.[11]

Q. 34. *What is adoption?*
A. Adoption is an act of God's free grace,[12] whereby we are received into the number, and have a right to all the privileges of the sons of God.[13]

Q. 35. *What is sanctification?*
A. Sanctification is the work of God's free grace,[14] whereby we

---

1 Acts 2:37
2 Acts 26:18
3 Ezekiel 36:26–27
4 John 6:44–45
5 Romans 8:30
6 Ephesians 1:5
7 1 Corinthians 1:30
8 Ephesians 1:17
9 2 Corinthians 5:21
10 Romans 5:19
11 Galatians 2:16
12 1 John 3:1
13 John 1:12; Romans 8:17
14 2 Thessalonians 2:13

are renewed in the whole man after the image of God,[1] and are enabled more and more to die unto sin, and live unto righteousness.[2]

Q. 36. *What are the benefits which in this life do accompany or flow from justification, adoption, and sanctification?*
A. The benefits which in this life do accompany or flow from justification, adoption, and sanctification, are, assurance of God's love, peace of conscience, joy in the Holy Spirit,[3] increase of grace,[4] and perseverance therein to the end.[5]

Q. 37. *What benefits do believers receive from Christ at death?*
A. The souls of believers are at their death made perfect in holiness,[6] and do immediately pass into glory;[7] and their bodies, being still united to Christ,[8] do rest in their graves[9] until the resurrection.[10]

Q. 38. *What benefits do believers receive from Christ at the resurrection?*
A. At the resurrection, believers, being raised up in glory,[11] shall be openly acknowledged and acquitted in the day of

---

1 Ephesians 4:24,
2 Romans 8:1
3 Romans 5:1-2, 5
4 Proverbs 4:18
5 1 John 5:13
6 Hebrews 12:23
7 Philippians 1:23
8 1 Thessalonians 4:14
9 Isaiah 57:2
10 Job 19:26
11 1 Corinthians 15:43

judgment,[1] and made perfectly blessed in the full enjoying of God[2] to all eternity.[3]

Q. 39. *What is the duty which God requires of man?*
A. The duty which God requires of man, is obedience to his revealed will.[4]

Q. 40. *What did God at first reveal to man for the rule of his obedience?*
A. The rule which God at first revealed to man for his obedience, was the moral law.[5]

Q. 41. *Where is the moral law summarized?*
A. The moral law is summarized in the Ten Commandments.[6]

Q. 42. *What is the sum of the Ten Commandments?*
A. The sum of the Ten Commandments is, to love the Lord our God with all our heart, with all our soul, with all our strength, and with all our mind; and our neighbor as ourselves.[7]

Q. 43. *What is the preface to the Ten Commandments?*
A. The preface to the Ten Commandments is in these words, I am the Lord your God, who brought you out of the land of Egypt, out of the house of slavery.[8]

Q. 44. *What does the preface to the Ten Commandments teach us?*
A. The preface to the Ten Commandments teaches us, that

---

1 Matthew 10:32
2 1 John 3:2
3 1 Thessalonians 4:17
4 Micah 6:8
5 Romans 2:14-15
6 Deuteronomy 10:4; Matthew 19:17
7 Matthew 22:37-40
8 Exodus 20:2

because God is the Lord, and our God, and Redeemer, therefore we are bound to keep all his commandments.[1]

Q. 45. *Which is the first commandment?*
A. The first commandment is, You shall have no other gods before me.

Q. 46. *What is required in the first commandment?*
A. The first commandment requires us to know[2] and acknowledge God to be the only true God, and our God;[3] and to worship and glorify him accordingly.[4]

Q. 47. *What is forbidden in the first commandment?*
A. The first commandment forbids the denying,[5] or not worshipping and glorifying, the true God as God,[6] and our God;[7] and the giving of that worship and glory to any other, which is due to him alone.[8]

Q. 48. *What are we specially taught by these words 'before me' in the first commandment?*
A. These words before me in the first commandment teach us, that God, who sees all things, takes notice of, and is much displeased with, the sin of having any other god.[9]

Q. 49. *Which is the second commandment?*
A. The second commandment is, You shall not make for yourself a carved image, or any likeness of anything that is in heaven above, or that is in the earth beneath, or that is in the water under the earth. You shall not bow down to them nor serve them; for I the LORD your God am a jealous God, visiting

---

[1] Deuteronomy 11:1; Luke 1:74-75
[2] 1 Chronicles 28:9
[3] Deuteronomy 26:17
[4] Matthew 4:10
[5] Psalms 14:1
[6] Romans 1:20-21
[7] Psalms 81:11
[8] Romans 1:25
[9] Psalms 44:20-21

the iniquity of the fathers on the children to the third and the fourth generation of those who hate me; and showing steadfast love to thousands of those who love me and keep my commandments.

Q. 50. *What is required in the second commandment?*
A. The second commandment requires the receiving, observing,[1] and keeping pure and entire, all such religious worship and ordinances as God has appointed in his Word.[2]

Q. 51. *What is forbidden in the second commandment?*
A. The second commandment forbids the worshipping of God by images,[3] or any other way not appointed in his Word.[4]

Q. 52. *What are the reasons annexed to the second commandment?*
A. The reasons annexed to the second commandment are, God's sovereignty over us,[5] his propriety in us,[6] and the zeal he has to his own worship.[7]

Q. 53. *Which is the third commandment?*
A. The third commandment is, You shall not take the name of the Lord your God in vain, for the Lord will not hold him guiltless who takes his name in vain.

Q. 54. *What is required in the third commandment?*
A. The third commandment requires the holy and reverent use

---

[1] Deuteronomy 32:46; Matthew 28:20
[2] Deuteronomy 12:32
[3] Deuteronomy 4:15–16
[4] Colossians 2:18
[5] Psalms 95:2–3
[6] Psalms 45:11
[7] Exodus 34:14

of God's names,[1] titles, attributes,[2] ordinances,[3] Word,[4] and works.[5]

Q. 55. *What is forbidden in the third commandment?*
A. The third commandment forbids all profaning or abusing of anything whereby God makes himself known.[6]

Q. 56. *What is the reason annexed to the third commandment?*
A. The reason annexed to the third commandment is, that however the breakers of this commandment may escape punishment from men, yet the Lord our God will not let them escape his righteous judgment.[7]

Q. 57. *Which is the fourth commandment?*
A. The fourth commandment is, Remember the Sabbath day, to keep it holy. Six days you shall labour, and do all your work, but the seventh day is a Sabbath to the Lord your God. On it you shall not do any work, you, nor your son, nor your daughter, your male servant, nor your female servant, nor your livestock, nor the sojourner who is within your gates. For in six days the Lord made heaven and earth, the sea, and all that is in them, and rested on the seventh day. Therefore the Lord blessed the Sabbath day and made it holy.

Q. 58. *What is required in the fourth commandment?*
A. The fourth commandment requires the keeping holy to God

---

[1] Psalms 29:2
[2] Revelation 15:3-4
[3] Ecclesiastes 5:1
[4] Psalms 138:2
[5] Job 36:24
[6] Malachi 2:2
[7] Deuteronomy 28:58-59

such set times as he has appointed in his Word; expressly one whole day in seven, to be a holy Sabbath to himself.[1]

Q. 59. *Which day of the seven has God appointed to be the weekly Sabbath?*
A. From the beginning of the world to the resurrection of Christ, God appointed the seventh day of the week to be the weekly Sabbath;[2] and the first day of the week ever since, to continue to the end of the world, which is the Christian Sabbath.[3]

Q. 60. *How is the Sabbath to be sanctified?*
A. The sabbath is to be sanctified by a holy resting all that day, even from such worldly employments and recreations as are lawful on other days;[4] and spending the whole time in the public and private exercises of God's worship,[5] except so much as is to be taken up in the works of necessity and mercy.[6]

Q. 61. *What is forbidden in the fourth commandment?*
A. The fourth commandment forbids the omission, or careless performance of the duties required,[7] and the profaning the day by idleness, or doing that which is in itself sinful,[8] or by unnecessary thoughts, words, or works, about our worldly employments or recreations.[9]

Q. 62. *What are the reasons annexed to the fourth commandment?*
A. The reasons annexed to the fourth commandment are, God's allowing us six days of the week for our own employments,[10]

---

1 Leviticus 19:30; Deuteronomy 5:12
2 Genesis 2:3
3 Acts 20:7; Revelation 1:10
4 Leviticus 23:3
5 Psalm 92:1-2
6 Matthew 12:11-12
7 Malachi 1:13
8 Ezekiel 23:38
9 Isaiah 58:13
10 Exodus 31:15-16

his challenging a special propriety in the seventh,[1] his own example,[2] and his blessing the Sabbath day.[3]

Q. 63. *Which is the fifth commandment?*
A. The fifth commandment is, Honour your father and your mother, that your days may be long in the land that the LORD your God is giving you.

Q. 64. *What is required in the fifth commandment?*
A. The fifth commandment requires the preserving the honour, and performing the duties, belonging to everyone in their several places and relations, as superiors,[4] inferiors,[5] or equals.[6]

Q. 65. *What is forbidden in the fifth commandment?*
A. The fifth commandment forbids the neglecting of, or doing anything against, the honour and duty which belongs to everyone in their several places and relations.[7]

Q. 66. *What is the reason annexed to the fifth commandment?*
A. The reason annexed to the fifth commandment is, a promise of long life and prosperity (as far as it shall serve

---

[1] Leviticus 23:3
[2] Exodus 31:17
[3] Genesis 2:3
[4] Ephesians 5:21-22; 6:1, 5; Romans 13:1
[5] 1 Peter 3:16; Acts 25:10
[6] Romans 12:10
[7] Romans 13:7-8

for God's glory and their own good) to all such as keep this commandment.[1]

Q. 67. *Which is the sixth commandment?*
A. The sixth commandment is, You shall not murder.

Q. 68. *What is required in the sixth commandment?*
A. The sixth commandment requires all lawful endeavors to preserve our own life,[2] and the life of others.[3]

Q. 69. *What is forbidden in the sixth commandment?*
A. The sixth commandment forbids the taking away of our own life,[4] or the life of our neighbour,[5] unjustly, or whatsoever is related thereunto.[6]

Q. 70. *Which is the seventh commandment?*
A. The seventh commandment is, You shall not commit adultery.

Q. 71. *What is required in the seventh commandment?*
A. The seventh commandment requires the preservation of our

---

1 Ephesians 6:2–3
2 Ephesians 5:28–29
3 Psalm 82:3–4; Job 29:13
4 Acts 16:28
5 Genesis 9:6
6 Proverbs 24:11–12

own[1] and our neighbour's chastity,[2] in heart,[3] speech,[4] and behaviour.[5]

Q. 72. *What is forbidden in the seventh commandment?*
A. The seventh commandment forbids all unchaste thoughts,[6] words,[7] and actions.[8]

Q. 73. *Which is the eighth commandment?*
A. The eighth commandment is, You shall not steal.

Q. 74. *What is required in the eighth commandment?*
A. The eighth commandment requires the lawful procuring [obtaining] and furthering the wealth and outward estate of ourselves[9] and others.[10]

Q. 75. *What is forbidden in the eighth commandment?*
A. The eighth commandment forbids whatsoever does, or may, unjustly hinder our own,[11] or our neighbour's wealth or outward estate.[12]

Q. 76. *Which is the ninth commandment?*
A. The ninth commandment is, You shall not bear false witness against your neighbour.

Q. 77. *What is required in the ninth commandment?*
A. The ninth commandment requires the maintaining and promoting of truth between man and man,[13] and of our

---

1 1 Thessalonians 4:4
2 Ephesians 5:11-12
3 2 Timothy 2:22
4 Colossians 4:6
5 1 Peter 3:2
6 Matthew 5:28
7 Ephesians 5:4
8 Ephesians 5:3
9 Romans 12:17; Proverbs 27:23
10 Leviticus 25:35; Philippians 2:4
11 1 Timothy 5:8
12 Proverbs 28:19; 21:6; Job 20:19-20
13 Zechariah 8:16

own[1] and our neighbour's good name,[2] especially in witness-bearing.[3]

Q. 78. *What is forbidden in the ninth commandment?*
A. The ninth commandment forbids whatsoever is prejudicial to truth, or injurious to our own, or our neighbour's, good name.[4]

Q. 79. *Which is the tenth commandment?*
A. The tenth commandment is, You shall not covet your neighbour's house; you shall not covet your neighbour's wife, or his male servant, or his female servant, or his ox, or his donkey, or anything that is your neighbour's.

Q. 80. *What is required in the tenth commandment?*
A. The tenth commandment requires full contentment with our own condition,[5] with a right and charitable frame of spirit toward our neighbour, and all that is his.[6]

Q. 81. *What is forbidden in the tenth commandment?*
A. The tenth commandment forbids all discontentment with our own estate,[7] envying or grieving at the good of our neighbour,[8] and all inordinate motions and affections to anything that is his.[9]

Q. 82. *Is any man able perfectly to keep the commandments of God?*
A. No mere man, since the fall, is able in this life perfectly to

---

1   1 Peter 3:16
2   3 John 12
3   Proverbs 14:5, 25
4   Psalms 15:3; Job 27:5; Romans 3:13
5   Hebrews 13:5
6   Romans 12:15; 1 Corinthians 13:4–6
7   1 Corinthians 10:10
8   Galatians 5:26
9   Colossians 3:5

keep the commandments of God,[1] but does daily break them in thought,[2] word,[3] and deed.[4]

Q. 83. *Are all transgressions of the law equally heinous?*
A. Some sins in themselves, and by reason of several aggravations, are more heinous in the sight of God than others.[5]

Q. 84. *What does every sin deserve?*
A. Every sin deserves God's wrath and curse, both in this life, and that which is to come.[6]

Q. 85. *What does God require of us, that we may escape his wrath and curse, due to us for sin?*
A. To escape the wrath and curse of God, due to us for sin, God requires of us faith in Jesus Christ, repentance unto life,[7] with the diligent use of all the outward means whereby Christ communicates to us the benefits of redemption.[8]

Q. 86. *What is faith in Jesus Christ?*
A. Faith in Jesus Christ is a saving grace,[9] whereby we receive[10] and rest upon him alone for salvation,[11] as he is offered to us in the gospel.[12]

Q. 87. *What is repentance unto life?*
A. Repentance unto life is a saving grace,[13] whereby a sinner, out

---

1 Ecclesiastes 7:20
2 Genesis 8:21
3 James 3:8
4 James 3:2
5 John 19:11
6 Galatians 3:10; Matthew 25:41
7 Acts 20:21
8 Proverbs 2:1-5
9 Hebrews 10:39
10 John 1:12
11 Philippians 3:9
12 Isaiah 33:22
13 Acts 11:18

of a true sense of his sin,[1] and apprehension of the mercy of God in Christ,[2] does, with grief and hatred of his sin, turn from it unto God,[3] with full purpose of, and endeavor after, new obedience.[4]

Q. 88. *What are the outward means whereby Christ communicates to us the benefits of redemption?*
A. The outward and ordinary means whereby Christ communicates to us the benefits of redemption are, his ordinances, especially the Word, sacraments, and prayer; all of which are made effectual to the elect for salvation.[5]

Q. 89. *How is the Word made effectual to salvation?*
A. The Spirit of God makes the reading, but especially the preaching, of the Word, an effectual means of convincing and converting sinners,[6] and of building them up in holiness and comfort,[7] through faith, unto salvation.[8]

Q. 90. *How is the Word to be read and heard, that it may become effectual to salvation?*
A. That the Word may become effectual to salvation, we must practise the preaching and reading of the Word with diligence,[9] preparation,[10] and prayer;[11] receive it with faith[12]

---

1 Acts 2:37
2 Joel 2:13
3 Jeremiah 31:18–19
4 Psalms 119:59
5 Acts 2:41–42
6 Psalm 19:7
7 1 Thessalonians 1:6
8 Romans 1:16
9 Proverbs 8:34
10 1 Peter 2:1–2
11 Psalms 119:18
12 Hebrews 4:2

and love,[1] lay it up in our hearts,[2] and practise it in our lives.[3]

Q. 91. *How do the sacraments become effectual means of salvation?*
A. The sacraments become effectual means of salvation, not from any virtue in them, or in him who administers them;[4] but only by the blessing of Christ, and the working of his Spirit in them that by faith receive them.[5]

Q. 92. *What is a sacrament?*
A. A sacrament is a holy ordinance instituted by Christ;[6] wherein, by sensible signs, Christ, and the benefits of the new covenant, are represented, sealed, and applied to believers.[7]

Q. 93. *Which are the sacraments of the New Testament?*
A. The sacraments of the New Testament are, baptism,[8] and the Lord's Supper.[9]

Q. 94. *What is baptism?*
A. Baptism is a sacrament, wherein the washing with water in the name of the Father, and of the Son, and of the Holy Spirit,[10] signifies and seals our ingrafting into Christ, and partaking of the benefits of the covenant of grace,[11] and our engagement to be the Lord's.[12]

Q. 95. *To whom is baptism to be administered?*
A. Baptism is not to be administered to any that are out of the visible church, till they profess their faith in Christ, and

---

1 2 Thessalonians 2:10
2 Psalm 119:11
3 James 1:25
4 1 Corinthians 3:7
5 1 Peter 3:21
6 Genesis 17:10
7 Romans 4:11
8 Mark 16:16
9 1 Corinthians 11:23–26
10 Matthew 28:19
11 Romans 6:3
12 Romans 6:4

obedience to him;[1] but the infants of such as are members of the visible church are to be baptised.[2]

Q. 96. *What is the Lord's Supper?*
A. The Lord's Supper is a sacrament, wherein, by giving and receiving bread and wine, according to Christ's appointment, his death is showed forth;[3] and the worthy receivers are, not after a corporal and carnal manner, but by faith, made partakers of his body and blood, with all his benefits, to their spiritual nourishment, and growth in grace.[4]

Q. 97. *What is required for the worthy receiving of the Lord's Supper?*
A. It is required of those who would worthily partake of the Lord's Supper, that they examine themselves of their knowledge to discern the Lord's body,[5] of their faith to feed upon him,[6] of their repentance,[7] love,[8] and new obedience;[9] lest, coming unworthily, they eat and drink judgment to themselves.[10]

Q. 98. *What is prayer?*
A. Prayer is an offering up of our desires unto God,[11] for things

---

[1] Acts 2:41
[2] Genesis 17:7, 10; Acts 2:38–39
[3] Luke 22:19–20
[4] 1 Corinthians 10:16
[5] 1 Corinthians 11:28–29
[6] 2 Corinthians 13:5
[7] 1 Corinthians 11:31
[8] 1 Corinthians 11:18, 20
[9] 1 Corinthians 5:8
[10] 1 Corinthians 11:27
[11] Psalms 62:8

agreeable to his will,[1] in the name of Christ,[2] with confession of our sins,[3] and thankful acknowledgment of his mercies.[4]

Q. 99. *What rule has God given for our direction in prayer?*
A. The whole Word of God is of use to direct us in prayer;[5] but the special rule of direction is that form of prayer which Christ taught his disciples, commonly called the Lord's Prayer.[6]

Q. 100. *What does the preface of the Lord's Prayer teach us?*
A. The preface of the Lord's Prayer, which is, Our Father in heaven, teaches us to draw near to God with all holy reverence and confidence,[7] as children to a father,[8] able and ready to help us;[9] and that we should pray with and for others.[10]

Q. 101. *What do we pray for in the first petition?*
A. In the first petition, which is, Hallowed be your name, we pray that God would enable us, and others, to glorify him in all that whereby he makes himself known;[11] and that he would dispose all things to his own glory.[12]

Q. 102. *What do we pray for in the second petition?*
A. In the second petition, which is, Your kingdom come, we pray that Satan's kingdom may be destroyed;[13] and that the kingdom of grace may be advanced,[14] ourselves and others

---

1 Romans 8:27
2 John 16:23
3 Daniel 9:4
4 Philippians 4:6
5 1 John 5:14
6 Matthew 6:9
7 Isaiah 64:9
8 Luke 11:13
9 Romans 8:15
10 Ephesians 6:18
11 Psalms 67:1-3
12 Romans 11:36
13 Psalm 68:1
14 Psalms 51:18

brought into it, and kept in it;[1] and that the kingdom of glory may be hastened.[2]

Q. 103. *What do we pray for in the third petition?*
A. In the third petition, which is, Your will be done in earth, as it is in heaven, we pray that God, by his grace, would make us able and willing to know, obey,[3] and submit to his will in all things,[4] as the angels do in heaven.[5]

Q. 104. *What do we pray for in the fourth petition?*
A. In the fourth petition, which is, Give us this day our daily bread, we pray that of God's free gift we may receive a competent portion of the good things of this life,[6] and enjoy his blessing with them.[7]

Q. 105. *What do we pray for in the fifth petition?*
A. In the fifth petition, which is, And forgive us our debts, as we also have forgiven our debtors, we pray that God, for Christ's sake, would freely pardon all our sins;[8] which we are the rather encouraged to ask, because by his grace we are enabled from the heart to forgive others.[9]

Q. 106. *What do we pray for in the sixth petition?*
A. In the sixth petition, which is, And lead us not into

---

1 2 Thessalonians 3:1; Romans 10:1
2 Revelation 22:20
3 Psalm 119:34-36
4 Acts 21:14
5 Psalms 103:20, 22
6 Proverbs 30:8
7 Psalm 90:17
8 Psalms 51:1
9 Matthew 6:14

temptation, but deliver us from evil, we pray that God would either keep us from being tempted to sin,[1] or support and deliver us when we are tempted.[2]

Q. 107. *What does the conclusion of the Lord's Prayer teach us?*
A. The conclusion of the Lord's Prayer, which is, For yours is the kingdom, and the power, and the glory, forever. Amen, teaches us to take our encouragement in prayer from God only,[3] and in our prayers to praise him, ascribing kingdom, power, and glory to him;[4] and, in testimony of our desire, and assurance to be heard, we say, Amen[5]

---

[1] Matthew 26:41; Psalms 19:13
[2] Psalm 51:10, 12
[3] Daniel 9:18-19
[4] 1 Chronicles 29:11, 13
[5] Revelation 22:20

The Creeds

The Apostles' Creed

I believe in God the Father Almighty, Maker of heaven and earth.

And in Jesus Christ, His only Son, our Lord; who was conceived by the Holy Spirit, born of the Virgin Mary; suffered under Pontius Pilate, was crucified, dead, and buried; He descended into hell; the third day He rose again from the dead; He ascended into heaven, and sits on the right hand of God the Father Almighty; from thence He shall come to judge the living and the dead.

I believe in the Holy Spirit; the holy catholic church, the communion of saints; the forgiveness of sins; the resurrection of the body; and the life everlasting. Amen.

The Nicene Creed (AD 381)

I believe in one God, the Father Almighty, Maker of heaven and earth, and of all things visible and invisible.

And in one Lord Jesus Christ, the only-begotten Son of God, begotten of the Father before all worlds; God of God, Light of Light, very God of very God; begotten, not made, being of one substance with the Father, by whom all things were made.

Who, for us men and for our salvation, came down from heaven, and was incarnate by the Holy Spirit of the virgin Mary, and was made man; and was crucified also for us under Pontius Pilate; He suffered and was buried; and the third day He rose again, according to the Scriptures; and ascended into heaven, and sits on the right hand of the Father; and He shall come again, with glory, to judge the living and the dead; whose kingdom shall have no end.

And I believe in the Holy Spirit, the Lord and Giver of Life; who proceeds from the Father and the Son; who with the Father and the Son together is worshiped and glorified; who spoke by the prophets.

And I believe in one holy catholic and apostolic Church. I acknowledge one baptism for the remission of sins; and I look for the resurrection of the dead, and the life of the world to come. Amen.

The Athanasian Creed

Whoever will be saved, before all things it is necessary that he hold the catholic faith. Which faith except every one do keep whole and undefiled, without doubt he shall perish everlastingly.

   And the catholic faith is this, that we worship one God in Trinity, and Trinity in Unity; neither confounding the Persons, nor dividing the Substance. For there is one Person of the Father, another of the Son, and another of the Holy Spirit. But the Godhead of the Father, of the Son, and of the Holy Spirit is all one: the glory equal, the majesty coeternal. Such as the Father is, such is the Son, and such is the Holy Spirit. The Father uncreated, the Son uncreated, and the Holy Spirit uncreated. The Father incomprehensible, the Son incomprehensible, and the Holy Spirit incomprehensible. The Father eternal, the Son eternal, and the Holy Spirit eternal. And yet they are not three Eternals, but one Eternal. As there are not three Uncreated nor three Incomprehensibles, but one Uncreated and one Incomprehensible. So likewise the Father is almighty, the Son almighty, and the Holy Spirit almighty. And yet they are not three Almighties, but one Almighty. So the Father is God, the Son is God, and the Holy Spirit is God. And yet they are not three Gods, but one God. So likewise the Father is Lord, the Son Lord, and the Holy Spirit Lord. And yet not three Lords, but one Lord. For like as we are compelled by the Christian verity to acknowledge every Person by Himself to be God and Lord, So are we forbidden by the catholic religion to say, There be three Gods, or three Lords.

The Father is made of none: neither created nor begotten. The Son is of the Father alone; not made, nor created, but begotten. The Holy Spirit is of the Father and of the Son: neither made, nor created, nor begotten, but proceeding. So there is one Father, not three Fathers; one Son, not three Sons; one Holy Spirit, not three Holy Spirits. And in this Trinity none is before or after other; none is greater or less than another; But the whole three Persons are coeternal together, and coequal: so that in all things, as is aforesaid, the Unity in Trinity and the Trinity in Unity is to be worshipped. He, therefore, that will be saved must thus think of the Trinity.

Furthermore, it is necessary to everlasting salvation that he also believe faithfully the incarnation of our Lord Jesus Christ. For the right faith is, that we believe and confess that our Lord Jesus Christ, the Son of God, is God and Man; God of the Substance of the Father, begotten before the worlds; and Man of the substance of His mother, born in the world; Perfect God and perfect Man, of a reasonable soul and human flesh subsisting. Equal to the Father as touching His Godhead, and inferior to the Father as touching His manhood; Who, although He be God and Man, yet He is not two, but one Christ: One, not by conversion of the Godhead into flesh, but by taking the manhood into God; One altogether; not by confusion of Substance, but by unity of Person. For as the reasonable soul and flesh is one man, so God and Man is one Christ; Who suffered for our salvation; descended into hell, rose again the third day from the dead; He ascended into heaven; He sits on the right hand of the Father, God Almighty; from whence He shall come to judge the living and the dead. At whose coming all men shall rise again with their bodies, and shall give an account of their own works. And they that have done good shall go into life everlasting; and they that have done evil, into everlasting fire.

This is the catholic faith; which except a man believe faithfully and firmly, he cannot be saved.

The Definition of the Council of Chalcedon (AD 451)

Therefore, following the holy fathers, we all with one accord teach men to acknowledge one and the same Son, our Lord Jesus Christ, at once complete in Godhead and complete in manhood, truly God and truly man, consisting also of a reasonable soul and body; of one substance with the Father as regards his Godhead, and at the same time of one substance with us as regards his manhood; like us in all respects, apart from sin; as regards his Godhead, begotten of the Father before the ages, but yet as regards his manhood begotten, for us men and for our salvation, of Mary the Virgin, the God-bearer; one and the same Christ, Son, Lord, Only-begotten, recognized in two natures, without confusion, without change, without division, without separation; the distinction of natures being in no way annulled by the union, but rather the characteristics of each nature being preserved and coming together to form one person and subsistence, not as parted or separated into two persons, but one and the same Son and Only-begotten God the Word, Lord Jesus Christ; even as the prophets from earliest times spoke of him, and our Lord Jesus Christ himself taught us, and the creed of the fathers has handed down to us.